Jesus of Hollywood

Jesus of Hollywood

ADELE REINHARTZ

OXFORD
UNIVERSITY PRESS

OXFORD
UNIVERSITY PRESS

Oxford University Press, Inc., publishes works that further
Oxford University's objective of excellence
in research, scholarship, and education.

Oxford   New York
Auckland   Cape Town   Dar es Salaam   Hong Kong   Karachi
Kuala Lumpur   Madrid   Melbourne   Mexico City   Nairobi
New Delhi   Shanghai   Taipei   Toronto

With offices in
Argentina   Austria   Brazil   Chile   Czech Republic   France   Greece
Guatemala   Hungary   Italy   Japan   Poland   Portugal   Singapore
South Korea   Switzerland   Thailand   Turkey   Ukraine   Vietnam

Copyright © 2007 by Oxford University Press, Inc.

Published by Oxford University Press, Inc.
198 Madison Avenue, New York, New York 10016

www.oup.com

First issued as an Oxford University Press paperback, 2009

Oxford is a registered trademark of Oxford University Press

Library of Congress Cataloging-in-Publication Data

Reinhartz, Adele, 1953–
Jesus of Hollywood / Adele Reinhartz.
   p. cm.
Includes bibliographical references and index.
ISBN 978-0-19-538338-6
1. Jesus Christ—In motion pictures. I. Title.
PN1995.9.J4R45 2006
791.43'651—dc22   2006014395

David Kinsley
April 25, 1939–April 25, 2000
In memoriam

Permissions

Preface

One does not have to be a biblical scholar to write a book about the Jesus movies. Indeed, there are many other sorts of academics who potentially have an interest in this subject and would be able to provide insights that may be lost on a biblical scholar. A film historian could situate these films in the context of the movie industry in North America and Europe or consider how the advances in technology have either added to or detracted from the power of these films. An art historian could look at how the Jesus movies utilize the masterpieces of Christian art in the appearance of Jesus and those who surround him, support him and oppose him, and in framing particular scenes such as the Flight to Egypt or the Last Supper. A specialist in popular culture could look at the films' use of "Hallmark" crèche images and other clichés and stereotypes. A music historian could analyze the presence, or absence, of Handel's Messiah, gospel music, or contemporary Middle Eastern cadences in the movies' soundtracks, as well as the mood created by the instrumentation and other musical elements. A theologian could study the faith claims implicit in these movies in the context of various theological streams in contemporary Christian society in North America and Western Europe.

As it happens, however, I am a scholar of the Christian scriptures, and my academic interests and education have shaped my approach to these movies. As will no doubt be clear to my readers, I have been fascinated in particular by the complicated relationship between these films and their sources, particularly the Gospels of

Matthew, Mark, Luke and John. But in the process I have been drawn into the orbits of the disciplines I have mentioned, for it is impossible to understand the Jesus movies without at least some attention to the two thousand years of meditation and imagination that has resulted in a rich tapestry of images, sounds, beliefs and ideas that have shaped this genre of film at least as much as the Gospels and other literary sources have done. No doubt specialists in those fields will find evidence of my amateur approach to their areas, and for this I apologize in advance. But the study itself has ignited my own interests, particularly in Christian art through the ages, and a profound appreciation for the impact of art on the way in which we visualize "the greatest story ever told."

I gratefully acknowledge the support of the Social Sciences and Humanities Research Council, as well as of McMaster University, Wilfrid Laurier University, the University of Ottawa, the Hebrew University, and their libraries. This book had its beginning during a year spent at the Institute for Advanced Studies at the Hebrew University of Jerusalem 2000–2001 and numerous short stays from 2001–2005, and the first draft was written in July 2004 while I was a resident at the lovely Villa Serbelloni in Bellagio, courtesy of the Rockefeller Foundation. My colleagues both at the Institute and at the Villa Serbelloni were wonderful dialogue partners and I learned much from conversations with them and from their feedback on my presentations.

Like all teachers, I have perhaps learned the most from my students. As a wandering academic, I have had the pleasure and privilege of sharing this material with numerous students at numerous institutions, whether in formal courses at McMaster University, Wilfrid Laurier University and the University of Cape Town Summer School, through occasional lectures at universities, colleges and divinity schools in North America, Europe, and Israel, or in the context of informal adult education at the Summer Institute of the National Havurah Committee, and numerous synagogues, churches, and other organizations. Most memorable, perhaps was my sole attempt at distance education, linking Wilfrid Laurier University with the Universities of Helsinki, Calgary, and Liverpool for an intensive transatlantic graduate course.

My friends and colleagues have been listening to me or reading my drafts patiently for several years now. I wish to express my appreciation in particular to Carl Holladay, W. Barnes Tatum, William R. Telford, Jan Willem van Henten, Richard Walsh, and Robin McL. Wilson, as well as to my editor, Cynthia Read, not only for her patience, but also for her insightful comments on the draft. Many thanks to Steven Scott and Jo Wilkinson. Eva Bach did numerous tasks, from checking transcriptions to organizing my files and creating bibliographic databases. Julia TerMaat, of Oxford University Press, guided me gently through the process of preparing the final manuscript complete with stills, and Gwen Colvin through the production process.

As always, I have my family to thank at every turn. My younger children, Simcha and Shoshana, joined me through my first run through many of these films, offering commentary that was occasionally useful and always entertaining. Mordechai Walfish helped to transcribe notes and compile an initial bibliography. My daughter Miriam-Simma and son-in-law Michael listened patiently at various points in the book and tried to work through some of the structural issues that the book presented. Most of all, I thank my husband Barry Walfish, who throughout many years kept his eyes open for any pertinent books that appeared on the shelves of Robarts Library at the University of Toronto, and went over the penultimate draft with his usual care and eye for detail.

Finally, I owe a major debt of gratitude to Jason Shim. Jason's genuine and unflagging interest in this project made it a pleasure to work with him for the past three years. Not only did Jason proofread and comment upon the entire manuscript, but his expertise in matters digital enabled me to work on this project whether I was in Hamilton, Jerusalem, or Bellagio, and made the many technical tasks involved in the preparation of the manuscript much easier. I could not have completed this book without his assistance.

This book is dedicated to David Kinsley. David was a relatively new professor in the Religious Studies Department at McMaster University when I arrived in 1975 to begin my MA. Throughout my years as a graduate student and, later, as a faculty member myself, we enjoyed a cordial and collegial relationship. But it was only in January 2000, when David was diagnosed with terminal lung cancer, that we truly became friends. David made it clear that he and his wife Cary welcomed visitors. I took him at his word, began to visit them at home on a weekly basis, and took my turn at driving David to the hospital for his radiation treatments. These visits were the high point of my week, a time of conversation and respite from a hectic schedule. Despite his illness and growing weakness, David retained his warmth, his interest in life, and his optimistic outlook on life and humankind. At this time "Jesus of Hollywood" was barely a glimmer in my mind and it was in conversations with David that the project began to take shape. He urged me to prepare a book proposal for Oxford, and I did so immediately, in the hope—gratefully realized—that I would have a book contract to show him before he left us. His memory is a blessing, for me and the many others who knew him.

Contents

PART I

The Genre

Jesus Movies as Biopics

I

Introduction: From Holy Scripture to Silver Screen

Just as the Bible is the best-selling book of all time, so is Jesus the most popular movie subject in the history of cinema. In the hundred years or more since the inception of the film industry, well over a hundred "biopics"—feature film biographies—have been made about Jesus. Indeed, it may well be the case that more people worldwide know about Jesus and his life story from the movies than from any other medium.[1]

Biographical films, though they are set in an historical era and have an historical individual as their subject, are fundamentally fictional narratives. Yet we as viewers have a mixed response to these films. On the one hand, we recognize the fictional nature of the biopics and we typically grant them a measure of artistic license to flesh out the story and the character of their subjects. At the same time, however, we also view them as "real" or historical and expect them to cohere with the facts as we know them.

This expectation is evident in the tendency of many viewers, including film critics and scholars, to assess these movies on the basis of their historicity.[2] At least part of the debate that raged around Mel Gibson's 2004 film *The Passion of the Christ* had to do with the degree to which it corresponded to the "facts." According to Gibson's media machine, even the late Pope John Paul II purportedly weighed in on the matter when he declared: "It is as it was."[3]

Our preoccupation with the historical dimension of these films suggests that despite our awareness of the fictional nature of the biopic genre we nevertheless expect that the "reel" life of Jesus as constructed in the Jesus biopics will reproduce, or, at least, overlap considerably with, Jesus' "real" life as it was lived in the first few decades of what we now call the Common Era, in a place we now call Israel. In other words, we expect "Jesus of Hollywood" to bear a direct resemblance to "Jesus of Nazareth."

Our tendency to hold the Jesus movies up to the lens of history is not mere misapprehension on our part. Indeed, our expectations of historicity are actively encouraged by these films themselves. Through their choice of subject (someone who is known to have existed), and the use of costumes (the familiar bathrobe and sandals outfit of the biblical epics), settings (the Middle East or locations that resemble the Middle East), and language (biblical-sounding English or ancient languages such as Hebrew or Aramaic), these films imply not only that they are telling a story about people who really existed, but also that they are telling a "true" story.[4] More than this, the Jesus movies explicitly assert their claim to historicity, often through the use of scrolled texts, titles, and/or narration. The 1912 silent movie *From the Manger to the Cross*, for example, announces itself as "a review of the saviour's life according to the gospel-narrative."

Despite such assertions, these films inevitably, and obviously, contain nonhistorical elements. Every Jesus biopic includes scenes and/or dialogue that are not found in their primary sources, the Gospels of Matthew, Mark, Luke, and John. Most invent speeches for Jesus, from everyday interactions with his mother and disciples, to cryptic sayings and pious discourses. Some films even attribute to Jesus the *bon mots* of other New Testament personalities, as when Max von Sydow's Jesus (*The Greatest Story Ever Told*) recites the apostle Paul's famous ode to love (1 Corinthians 13). They may create fictional characters, such as the scribe Zerah who masterminds Jesus' execution in Franco Zeffirelli's *Jesus of Nazareth*. And some films present subplots that are nowhere to be found in the ancient sources. Nicholas Ray's *King of Kings* links Judas and Barabbas and places them among the leadership of a militant Jewish group that seeks to exploit Jesus' charisma for the good of the revolution. Robert Young's *Jesus* has the youthful savior fall in love with Mary of Bethany. While some films consult the works of ancient historians such as Josephus Flavius, many draw heavily upon works of legend, liturgy, and imagination, such as the apocryphal gospels (*The Protoevangelium of James*), liturgy (the Apostles' Creed), art (Michelangelo's *Pietà*; Leonardo da Vinci's *The Last Supper*), fiction (*Ben-Hur*; *The Last Temptation of Christ*), and last but certainly not least, other Jesus movies.

Finally, and most telling, biopics utilize a common narrative template that dictates the ways in which information is extracted from their sources and packaged into a coherent narrative.[5] The biopic template situates its subject within a family and circle of friends to show how the hero's immediate circle as well as the broader social and political context either influences or responds to his or her growing capabilities and sense of mission. After establishing their subject's talents and accomplishments, biopics place him or her in an antagonistic relationship with an individual or group. Conflict ensues, inflicting physical and mental pain upon the hero. The conflict is resolved in a judicial trial that provides the occasion for an impassioned summation of the hero's primary message for the benefit of the viewing audience. The hero is sustained by a best friend and, somewhere along the line, falls in love. Throughout, the principle of causality tightly links the story elements.

Jesus movies use this same template for telling their hero's life story. Jesus interacts with his particular social and religious context, engages in conflict with hostile forces, and endures a trial. While Jesus, as a unique being, is not the sort of hero to have romantic interests or even close friends, these films occasionally have hints of romance, normally involving Mary Magdalene, and friendship, with Judas. Often, in the interest of causality filmmakers introduce or emphasize plot elements that are absent from the Gospel narratives, as in DeMille's *The King of Kings*, which presents Caiaphas' greed as the direct cause of Jesus' downfall.

If, despite these and numerous other distortions, we viewers believe the Jesus biopics to be "real," what is the harm? Perhaps none; after all, the historical fallacy is itself part of the biopic genre. As George Custen notes in his major study of the genre, "biopics are real not because they are believable. Rather one must treat them as real because despite the obvious distortions ... they are believed to be real by many viewers."[6]

Nevertheless, those who approach these fictional Jesus movies expecting history are bound to be disappointed. It is patently incorrect, for example, to suppose that Jesus and his Roman persecutors spoke Latin, as Gibson would have us think; it is well known that Greek was the lingua franca of the Romans in the Eastern empire. Nor should we believe that Judas tried to goad Jesus into sparking revolution against Rome, as *King of Kings* (1961) suggests.

If not history, what should moviegoers expect? Entertainment, of course. Whatever other motives filmmakers may have, their aim is to engage and entertain their viewers. In this regard too, the Jesus biopics often disappoint. On the one hand, their primary sources, the four Gospels, offer a larger-than-life hero, quotable quotes, and wondrous deeds. Even those who are not Christian can be riveted by the story of a man of humble origins who captivates his audience, challenges the authorities, suffers a painful death, and miraculously rises again. On the other hand, the power of the story is diminished by its overfamiliarity. The ending is predictable: Jesus is inevitably crucified, buried and resurrected. Worse, he himself talks too much and does too little to be effective in the visual medium of cinema[7] and as the Son of God, he is not permitted the foibles, failings, the false starts or true loves that induce us viewers to identify with and care about our movie heroes.

Furthermore, in their efforts to preserve Jesus' aura of sanctity, filmmakers use strategies that are more likely to bore than to entertain. The pace of these biopics is often agonizingly slow, apparently on the (dubious) assumption that reverence is best conveyed in slow motion. On numerous occasions, Franco Zeffirelli (*Jesus of Nazareth*) brings Jesus into extreme close-up, forcing us to stare intently at his mouth as he slowly and deliberately articulates his sacred saying. In his review of George Stevens's epic film critic John Simon quips:

> God is unlucky in *The Greatest Story Ever Told*. His only-begotten Son turns out to be a bore. This is not the fault of Max von Sydow, whose Christ is notable in bearing, beautifully spoken with a slight Swedish accent, and penetratingly handsome in a way that, despite the black wig, is 100 percent Aryan. What else could you expect from someone whose mother is Dorothy McGuire, her age and expression beatifically identical at the manger and at the cross? No, Sydow cannot be faulted; but George Stevens, who made the film, can.[8]

It would seem, then, that the Jesus films demonstrably fall short both as history and as entertainment. Yet people continue both to enjoy these films, and to view them at least to some extent as a source of information about the historical Jesus. Some use them as a vehicle for reflecting upon their own Christian faith. Others watch these films out of habit or tradition, particularly at Christmas and Easter time when many networks will screen one Jesus biopic or another.

I too watch these films avidly. For me they are neither history (for which I turn more readily to the numerous books on the historical Jesus) nor objects of sentiment (as a child my annual television calendar included *The Wizard of Oz* and *The Ten Commandments* but not *The Greatest Story Ever Told*). Nor do I find them absorbing and distracting as entertainment (for which I seek out thrillers and romantic comedies). Indeed, I first viewed these movies merely out of duty. Given that I had taken to showing one or two films a year in my undergraduate New Testament courses, I had to watch them too. I told myself that introducing film to my New Testament courses not only added variety but also demonstrated that interpretation takes place not just in commentaries, in classrooms or from pulpits, but also through art, literature, music and film. But

I soon had to acknowledge that my own interest in these films was much more focused: to see how they portrayed Jews and women. Specifically, I was curious about whether changing sensibilities regarding Jews and anti-Semitism after the Holocaust affected the depiction of Jews in the story of Jesus' condemnation and death, and whether the impact of the feminist movement could be discerned in the portrayal of the women in Jesus' life, as it could in the lives of real women throughout the latter third of the twentieth century. In other words, what made these movies both interesting and fun for me was the act of viewing them as reflections, however imperfect or dim, of trends within our own society and culture.

Jesus movies of course are by no means unique in their use of the past as a vehicle for contemplating the present. Indeed, this tendency is characteristic of the historical film more generally. As film historian Leger Grindon notes:

> From the earliest days of their artistic practice, film-makers have engaged in the centuries-old tradition of grappling with the present by writing about the past.... [Historical film is a] means by which the cinema associated past events with contemporary issues that it seeks to explain.... The historical film indulges its contact with the immediate and generally refuses the past its distinct and foreign character. As a result, history in the cinema is seldom disinterested, but rather constitutes an address to the present.[9]

The very idea of making a Jesus movie implies the filmmaker's conviction that Jesus and his story continue to be meaningful.

That the Jesus movies draw upon and speak directly to our own cultural experiences is evident in their numerous references to well-known cultural products and historical events. In Young's *Jesus*, Joseph takes the young Jesus and his cousin John (the future Baptist) on their first visit to Jerusalem. As the city comes into view, Joseph points to the Temple and exclaims, "Jesus, John, we're not in Nazareth anymore." Viewers will recognize this as a paraphrase of Dorothy's famous line in *The Wizard of Oz*: "I don't think we're in Kansas anymore, Toto." The physical setting of *The Greatest Story Ever Told* recalls the classic Western films. Like the "bad guys" who rode into the western frontier terrorizing decent, God-fearing settlers in films like *Pale Rider* and *Shane*, the Romans rode into the dusty villages of the Galilee, striking fear into the local Jewish population.[10] In the dream sequence of *The Last Temptation of Christ*, Jesus reminds Paul, "We marched on Jerusalem," recalling the famous civil rights march on Washington in 1963. All films draw extensively upon familiar works of western religious art and music. Leonardo's *The Last Supper* often dictates the seating plan of the biopic Jesus and his disciples at their final meal

FIGURE 1a. Leonardo Da Vinci's *The Last Supper* (Alinari/Art Resource, New York)

(figures 1a, 1b), and the *Hallelujah Chorus* from Handel's oratorio, *The Messiah*, is the sound track to Jesus' most spectacular miracle—the raising of Lazarus— and even his own resurrection.[11]

But more than simply quoting from or alluding to the icons of western culture, the Jesus movies probe our deeper societal preoccupations, including gender roles, sexuality, and politics. Even as the Jesus biopics play out our society's fascination with Jesus as a historical and religious figure, they also address our own fears and anxieties, our comforts and joys, our beliefs and values.[12]

How do movies about the past address concerns of the present? The answer lies in their approach to and manipulation of their primary sources. In the case of the Jesus story, the primary sources are the Gospels of Matthew, Mark, Luke, and John, the first four books of the New Testament. It might seem a simple task to turn these sacred books into film; certainly they would appear to be less daunting than other works that have been successfully adapted to film, such as Tolstoy's *War and Peace* or the novels of Jane Austen. But while the Gospels are relatively short and straightforward from a narrative perspective, they nevertheless pose a number of serious challenges to the task of film adaptation.

In the first place, the Gospels do not present a single story of Jesus, but four different accounts. Filmmakers, like scholars, must grapple with the question of whether and how to resolve the contradictions among these versions of Jesus' biography.[13]

Second, the Gospels assert that Jesus of Nazareth is not only a human being but also the Son of God, the Messiah, the universal Savior. Jesus' sacred

FIGURE 1b. The Last Supper in *The Greatest Story Ever Told*

status within Christianity requires filmmakers to walk a fine line between creativity and reverence. On the one hand, they must fashion a plausible narrative of Jesus' life that will be accessible and compelling to their audiences. On the other hand, they risk boycott or financial failure if they stray too far from the portrait of Jesus that Christians, who constitute their principal viewers, recognize and accept.

A third problem is posed by the nature of the Gospels as literary texts. Not only do the Gospels vary with respect to the details and sequence of events in Jesus' life, but they also leave countless gaps. As narratives, the Gospels fail to provide filmmakers with the detailed biographical information that they need to tell the story effectively. What was Jesus up to from the age of twelve, when he taught the elders in the Temple (Luke 2:46), to the age of thirty or so, when he appears as an illness-healing, miracle-making, demon-exorcising itinerant preacher? What did he feel toward Joseph, his mother's husband? Did he drop in on his family when passing through the Galilee? Did he have any intimate relationships and, if so, with whom? What were his everyday likes and dislikes, his habits and pleasures?

Nor do the Gospels unequivocally address the major theological and historical questions with which scholars and ordinary believers alike must grapple: Did Jesus see himself as the Son of God and the Messiah, and, if so, what did these names mean to him? And what exactly happened in the days and hours leading to his execution, and in the three days that followed?

Furthermore, the Gospels provide precious few visual and aural clues for Jesus' cinematic portrayal. They do not tell us what Jesus and his family, friends, and opponents looked like, how they lived, what they wore, or what music they enjoyed. With regard to historical background, the Gospels refer to but do not fully describe a society characterized by complicated relationships within and among a variety of ethnic, political, and religious groups.

Gaps also exist between the Gospel accounts and other sources that pertain to the period and events that they recount. For example, Matthew's portrayal of Pilate as a fair-minded, even softhearted ruler who listens to his wife's concerns (Matthew 27:19) contradicts other ancient sources, which present Pilate as ruthless and cruel (e.g. Philo's *Legatio ad Gaium*, 300–301). Elements of the Gospels clash with contemporary sensibilities. This is nowhere more obvious than in their portrayal of the Jews as the ones who bear moral responsibility for Jesus' death despite the fact that it was Pilate who condemned him.

The sheer number and variety of such gaps and contradictions might well sabotage any attempt to transform "Jesus of Nazareth" into "Jesus of Hollywood." But as I will argue in the pages that follow, it is these very gaps that allow and even account for the variety and sheer number of cinematic Jesuses. The Gospels' silence allows filmmakers to fill the void with their own creativity. In the space created by the Gospels' gaps, filmmakers can insert the details and the causal links between events required to fill out the characters and to fashion a connected, plausible narrative that tells the story of Jesus within the limited time and budget at their disposal.

The fact that filmmakers reshape Jesus' story to reflect the concerns of their own times should not be condemned as a distortion of the past merely for the sake of entertainment and box office appeal, though these factors are not irrelevant. Rather, the varieties of Jesus on the silver screen testify to the conviction that Jesus remains relevant to our society; there is an ongoing need to tell and retell this story, in Hollywood and in other international cinematic centers in which commercial films are made. Viewing the Jesus movies as a vehicle through which filmmakers reflect upon their own time and place not only makes these movies more interesting and more fun but also allows us to see them as a starting point for understanding ourselves.

This book focuses on the interplay between "Jesus of Nazareth" and "Jesus of Hollywood." Throughout I will argue that the Jesus of the biopics reflects our own societies and cultures more than he illuminates the historical Jesus whose story these movies purport to tell.

Before we begin, two methodological considerations are in order. The first pertains to "Jesus of Nazareth." Filmmakers and historical-Jesus researchers alike must make sense of multiple and inconsistent sources in order to create a single, coherent, and persuasive narrative line. But whereas New Testament scholars absorb from their first year of studies the taboo of using one Gospel to interpret, amplify, or correct a problem that arises in another Gospel, film-makers are under no such constraint. The fact that most Jesus biopics blur the differences among the Gospels has significant methodological implications for the present study. In order to consider the ways in which the films fill in the gaps within the Gospel accounts, some degree of comparison between the films and the Gospels is required. The initial reflex of a New Testament scholar would be to respect the integrity of each individual Gospel through-out this comparison.[14] But to do so in a thematic study such as this one would undermine the exercise as a whole. The harmonizing approach used in most Jesus biopics requires us also to smooth over the differences among the Gospels and thus to compare the films to a constructed composite of the Gospels in which details are pulled from all four sources with little regard to their original context. This approach goes against the basic instincts of this writer, as it surely will for some readers of this book, but it is warranted, even required, by the ways in which the filmmakers themselves approach their sources.

The second methodological point pertains to "Jesus of Hollywood." The title of the present book notwithstanding, our study is not limited to films produced in Hollywood. Rather, "Hollywood" serves as shorthand for the com-mercial film industry in general. In using this term, my intention is neither to homogenize nor to overlook the distinctions within and among the American, Canadian, European, and other global film industries. Indeed, participants in non-American film rightly point to the profound differences in style and sen-sibility among the national cinemas. Nonetheless, it can be argued that, in com-mon parlance, "Hollywood" symbolizes commercial cinema's mass appeal, marketing strategies, and financial impetus. Furthermore, in the case of the Jesus films, it is the Hollywood films that have established the norms and con-ventions that other cinemas have adopted, adapted, and critiqued.[15]

This book builds on the work of others, including the helpful catalogue of Jesus films by Roy Kinnard and Tim Davis, entitled *Divine Images: A History of Jesus on the Screen*; studies of the major films by Baugh; Stern, Jefford, and De Bona; Tatum; and Zwick;[16] Babington and Evans' superb work on the epic genre; and the recent, insightful works by Walsh and by Christianson, Francis, and Telford.[17] My debts to these and other studies will be evident throughout these pages.

We begin, in the following chapter, by examining the ways in which the Jesus film genre simultaneously stakes and also undermines its claim to historical accuracy. The subsequent chapters trace the transformation of Jesus of Nazareth to Jesus of Hollywood via the common biopic template, looking specifically at his relationships with the key people in his life: his family, his friends, and his foes. Through these relationships we will see clearly just how the Jesus biopics construct the historical context into which he was born, his conflict with the powers that be, and the climactic trial that results in his condemnation. Throughout, the study will draw attention to the gaps and contradictions with which filmmakers must contend, and reflect upon what Jesus of Hollywood can tell us about the preoccupations of our own society over the hundred-year history of the cinema.

But first...a few words about the movies themselves.

The Jesus Movies: A Brief History

Jesus biopics span all eras and genres of cinema, on big screen and small. The majority attempt to give a full biography of Jesus, whereas others cover only a portion of Jesus' life, most frequently the events of Jesus' Passion from the betrayal to the resurrection.[18]

Jesus also appears in two types of films that are outside the biopic genre as such. One is the so-called peplum movie, otherwise known as the "sword-and-sandal" movie.[19] In these films, Jesus appears briefly within the fictional story of another character who may be purely imaginary (Demetrius, Judah Ben-Hur) or whose appearances in the Gospel provide us with virtually no information (Salome, Barabbas). Because they are fictional, peplum films develop a pious Christian theme while avoiding the historical problems associated with the Jesus genre *per se*. Examples include *Ben-Hur* (1925, 1959), *Salome* (1923, 1953), *The Big Fisherman* (1959, featuring Peter), and *Barabbas* (1962).

A second type is the "Passion play" movie. Passion play films present a fictional frame narrative about the preparation and performance of a Passion play; scenes from the Passion play itself are usually presented as well. Examples include *Jesus of Montreal* (1989) and *The Master and Margareth* (*Master i Margarita*, Russia, 1994). *Jesus Christ Superstar* technically belongs to this subgroup, in that occasional details remind us that we are watching a group of actors stage a Passion play, but there is no narrative associated with the contemporary frame. At the opposite end of the spectrum is the 1957 French/Italian film, *Celui Qui Doit Mourir* (*He Who Must Die*), which focuses so intensely on the frame narrative that the actual Passion play is never performed.

The Silent Era

The first known example of a Jesus movie is *The Passion Play at Oberammergau* (1898). While it claimed to be an authentic film of the Passion play performed periodically at Oberammergau, Germany,[20] this nineteen-minute movie was actually staged and filmed on the roof of the Grand Central Palace in New York, using props and costumes that had been created for a New York stage production that was shut down before its first performance. Even after the public learned that this movie was a "faked re-creation" of the Oberammergau production, the film remained immensely popular.[21]

The Passion Play at Oberammergau and other early silent films about Jesus, such as *From the Manger to the Cross* (1913) and *Christus* (1917), present a series of slow-moving tableaux. These tableaux are often set up in imitation of popular devotional paintings or of famous paintings by Leonardo Da Vinci, Donatello, and Rembrandt.[22] Jesus is invariably a tall, bearded, solemn and majestic figure whose piercing gaze is accentuated by a ring of black eye-liner. His white-robed figure is well-lit in contrast to his surroundings, creating a halo effect that reverently evokes Jesus' sanctity. These films presume the viewer's knowledge of the Gospels or at least of the general story line. Their goal is not to create a complex or unified narrative, but to illustrate the relevant Gospel scenes.

Some silent Jesus movies move beyond such formulaic presentations to emphasize specific aspects of Jesus' life. The 1921 German film *Der Galiläer* (*The Galilean*) goes further than most other movies of this period in its use of standard anti-Semitic tropes. Its Jewish characters are caricatures—physically repugnant, hate-mongering, avaricious, and ridiculous. The 1923 film *INRI*, reissued as a "talkie" in 1934 (as *The Crown of Thorns*), fleshes out the character of Jesus' mother, transforming her from a virginal maiden to a resourceful, adventurous, and assertive woman who will go to any lengths to be with her son in his moment of need.

The most interesting Jesus-related film of this period is D. W. Griffith's classic, *Intolerance* (1916). This film may have been intended to compensate for, or perhaps to undo, the damage done to Griffith's reputation by his magnum opus, *The Birth of a Nation* (1915), which, even as its brilliance was acknowledged, was also condemned for its highly positive portrayal of the Ku Klux Klan.[23] *Intolerance* weaves the story of Jesus together with three other narratives to illustrate the struggle between tolerance and intolerance through the ages. The central narrative thread is "The Modern Story," which relates the trials and tribulations that an intolerant, pious, and meddling group of powerful women called "the Uplifters" inflict upon a young, sweet couple called "the Boy and the

Dear One." Though brief, "The Judean Story" is crucial to Griffith's theme. Jesus' enemies among the Pharisees are portrayed as the prototype of the intolerant Uplifters of the Modern Story, while Jesus' crucifixion is directly compared to the travails of the Boy and the Dear One.[24]

The most famous Jesus film of the silent period is Cecil B. DeMille's *The King of Kings* (1927). In contrast to earlier films, DeMille's movie paid attention to character development and causality, creating a coherent plot and several subplots. Its intertitles not only quote from scripture and provide background information, but also convey witty dialogue as well as the narrator's commentary on the characters and events that it portrays. DeMille's work had a major influence on the Jesus biopic genre, and we shall return to it frequently throughout the present study.

With the exception of DeMille's film, the silent Jesus is often not much more than an animated version of the illustrated Jesus found in Bible storybooks and devotional literature. No doubt the limitations of the silent genre itself, which was superseded soon after DeMille's film was released, contributed to this cardboard treatment. But reluctance to offend public mores also played a part. Filmmakers met the challenge of portraying the son of God by stripping him of all human affect and robbing him of the ability to engage in normal human relationships and behavior.

Hiatus

The first major talkie about Jesus was the 1935 French film, *Golgotha*, directed by Julien Duvivier and released in the United States as *Ecce Homo* (*Behold the Man*). While critically acclaimed, this film did not receive the same attention internationally as did DeMille's silent classic and the later epics. Indeed, after DeMille's film the Jesus biopic machine in Hollywood went into hiatus. No major movie about Jesus was released for over thirty years, until the early 1960s.[25] True, there were films such as *The Robe* (1953) and *Ben-Hur* (1959) that depict scenes from Jesus' life, such as the Last Supper or the Passion, in the course of telling a fictional tale. But from DeMille's 1927 classic *The King of Kings* (1927) until Samuel Ray's *King of Kings* (1961), Hollywood studiously avoided placing Jesus at the center of a film.[26]

Some commentators attribute this lengthy silence to the extraordinary success of DeMille's *The King of Kings*. This film, they argue, left no room for competitors until narrative and technological norms had undergone significant change.[27] While DeMille's success may have been one factor, surely movie censorship played a role.[28] In 1930, the Motion Picture Producers and Distributors of America adopted a Production Code, which, in 1934, was endorsed and promoted by the powerful Catholic Legion of Decency.[29] From 1930 to 1966, no film could appear in American movie theatres unless it was certified by the Production Code Administration (PCA). Films which did not conform to the Code were subject to censorship.

The Code contained detailed guidelines on a wide range of issues that were seen as pertinent to American values.[30] For example, the Code forbade films to question marriage as an institution, or to portray "impure" love as attractive and beautiful. Films were not permitted to depict "ministers of religion" as comic characters or as villains "because the attitude taken toward them may easily become the attitude taken toward religion in general." Films were to present "correct standards of life" and to "hold up for admiration high types of characters" as well as to "present stories that will affect lives for the better."

The Production Code required a high standard of reverence in any representations of Jesus and forbade filmmakers from "throwing ridicule" on any religious faith. According to James Skinner, film was singled out as a medium that needed controlling due to the extraordinary power of the visual image. But criticism of the film media also stemmed in part from discomfort with the major role that immigrant Jews were playing in the film industry. "The increasing domination of the motion picture business by Jews, who had largely replaced the mostly white Anglo-Saxon pioneers, caused an escalation in criticism that had nasty undertones of racial and religious intolerance."[31] Controlling the content of the movies would also limit the appeal and hence the financial success of these less-than-desirable elements in American society.

Censorship was not limited to the United States. The British Board of Film Censors, founded in 1912, banned the visual depiction of Jesus. The ban was not lifted until after World War II. DeMille's *The King of Kings* could be screened in London only after a special license was obtained; Jesus was edited out of films such as *Golgotha* (1935) that were produced elsewhere but distributed in England.[32] This may also have been the reason for the absence of a "full frontal" view of Jesus in *Ben-Hur* which, though made in the United States, was also intended for British distribution.

The Epics

The cinematic Jesus did not fare much better in the first sound film about him, the little known 1935 French production *Golgotha*, also called *Ecce Homo* (*Behold the Man*). But when Jesus reappeared in the epic films of the early 1960s, he was treated in a much more dramatic if still highly reverential manner. Two major epics were released in relatively short order: *King of Kings*, directed by Nicholas Ray (1961), and *The Greatest Story Ever Told*, directed by George

Stevens (1965). Like DeMille's film, these movies emphasize causality; they fill in the gaps in the Gospel accounts in order to unify and clarify the plot. Their settings are grand and the cast of characters long. Their two Jesus figures, however, are very different from one another. The Jesus of *King of Kings* was an attractive youth (Jeffrey Hunter) who broke the mold of solemn Jesus figures and thereby spawned the film's derisive nickname, "I Was a Teenage Jesus."[33] The star of *The Greatest Story Ever Told*, Max von Sydow, was a gaunt, as yet unknown European actor who took Son-of-God solemnity to new heights. In contrast to most movie Jesuses, Sydow remains well groomed and perfectly coiffed throughout all his trials and tribulations.

The epic peplum films of this era were generally set in the period immediately after Jesus' death. The most famous film of this type, and an all-time cinematic classic, is *Ben-Hur* (1959, a remake of the original silent movie from 1925). The main plot traces the conflict between Judah Ben-Hur, a Jewish prince, and Messala, a high-ranking Roman officer. Scenes from the Sermon on the Mount and the Passion remind us that the Jesus story is running in the background concurrently and occasionally intersecting with the main fictional plot.[34] Jesus, or more precisely, Christian faith, hovers over the entire film, mediated for both the hero and the viewer through the words of the beautiful and pious Esther, Ben-Hur's love interest.

Films like *Ben-Hur* present Jesus in a reverential manner while still including the features such as spectacle (notably, *Ben-Hur*'s famous chariot race) and romance that were de rigueur in this period. Yet they also qualify as religious movies in their own right. Although they do not focus primarily on Jesus' life story, they illustrate the power of the Christian message and posit some sort of immortality or afterlife for Jesus through the impact that he has on people's lives. *Ben-Hur*, along with *The Greatest Story Ever Told*, *Kings of Kings*, and DeMille's 1956 *The Ten Commandments*, are the classics of the biblical epic genre as a whole.[35]

The Musicals

Most Jesus movies, both before and after the studio era, are dramas, in keeping with the tragic plot structure of the Gospel narratives. The year 1973 saw two exceptions: the musicals *Jesus Christ Superstar* and *Godspell*.[36] Both of these films were sound recordings and Broadway stage productions before they appeared on the silver screen, and both were influenced by the Jesus movement of the 1960s and 1970s. They implicitly propose an answer to the question of how a "hippie" Jesus would look and sound.

Jesus Christ Superstar depicts the staging of a Passion play in the Negev desert in southern Israel. The film portrays Jesus as a (Super)star who, like

Hollywood movie stars, is surrounded by a cult of celebrity that distorts his message, neutralizes it, removes its substance, and renders it incapable of sustaining the burden of starstruck crowds. Stardom reduces Jesus to a publicity-driven Hollywood figure in danger of losing his sense of self and the raison d'être of his own mission. In this sense, even as it takes its place among other Jesus biopics, this musical can be seen as a critique of the Hollywood star system that both feeds and is fed by the biopic genre.

In contrast to the superficial and self-centered savior of *Superstar*, the Jesus of *Godspell* is a winsome clown, brimming with warmth, friendship, and ethical maxims. *Godspell* makes no attempt to be realistic. The clown Jesus is surrounded by a group of young men and women who frolic with him through the streets, parks, and back alleys of a strangely quiet New York City. With the exception of Jesus, the figures in the film are not matched one on one with figures known from the Gospels; the same actor, for example, assumes the roles of John the Baptist and Judas, while the others take on and cast off roles as needed. The narrative line is very loose, with no clear causal development or plot.

While the songs might be catchy, the musical genre is ill-equipped to handle the drama of the Jesus story. It is therefore not surprising that there have been no mainstream additions to this list since 1973.[37]

The Dramas

Most of the Jesus films made from 1966 to the present day have been feature dramas, produced for commercial release and/or television broadcast. While many are products of Hollywood, that is, the American movie machinery, some of the most compelling films have emerged in other countries. Perhaps the most highly regarded Jesus movie is Pier Paoli Pasolini's *Il Vangelo secondo Matteo* (*The Gospel According to Saint Matthew*, 1964). This Italian film, shot in black and white with a handheld camera, takes all of its dialogue and most of its narrative from the Gospel of Matthew. Pasolini's Jesus is a passionate, angry young man who leads his group of peasant disciples in protest against the injustices of the established religious and political authorities. Almost none of the actors are professionals. The role of Jesus' mother in her maturity is played by Pasolini's own mother; the disciples and crowds are played by rural villagers. Pasolini's Marxist perspective pervades the film, but for many viewers this does not detract from the power of the savior figure.

A lesser-known but fascinating Jesus movie is Roberto Rossellini's *The Messiah* (*Il Messias*, 1975), which due to distribution difficulties was never commercially released in North America.[38] Rossellini's film, like Pasolini's, evokes the simple rural life. Jesus, his mother, and his followers, both male and female, spend much of their time on the shores of the Sea of Galilee, where they fish, mend nets, bake and cook as they tell stories and share spiritual insights.

The American-made and/or produced feature films in the 1970s and later, such as Franco Zeffirelli's lengthy made-for-TV series *Jesus of Nazareth* (1977), John Heyman's *Jesus* (1979), and Robert Young's miniseries by the same name (*Jesus*, 1999), exhibit the main features of the studio biopic that Custen has identified. Similarly, the British animated film, *The Miracle Maker* (2000), though novel with regard to its medium, remains quite conventional in its narrative. This film uses sophisticated stop-motion, computer, and traditional two-dimensional animation techniques to tell the story from the point of view of Jairus' daughter, a young girl whom Jesus raises from the dead or near dead, according to Mark 5:22–43.[39] This film borrows significantly from Zeffirelli's magnum opus, but attempts to tell the story in a way that is more accessible to young people.

Spoofs of the Jesus Biopic Genre

The clichés of the Jesus movie genre inspired a number of spoofs, the best known and loved of which is *Monty Python's Life of Brian*. Though it is a "Brian" movie and not a "Jesus" movie, *Life of Brian* both uses and mocks the clichés of the genre.[40] The fictional Brian is an unintentional and reluctant messiah whose life parallels Jesus' biography in its public nature and tragic death, without the reverence, sanctity, and perfection of the hero or the virginity of his mother. Despite the fictional premise of the spoof, *Life of Brian* is meticulously researched and gleefully intelligent. The film spares no one, except for Jesus himself. Its hilarious darts are aimed at the conventions of Jesus' portrayal in film and popular culture, as well as at targets such as the British school system.

A second, lesser-known spoof, Luis Bunuel's *La Voie Lactée* (*The Milky Way*, 1969), concerns two pilgrims from France who go on pilgrimage to Santiago de Compostela and have some theological adventures along the way, including flashbacks to first-century Palestine.[41] Bunuel's main targets are Catholic theology and popular belief, but the biopic Jesus also comes in for his share of ridicule.

Recent Contributions

The last twenty-five years have seen four major additions to the corpus of Jesus films that differ considerably from one another and vary in their adherence to the conventions of the biopic genre. Martin Scorsese's *The Last Temptation of Christ* (1988) opens with a scrolling text asserting that the film is based not on the Gospels but on the novel by Nikos Kazantzakis. This claim is somewhat disingenuous, in that the film involves the same cast of characters and narrative line as other Jesus biopics. By disclaiming historicity, however, Scorsese is free to explore areas that conventional Jesus movies leave untouched. In the final section of the film, Jesus, while still alive, is led down from the cross by a young, red-haired girl claiming to be his guardian angel. He marries, has children, and lives to a ripe old age. Only at the end do we learn that this sequence is a dream or hallucination; Jesus dies on the cross in this film as in every other Jesus biopic. But the mere suggestion that Jesus may have desired sexual intimacy and the domestic life was enough to trigger protests, angry letters, and editorials even before the film was released.[42]

The following year saw the release of the Quebec-made *Jesus of Montreal* (1989) directed by Denys Arcand. The film portrays a group of actors that has been commissioned by the priest of St. Joseph's Oratory in Montreal to refresh the Passion play that has been performed on the church grounds for decades. In the process of preparing and performing the play, the actors themselves take on the personas of the characters in the Gospel story. This blurring of identity is typical among actors who stage a Passion play, as the experience of the villagers in Oberammergau, the site of the most well-known Passion play, suggests. James Shapiro comments:

> ... in Oberammergau people don't say someone *acted* or *played the part of* Caiaphas; they say he *was* Caiaphas; in the minds of many of the performers—and of their fellow villagers—acting goes well beyond ordinary impersonation. When a cyclist whizzes by, a local is likely to tell a visitor, "There goes Pilate." Everyone seems to know who had which of the hundred or so speaking parts in the play, and how well they performed, going back decades. And they are frank in their judgments. It's like living in a village populated entirely by theater critics.[43]

Arcand's film is the most thoroughly allegorical of the Jesus biopic genre. Virtually every detail of the Gospel stories, and many aspects of New Testament and historical Jesus scholarship are present, or, more accurately, concealed, for the knowledgeable viewer to discern.

More recently, Philip Saville directed *The Gospel of John* (2003). This film has the distinction of being the only full-length feature in which every single word of a Gospel, in this case, the Good News Bible version of the Fourth Gospel, is spoken. At the same time, it tries to overcome the liability of many Jesus movies, namely, an overabundance of words. This is a challenge particularly with regard to the Gospel of John, in which Jesus often discourses at extraordinary length virtually uninterrupted by any dialogue or action. Thanks to the skill of the camera operators and the actor, this Jesus manages—if barely—to keep our attention throughout the nearly five chapters of farewell speeches that John inserts between the final supper and the betrayal in the garden (John 13–17).[44]

Finally, we must not overlook Mel Gibson's *The Passion of the Christ* (2004, released in slightly altered form in 2005). Like *The Passion Play at Oberammergau, Golgotha,* and *Jesus Christ Superstar,* Gibson's film is an account of Jesus' final hours. Its heavy-handed violence and its negative representations of the Jewish authorities touched off a major controversy that may well have contributed to its box-office success. Viewers who do not already know the story in some detail may well be puzzled by the plotline of the film; on its own, the film does not provide enough information for viewers to know what Jesus has done to raise the ire of Jews and Romans alike or why he is subjected to such violence culminating in death on the cross. In this regard Gibson's film resembles the early silent movies much more than it does the epics or later dramas. It seems that we have come full circle, from the faked *Passion Play at Oberammergau* to the overwrought *Passion of the Christ.*

Conclusion

As Richard Wightman Fox has noted, it is Jesus' fate to be "perpetually reborn in one culture after another.... His incarnation guaranteed that each later culture would grasp him anew for each would have a different view of what it meant to be human. Jesus had to be reborn if he was going to inspire or even make sense to people in every era."[45] Our study of Jesus' celluloid incarnations through the last hundred years and more will look at how the Jesus biopics, like other biographical films, reshape the past in the image of the present, out of conviction that the past, or their versions thereof, continues to be relevant for audiences today.

2

History and Anti-History

What is the connection between the "reel" world of the biopic and the "real" world of its subject? Here is Cecil B. DeMille's answer:

> The events portrayed by this picture occurred in Palestine nineteen centuries ago, when the Jews were under the complete subjection of Rome—even their own High Priest being appointed by the Roman procurator.
>
> Cecil B. DeMille

The King of Kings, says DeMille, portrays real events that occurred in a specific place (Palestine) and historical era (when the Jews were under Roman subjugation). Other features of the title statement, such as its placement at the film's opening, its didactic tone, its faintly Gothic font, and DeMille's famous and, by Hollywood standards, authoritative signature, bolster its claim to historicity.

The epics of the 1950s and early '60s similarly proclaim the historicity of their accounts, often through a solemn and sonorous "voice-of-God" narrator.[1] The unidentified but eminently recognizable narrator of *King of Kings*, Orson Welles, states the following "facts":

> And it is written, that in the year 63 BC the Roman Legions like a scourge of locusts poured through the east laying waste to the land of Canaan and the kingdom of Judea. Rome's

imperial armies went unto the hills and struck Jerusalem's walls in a three-month siege. Reaching the gates, these legions laid the dust of battle in a shower of blood.

When it comes to the political and religious background of Jesus' life, the Jesus biopics often draw on the work of the ancient historian Josephus Flavius. But in their accounts of the events of Jesus' life as such, they rely on the Gospels of Matthew, Mark, Luke, and John, on the assumption that these canonical texts preserve reliable historical information. If the Gospels are historical accounts, then a film based on these Gospels will also be historical, or close enough. Roberto Rossellini, the director of the 1975 Italian film *The Messiah* (*Il Messias*), explains:

> I do not want to invent, or to interpret the Old and New Testaments— but just to present it in "quotes." I attempt to reconstruct every- thing accurately—you have to do this precisely and objectively in order to portray the truth. *The Messiah* will thus present the historical Jesus as portrayed in the Four Gospels through an accurate devel- opment of the principal events of his life.[2]

The moviegoing audience may well share the filmmakers' assumptions that the Gospels are history. As Mark Goodacre notes with regard to Gibson's *The Passion of the Christ*:

> ... the distinction between "historically accurate" and "faithful to Scripture" is a distinction that would make little sense to many of its Christian viewers. For the fundamentalist, historical accuracy is di- rectly continuous with faithfulness to Scripture, and any attempt to differentiate them would be at best simply academic.[3]

To be sure, belief in the accuracy of the Gospels is fostered by the Gospels themselves. The Gospels of Luke and John in particular assert their own his- toricity. The Gospel of Luke begins with a brief prologue addressed to Theo- philus, an individual who may have been the author's patron:[4]

> Since many have undertaken to set down an orderly account of the events that have been fulfilled among us, just as they were handed on to us by those who from the beginning were eyewitnesses and ser- vants of the word, I too decided, after investigating everything care- fully from the very first, to write an orderly account for you, most excellent Theophilus, so that you may know the truth concerning the things about which you have been instructed.[5]

Luke's prologue suggests that his "orderly account" is "the truth" based on careful investigation of the facts.[6] The Gospel of John emphasizes the reliability of the witness whose testimony it claims to record: "He who saw this has testified so that you also may believe. His testimony is true, and he knows that he tells the truth" (John 19:35). This witness, the so-called Beloved Disciple, "is the disciple who is testifying to these things and has written them, and we know that his testimony is true" (John 21:24).

The Gospels and History

Despite such explicit statements, there is good reason to question the historical accuracy of the Gospel narratives. In the first place, the Gospels contradict each other frequently in ways that cannot easily be resolved. For example, did Jesus' ministry take place over a year-long period, beginning in Galilee and culminating with his trip to Jerusalem immediately before the Passover, as the Gospels of Matthew, Mark, and Luke (collectively known as the Synoptic Gospels) suggest? Or did Jesus travel numerous times between Galilee and Jerusalem, preaching and doing signs and wonders for two and a half or even three years, as the Gospel of John would have us believe?

The length of the ministry is a minor challenge compared to other chronological discrepancies. The presence or absence of specific events in particular gospels can be accommodated on the basic principle that no book could possibility contain *all* of Jesus' deeds (cf. John 20:30–31). But what does one do about events that are recounted in all four Gospels but at different points in the narrative? The Synoptics place Jesus' "Temple tantrum" ("the cleansing of the Temple")[7] at the end of his ministry, implying that this violent act precipitated the fatal plot against Jesus. In John, however, Jesus evicts the moneychangers during the first Passover of his three-year ministry (2:13–22). While this act garners him some attention, it does not directly lead to overt hostility or violence against him. For the Fourth Evangelist, it is the resurrection of Lazarus (John 11), an act absent from the Synoptics, that is the catalyst for the plot against Jesus (cf. 11:47–53).

Perhaps the most significant and irreconcilable difference concerns the chronology of the Passion. All Jewish festivals begin at sundown; the evening meal is, in effect, the first meal of the new day. For the Synoptics, the Last Supper is necessarily a Passover *seder* (ceremonial meal), for it takes place on the first evening of Passover (e.g., Mark 14:12–16). In John, however, the final dinner takes place the night before Passover eve and therefore is not a Passover seder (John 13:1–4). Indeed, John takes care to note that Jesus' body had to be removed from the cross before sundown in order not to interfere with the onset of the Passover festival (19:31). For both John and the Synoptics, the association with Passover is important, as Passover is the season when the Jewish people look back to the exodus from Egypt and ahead to the moment when God will once more intervene in history to redeem God's people. For believers in Jesus, his coming is this very intervention, and their faith in Jesus as the Messiah has assured them of salvation. In this broad sense, it does not matter much whether the crucifixion took place on the Passover itself or on the previous day.

But this chronological detail does affect the question of the origins of the Eucharist. Whereas the Synoptic Gospels have Jesus identify the bread and wine consumed during the Passover seder as his own body and blood, John does not associate the Eucharist with Jesus' final Passover. Instead, Jesus' declaration that his followers must consume his body and blood comes in the "bread of life" discourse that Jesus delivers after the miracle of the loaves and fishes. This event is said to have taken place at or around the time of Passover (John 6:4), but it is most definitely not a "last supper," nor is it an intimate meal with the disciples alone. Rather it is a public feast for thousands of men, women, and children who eat their fill of bread and fish.[8] Here, then, are contradictions that cannot be resolved.[9] Historians and filmmakers alike must make their choices.

A second factor is the obvious literary relationship among the three Synoptic Gospels. At first blush it might seem that the relative consistency among the three Synoptic Gospels means that they are more historically accurate than John's lone voice.[10] But the strong similarities among all three both in their content and in the order of events they describe can be explained only on the grounds of literary dependence. Indeed, many scholars believe that the authors of Matthew and Luke used Mark's Gospel, or an earlier version thereof, as the main source for the narrative portions of their own compositions. Similarly, the substantial amount of word-for-word agreement between Matthew's and Luke's versions of Jesus' sayings suggests to many scholars that they had access to a second literary source, no longer extant. This source is usually referred to as "Q" (from the German "Quelle," meaning "source").[11] Whether one holds by this two-source hypothesis or by some other theory, the fact remains that these literary features imply considerable literary interdependence among the Synoptic Gospels; it is extremely unlikely that they are three discrete accounts of the life of Jesus, written without knowledge of the others.[12]

Perhaps, then, Mark, which, according to the two-source hypothesis is the earliest gospel, may also be our best historical source. Unfortunately, this is also unlikely. Mark, like the other Gospels, tells Jesus' story from a particular, theological perspective that shapes the narrative.[13] In Mark's case, the controlling theme is that of the "messianic secret."[14] In Mark 1:44–45, for example, Jesus heals a leper, warns him sternly, and then sends him away with solemn instructions to keep the matter to himself: "See that you say nothing to anyone; but go, show yourself to the priest, and offer for your cleansing what Moses commanded, as a testimony to them." But the newly healed leper could not resist: "He went out and began to proclaim it freely, and to spread the word, so that Jesus could no longer go into a town openly, but stayed out in the country; and people came to him from every quarter" (1:44–45). Mark's Gospel asserts that most human beings, like the healed leper, did not understand the significance of Jesus' deeds during his lifetime, nor did they comprehend his messianic identity until after his death. Mark tells his story not so much in order to provide a straightforward history as to emphasize the theme of messianic secrecy.

Gospels and the Biopics

How, then, do filmmakers navigate among these contradictory, fragmentary, and theologically motivated sources? The path of least resistance is to choose only one of the four Gospels as a source text, thereby eliminating the need to negotiate among the various Gospel portraits of Jesus. Philip Saville's *The Gospel of John* follows this line most consistently. His film reproduces virtually every word of the Good News translation of the Fourth Gospel, and in doing so depicts every act and deed recorded in that Gospel, in the order in which it appears in the written text. For *The Gospel According to Saint Matthew*, Pasolini similarly did not create any dialogue but used only what he found in the Gospel of Matthew. Unlike Saville, however, Pasolini omitted and rearranged some of his source material.[15] Heyman's *Jesus* is based primarily on the Gospel of Luke, but it does not refrain from quoting or paraphrasing text from other books of the New Testament nor from inventing material out of whole cloth.[16]

The one-Gospel approach can relax the claim to historicity by allowing filmmakers to focus on the cinematic interpretation of a single source text rather than the construction of the historical figure of Jesus as such. Gone is the need to resolve contradictory plot lines and, for Saville and Pasolini, the responsibility of creating plausible dialogue.

This path, however, still leaves a multitude of choices with regard to the visual and aural elements that are arguably far more important than dialogue in conveying the mood and message of any film. Jesus, his family, his compatriots, and his enemies must still be portrayed visually, and the film must still have a soundtrack.

Pasolini in particular makes effective use of visual elements, which occasionally reframe or even subvert the literal meaning of the words or the context in which they are to be found in the Gospel of Matthew. For example, Herod's slaughter of infant boys, which Matthew describes as Herod's plot to ensure Jesus' death, is in Pasolini's movie perpetrated by the Roman army, as is apparent from their uniforms. Pasolini also invents entire scenes that are unaccompanied by dialogue, as when the Holy Family takes a rest stop at a stony beach on their way from Egypt back home to Nazareth. In this way he can technically stay true to his commitment to Matthew's text while exercising his own creativity. The camera work also adds detail and perspective. Whereas Matthew tells the story of the annunciation strictly from Joseph's point of view, Pasolini uses the camera to focus our attention on the confused emotions of the young, beautiful, and very pregnant, Mary. The soundtrack, which includes a broad range of music from classical (e.g. J. S. Bach, *St. Matthew's Passion*) to gospel (Odetta, singing "Sometimes I Feel Like a Motherless Child"), creates mood and adds depth throughout the film.

Despite its appeal, most filmmakers eschew the one-Gospel approach, opting instead to harmonize all four Gospels into a single narrative.[17] Many films side-step the contradictions between the Synoptic and Johannine traditions with respect to the length of Jesus' ministry by being vague as to its duration and geographical setting (Galilee or Judea). They freely harmonize the various versions of the same stories by drawing elements from each version. For example, the cinematic versions of Jesus' birth story combine Matthew's shining star and magi with Luke's manger and shepherds, to arrive at a stereotypical image that owes as much to Hallmark as to the New Testament. (This sequence is spoofed brilliantly in *Monty Python's Life of Brian*, in which the magi mistakenly come to the wrong manger to offer their lucrative gifts of gold, frankincense, and myrrh.) Harmonizing movies also use events that are unique to each tradition. For example, they almost always include the raising of Lazarus as Jesus' most spectacular miracle (John 11), though it is recounted only in John, and the Sermon on the Mount, Jesus' most famous discourse, though it occurs only in Matthew (Matthew 5–7).

A number of related motives guide the process of selection. One is simply the need to create a plausible and recognizable plot line. This need is less evident in the early silent movies that present Jesus' life as a series of living tableaux, for viewers are expected to fill in the gaps themselves. But Jesus films from the latter part of the silent era to the present day generally attempt to place events in a cause-effect relationship, according to cinematic convention.

For this reason, for example, Jesus biopics often trace Mary Magdalene's devotion to Jesus to his exorcism of her seven demons (cf. Luke 8:2–3) or (in films in which she is identified as the adulterous woman of John 7:53–8:10) to his intervention on her behalf when she is threatened with stoning.

A second factor affecting filmmakers' selections from the Gospel materials is, of course, the main message they want to convey (e.g., "Jesus is love"), as well as those they may want to avoid (e.g., "Pharisees are hypocrites"). For example, Jesus' diatribe against the Pharisees in Matthew 23 is avoided, curtailed, or softened in almost all of these movies. Where it is recited at any length at all, as in the films by Pasolini and Arcand, it is reinterpreted and redirected to a contemporary target, the Italian state in the case of Pasolini, and the Catholic clergy in Quebec in the case of Arcand.

A third factor is the audience's expectations. While the Gospels of Matthew, Mark, Luke, and John are canonical in their entirety, there are some parts that are better known and better loved than others. The wedding at Cana, the Sermon on the Mount, the feeding of the multitudes, the raising of Lazarus, the cleansing of the Temple, and, of course, the Passion, are the mainstays of any Jesus biopic of the harmonizing variety. Including these high spots helps to support the claim to historicity and completeness; even viewers who are not very familiar with the New Testament will recognize these events and may well believe them to be historical.

The more nuanced understanding of the relationship between the Gospels and history that scholars have long advocated has been taken to heart by at least some filmmakers. Denys Arcand, director of *Jesus of Montreal,* has the narrators of his Passion play categorically declare: "Disciples lie; they embellish." Yet on the whole, scholarly skepticism does not seem to have penetrated very deeply into the entertainment world, if Mel Gibson's comments are any indication. In an ABC interview with Diane Sawyer (February 18, 2004), Gibson repeatedly states that his movie bases itself squarely on the Gospels. While he does not deny that his film, and his own religiosity, are profoundly influenced by *The Dolorous Passion of Our Lord Jesus Christ,* by Anne Catherine of Emmerich (1833), he insists: "I didn't do a book [sic] on Anne Catherine Emmerich's Passion. . . . I did a book [sic] according to the Gospels." For Gibson, this means that his film also accords with the historical facts, since, in his view, the Bible is literally, historically true, in every respect. "You either accept the whole thing or don't accept it at all," he told Diane Sawyer.

In claiming to portray historical events, Jesus movies conform entirely to the conventions of the biopic genre as a whole. But a number of Jesus films strain at the limits of the genre, raising the question of whether they are within or outside its boundaries. Several films claim not only to be historical but also portray themselves as a meaningful foundation for Christian faith. The 1923 silent film INRI, for example, declares at the outset:

> INRI wants to speak in the simple language which appeals to all hearts. The teaching of Jesus is placed before everyone, rich and poor, great and humble; it is Love one another, even at the price of a great Sacrifice. It wants to lead the spectator's soul to the great aim which is common to all men and nations, the will to mutual help, the human love. Peace on Earth.

DeMille's *The King of Kings* begins with a similar declaration: "This is the story of Jesus of Nazareth.... He, Himself, commanded that His message be carried to the uttermost parts of the earth. May this portrayal play a reverent part in the spirit of that great command."

The most explicitly evangelical film is *Jesus* (1979; produced by John Heyman). The film concludes with a lengthy epilogue that addresses the viewers directly and urges them to pledge faith to Jesus, then and there, by repeating a faith formula that the narrator proceeds to recite. Even films that do not aim to propagate Christian faith generally portray believers in a positive light and may serve, if not to convert viewers, at least to reinforce their Christian faith.

Second, a small number of films make no claim at all to historicity. *Godspell* and *Jesus Christ Superstar* focus only on their subject's contemporary relevance. Peplum films such as *Ben-Hur*, *The Robe*, and *Quo Vadis* set out to tell a completely fictional tale.[18]

The Gospel of John, released just months before Gibson's film, does not explicitly query the historicity of the Fourth Gospel, but provides its viewers with an introductory text that scrolls down the screen prior to the opening scene:

> The Gospel of John was written two generations after the crucifix-
> ion of Jesus Christ. It is set in a time when the Roman Empire
> controlled Jerusalem. Although crucifixion was the preferred Roman
> method of punishment, it was not one sanctioned by Jewish law.
> Jesus and all his early followers were Jewish. The Gospel reflects
> a period of unprecedented polemic and antagonism between the
> emerging church and the religious establishment of the Jewish peo-
> ple. This film is a faithful representation of that Gospel.

Here there is no claim to historicity, but neither is there a denial thereof. The distinction between fidelity to scripture and fidelity to history, however, may well be lost on viewers who are not already familiar with the difficulties involved in using the Gospels as sources for historical Jesus research.

Most iconoclastic, however, are two films that challenge both the possibility and even the necessity of arriving at the historical facts about Jesus' life. Scorsese's 1988 *The Last Temptation of Christ* is an explicitly fictional account based on Nikos Kazantzakis' 1951 novel by the same name. Denys Arcand's *Jesus of Montreal*, which appeared one year later, mounts a powerful critique of the view of the Gospels as history. It may be pure coincidence that these films appeared so closely together. It is possible, however, that both filmmakers were aware of the controversies in historical Jesus research, which were receiving considerable media attention at the time.[19] At stake in these controversies was precisely the question of whether or to what extent it was possible to derive reliable historical information about Jesus from the Gospel accounts, an issue that comes to the fore in these two movies.

The Last Temptation of Christ

Like the early silent films, *The Last Temptation of Christ* opens with a scrolled text that instructs the reader as to its purpose. But in contrast to films like *INRI* and *The King of Kings*, Scorsese's film explicitly disavows any attempt either to recreate the historical Jesus or to encourage faith. The opening text stresses that the film is an adaptation not of the Gospels but of Nikos Kazantzakis's novel *The Last Temptation*.

> The dual substance of Christ—the yearning, so human, so superhuman, of man to attain God...has always been a deep inscrutable mystery to me. My principle [sic] anguish and source of all my joys and sorrows from my youth onward has been the incessant, merciless battle between the spirit and the flesh...and my soul is the arena where these two armies have clashed and met....This film is not based upon the Gospels but upon this fictional exploration of the eternal spiritual conflict.

As we have noted, the text's explicit dissociation of the movie from the Gospels is somewhat disingenuous. But it does prepare the viewer for a Jesus who, in his transparent weaknesses and torment, differs fundamentally from other cinematic Jesus figures, and from the Jesus of the Gospels as well.

Scorsese explicitly disengages history from scripture in the final dream sequence, in which a middle-aged Jesus, now a husband and father, comes face to face with the apostle Paul preaching in the village square. In an impassioned sermon, Paul recounts his own personal journey toward faith in Jesus as the Messiah; he describes the road to Damascus and his vision of Jesus, who spoke to him and persuaded him to stop persecuting the church and become his apostle:

> He [Jesus] made me see ... and he put his hands on me and I opened my eyes, and I was baptized and became Paul! And now I bring the good news to you! And it's about Jesus of Nazareth. He was not the son of Mary, he was the son of God! His mother was a virgin and the angel Gabriel came down and put God's seed in her womb, that's how he was born. And he was punished for our sins. *Our* sins. Then he was tortured and crucified, but three days later he rose up from the dead and went up to heaven. Death was conquered, Amen. Do you understand what that means? He conquered death! All our sins were forgiven and now the world of God is open to every one of us, to everybody!

Jesus confronts Paul angrily:

> Did you ever see this Jesus of Nazareth? After he came back from the dead, I mean with your own eyes?...I was never crucified, I never came back from the dead, I'm a man like everybody else!...Why are you telling these lies?...Don't try and tell me what happened to me because I know. I live like a man now, I work, eat, have children, I enjoy my life. For the first time I'm enjoying it. Do you understand what I'm saying? So don't go around telling lies about me or I'll tell everybody the truth!

Paul responds, in a conciliatory tone:

> Wait just a minute, what's the matter with you? Look around you, look at all these people. Look at their faces. Do you see how unhappy they are? Do you see how much they're suffering? Their only *hope* is the resurrected Jesus. I don't care whether you're Jesus or not! The resurrected Jesus will save the world and that's what matters....I created the truth out of what people needed, and what they believed. If I have to crucify you to save the world then I'll crucify you, and if I have to resurrect you then I'll do that too, whether you like it or not....You see, you don't know how much people need God, you don't know how happy he can make them. He can make them happy to do anything, he can make them happy to die, and

they'll die. All for the sake of Christ. Jesus Christ. Jesus of Nazareth, the Son of God, the Messiah. Not you, not for your sake (*pause*). You know, I'm glad I met you. Because now I can forget all about you. My Jesus is much more important and much more powerful. Thank you. It was a good thing I met you.

Paul walks away. Jesus rejoins his family, picks up his youngest child and hugs him tightly.

Paul's encounter with Jesus both changes and deepens his own sense of his mission. It is only now that Paul truly comprehends that the Christian message has meaning regardless of whether Jesus was crucified or not. The film consigns the connection between fidelity to scripture and historical accuracy to irrelevance. Still unresolved, however, is the question that Jesus raises: Can or should faith be based on lies? Does the fact that the people need the good news that Paul preaches justify the creation of a false history? These questions, while significant, become ironic when Scorsese's Jesus awakens from his dream and finds himself dying on the cross after all.

Freeing himself from the constraints of the Jesus film genre allows Scorsese to tackle the paradox and complexity of the Christological claim that Jesus is both human and divine. His Jesus struggles to understand his own words, deeds, and nature, and more important, God's will for him. Not for him the facile acceptance of death that we see in most movies about Jesus. His subjective return to the cross after his dream of surrender to the "last" temptation of domesticity marks a profound transformation and joyful subjection to God's will and confirmation, at long last, of his own divine sonship.

In the final analysis, this film queries the link between scripture and history but refrains from dismantling it. The biography of Scorsese's Jesus uses the same template as do the other Jesus biopics—he interacts with the social context into which he born, and has meaningful, if difficult, relationships with family and friends; he overcomes temptation in the desert, heals and preaches, confronts his enemies, and dies on the cross.[20] What differs is the emphasis on Jesus' anguished self-doubt. Scorsese's Jesus grows into his identity as Son of God, fully realizing it only at the moment of death, which for him, more than for other cinematic saviors, is a moment of sweet victory and peace.

Jesus of Montreal

Far more iconoclastic is Denys Arcand's *Jesus of Montreal*. This film presents a two-layered narrative: the fictional story of a group of actors struggling to make ends meet in late-twentieth-century Montreal, and the Passion play that they prepare and perform on the grounds of St. Joseph's Oratory atop Mount Royal. By portraying the actors' role in constructing or creating the Passion play, the movie foregrounds the notion that history itself is a construct.

The movie is open to interpretation on many levels. Anyone familiar with the Gospel accounts will recognize that the lives of Daniel and his fellow actors closely parallel the story of Jesus and his disciples. The role of John the Baptist is played by an actor who deprecates his own talent and points instead to that of Jesus. Like the Baptist, this actor loses his head, in his case to a female advertising tycoon who uses his image to advertise a new perfume called "Wild Man" ("l'homme sauvage"). The actors share a final dinner of pizza and wine; others order "Lobster Magdalene" and "Virgin Marys" at a restaurant.

Arcand challenges the link between history and scripture in two ways. First, he deconstructs the historicity of the traditional Jesus story that is based on a harmony of the Gospels and enshrined in the Apostles' Creed, children's stories, and popular belief. The traditional Jesus story is tackled straight on in a scene in which Daniel and his troupe rehearse the prologue to their Passion play. Our attention is drawn to Daniel's attempts to bolster Mireille's confidence in her acting ability. But the content of the scene, that is, the script that the players read out, explicitly focuses on the impossibility of constructing Jesus' full story from the sources at our disposal.

> [This is] the story of the Jewish prophet Yeshu Ben Panthera whom we all call Jesus. Historians of the day, Tacitus, Suetonius, Pliny, Flavius Josephus, mention him only in passing. What we know was pieced together by his disciples a century later. Disciples lie; they embellish. We don't know where he was born, or his age when he died. Some say 24, others 50. But we do know that on April 7 in year 30, or April 27 in year 31, or April 3 in year 33 he appeared before the fifth Roman procurator of Judea, Pontius Pilate.

Having raised doubts about the historical accuracy of the traditional Jesus story, Arcand takes a second step. Using ancient sources other than the New Testament, he constructs an alternative history for Jesus that fundamentally challenge the belief in the uniqueness of Jesus' identity. This construction, the film insists, is based on rigorous academic research. Daniel consults an eminent theologian in the Faculty of Theology at the University of Montreal. The theologian is very secretive, due to the control that the archdiocese exerts over the Faculty of Theology. He refuses to meet openly with Daniel, but he agrees to an encounter in an underground parking lot, far from prying eyes. The theologian tells Daniel: "There have been discoveries in archaeology since Israel annexed the territories. Computer analyses of texts that are incredible and new translations of the Talmud. We are beginning to understand who he really was. . . . I photocopied some articles. . . . Please don't tell anyone. It could get me into trouble."[21] The scholar's speech implies an essential opposition between the objective, scholarly construction of Jesus' life and the story sanctioned and controlled by the Church. He also places great faith in the ability of new texts, translations, and archaeological finds to illuminate the truth about Jesus, "who he really was."

Immediately after this conversation, we look over Daniel's shoulder as he sits in the theology library poring over scientific drawings of the crucifixion.[22] No doubt Daniel's version of the Passion play will be true to unassailable historical sources, not the "lies" and embellishments authored by the disciples. In this way, Arcand's film stakes its claim to historicity, but it is a history detached emphatically from the canonical Gospels.

The fruits of Daniel's research are evident in the narration that accompanies the dramatized segments of the Passion play itself. In this narration, the two female actors, Constance and Mireille, provide the historical context within which the new Passion play would have us place Jesus' birth, ministry, and death.

The Passion play targets the Christian belief that Jesus was born of a virgin mother. Referring to noncanonical sources, the narrative suggests that Jesus was in fact the illegitimate son of a Jewish woman and a Roman soldier named Panthera.

> The Jews claimed Christ was a false prophet, born of fornication. They called him Yeshu Ben Panthera, "the son of Panthera." We've discovered an order to transfer a soldier from Carpernaum in 6 A.D. His name was Panthera. Jews always referred to a man as "his father's son"—unless he was illegitimate. [The narrator now "reads" a Hebrew text on a computer screen.] "When Jesus returned home the villagers cried out: 'Is not this the carpenter? The son of Mary?'"

Arcand builds an elaborate argument for the notion that Jesus was an illegitimate child. The components of the argument are as follows: Jesus was a Jew, therefore we should give credence to his description in Jewish sources as the son of Panthera.[23] This identification is supported by two other pieces of evidence: the Roman order regarding the soldier Panthera and Mark's note that the Jews considered Jesus to be an illegitimate child.

After proposing this alternative to the biblical version of Jesus' conception, the Passion play addresses Jesus' ability to do miracles. In this segment, Constance and Mireille place Jesus' signs and wonders in the context of the magicians and miracle-workers known to us from ancient sources such as Josephus and the Church Fathers:

> This story is 2000 years old. Back then people thought the earth
> was flat, that stars were lamps hung on the firmament. They be-
> lieved in evil spirits, demons, miraculous cures, resurrection of the
> dead. The East swarmed with prophets, charlatans, magicians...Ju-
> das of Galilee...Simon the Magician....Jesus was also a magician.
> He was said to have grown up in Egypt, the cradle of magic. His
> miracles were more popular than his sermons.[24]

Here the ancient belief in magic and resurrection is put in the same category as other false beliefs, thereby placing Jesus in the dubious company of ancient magicians.[25] It therefore implies that belief in miracles is false, even primitive, and that Jesus' magical abilities were by no means unusual.

Even the crucifixion was not unique. Daniel's Passion play does not deny that Jesus was crucified; indeed, this seems to be the sole element of the biblical story that the Passion play upholds as historically accurate. But, as in the previous segment, the play sets Jesus' experience within the broader context of Judea in the Greco-Roman world. Jesus' manner of death was only too common in the world in which he lived. "Prisoners were whipped to speed their death. There were crucifixions every week in Jerusalem. This one was nothing special."

The authority attached to the alternative history constructed in the Passion play depends not only on the narrated information and the logic of the argumentation but also on the visual and performative elements of the narrators' presentation. The two narrators, Constance and Mireille, employ a didactic tone of voice; they recite facts and figures that would be unknown to a general audience and they refer explicitly if imprecisely to the ancient sources that support these facts. They demonstrate the ways in which sources may be brought together to construct an historical argument. They even employ the latest technology (at least, the latest as of 1989), including a laptop computer that displays the sources in Hebrew, an ancient and therefore authoritative language, which they apparently have the ability to translate into French directly from the screen. The implication is that their version of Jesus' biography is based on exhaustive academic research conducted by learned scholars. Not coincidentally, these elements are features of the documentary film genre, to which Arcand is one of Canada's foremost contributors.[26]

This alternate history may well be credible both to the Passion play's audience on Mount Royal as well as to many viewers of the film itself. New Testament scholars and historians of early Christianity, however, are likely to find it highly dubious precisely because of its use, or, rather, misuse, of the primary materials. Although virtually all of the points that Arcand makes are to be found in the ancient sources, Arcand uses those sources without regard to their dating or ideological tendencies. It is true, for example, that some rabbis of the Talmud suppose Jesus to have been fathered by a Roman soldier named Panthera. But the reliability of the Talmud on this point is highly doubtful. The rabbinic sources postdate the time of Jesus by several centuries. The rabbis had a polemical interest in contradicting and even mocking the tradition that Jesus was born of a virgin mother. What better way than to state that his mother, far from being a virgin, was in fact a promiscuous woman?

Not only does Arcand use the ancient sources uncritically, but he virtually ignores the most important sources of all, namely, the Gospel accounts. Arcand's skepticism is justified up to a point. As we have seen, the Gospel accounts are certainly problematic from a historical point of view. Nevertheless, they cannot be dismissed as sources for the historical Jesus; indeed, they remain essential for any attempt to construct a credible account of his life, his preaching, and his death.

The narrative that Arcand creates is not so much a history as a pseudo-history, or, better, an anti-history. Its effect is not to provide a new narrative of Jesus' life but to subvert the very notion that Jesus has a unique biography. The narrative contextualizes Jesus to the point that his birth, activities, and death are subsumed by the common experiences of first-century Palestinian Jews. Like many other babies, he was born out of wedlock; like many other holy men, he was thought to have magical powers; like many other Jews, he died a miserable death on the cross.

Students of early Christianity, then, would take issue with Arcand's particular version of Jesus' life story. But one should not dismiss the film on these grounds. Arcand's anti-history, based on what from an historian's view is a misuse of ancient sources, should not be attributed to naiveté or ignorance. Arcand's portrait of Jesus' life serves as a powerful vehicle for the major themes of his film: the hypocrisy of the Catholic Church in Quebec and the degradation of art in a world where the bottom line means all.

History, Hypocrisy, and Art

Arcand's anti-history is the vantage point from which he launches his trenchant critique of the Catholic Church in Quebec. The notion that the church exerts tight, hypocritical control is explicit in the theologian's need for secrecy. Daniel's own experience shows that actors who work for the church are not any better off than renegade theologians. Father Leclerc, the priest who commissioned the revitalized Passion play, is incensed after its first performance precisely because it deconstructs the traditional Jesus story. "Are you out of your mind?" he shouts at Daniel after the first performance. "Christ, the natural son of a Roman soldier? The Virgin Mary, an unwed mother? Are you crazy?" Daniel tries to respond, "In the Bible...," but Leclerc interrupts him: "It can be made to say anything. I know, from experience. Lots of fascists go to mass. Communists recite the Sermon on the Mount. I'm a member of a Catholic order. This shrine has a board of trustees. Respected people. Get the picture?"

The priest is more interested in authority than in truth. The hierarchy of the church, "respected people," as he calls them, will not take kindly to a Passion play that departs so radically from the accepted Catholic view of Jesus' life.

For Arcand, hypocrisy is the fundamental flaw of the Catholic Church in Quebec. Father Leclerc exemplifies this hypocrisy. Even as he upbraids Daniel for transgressing the boundaries of acceptability in rewriting Jesus' biography, he violates his own vow of celibacy by having an affair with Constance, a member of Daniel's acting troupe. Thus Daniel addresses Jesus' passionate indictment of the hypocritical Pharisees in Matthew 23 against the Catholic Church and its priests who have cancelled all future performances of the Passion play. As Daniel/Jesus begins his discourse, the camera lingers on the exterior of St. Joseph's Oratory, an imposing edifice that symbolizes the powerful ecclesiastical institution that Daniel/Jesus is criticizing here. Daniel/Jesus addresses the priests themselves and calls upon the audience to bear witness to his accusations.

> Woe to you, Lawmakers. You laden men with grievous burdens
> but will not touch them with one finger. Beware of priests who
> desire to walk in long robes and love greetings in the markets, the
> highest seats in temples, the best rooms at feasts, who devour wi-
> dow's houses, pretending prayer. They shall receive a greater dam-
> nation. Whoever will be high among you let him be your servant.
> Whoever will be chief among you let him be your slave. Do not be
> called Rabbi or Reverend Father or Your Grace or Your Eminence,
> for one is your Master, who is in heaven and you are all brothers.

In rejecting the Catholic Church and its authority over the story of Jesus and the lives of its parishioners, however, the film does not reject Christian faith as such. Instead, it posits an unmediated encounter between Jesus and humankind. This mode of encounter is exemplified by a Haitian spectator who throws herself at Daniel/Jesus and exclaims: "Lord Jesus...I belong to you.

I'm yours. Forgive me, I've sinned. Speak to me, sweet Jesus...Forgive me, Jesus....Speak to me...I need you, I love you, I live for you." Her emotional connection is strong and palpable, as is her disgust when the security guard forcibly carries her back to her place in the audience. This woman's direct appeal to the actor Daniel as Jesus does not signify an inability to distinguish between the actor and his character, or between truth and drama. Rather, it shows that the Passion play's deconstruction of Jesus' traditional life story in no way diminishes the ability of Jesus to touch people's hearts directly, mediated by neither Gospel nor church.

This same point is accomplished through the gradual fusion of the actor Daniel with the persona of Jesus. Just as Jesus' words in the Passion play express compassion and provide hope for those around him, so does Daniel restore the *joie de vivre* of his fellow actors and provide them with a new, more positive way of seeing themselves. Finally, and on a more somber note, just as Jesus is crucified by the controlling and hypocritical powers of his own time and place, so is Daniel figuratively crucified—unjustly accused, if only accidentally killed—by the authorities of the church, who send police to arrest him while he is hanging on the cross in his role as the crucified Jesus.

In its critique of the Catholic Church, the film takes us with humor and drama on a sobering journey from optimism to pessimism. At the outset, it appears that the Catholic Church, represented by Father Leclerc, is able to sustain and support the rejuvenation of Christian faith by sponsoring a revision of the traditional Passion play. Leclerc's outrage at the unconventional results leads to the cancellation of the play and thus quite directly to Daniel's death. The Church cannot relinquish control over the story after all. The pessimism is not absolute, however, because of the ways in which people are moved both by the Passion play and by Daniel himself. The transplanting of his heart and corneas, though perhaps an overly literal and sentimental conclusion, symbolizes resurrection and ongoing hope and new life that Jesus, apart from the Catholic Church, can give to humankind.

Throughout the film a similar movement can be seen with respect to the second theme, the degradation of art. Daniel and the four members of his troupe, though trained actors, are all reduced to earning their living in other ways. The Passion play provides a medium through which they can regain their artistic dignity and self-respect, difficult as this is in a climate in which the profit motive reigns supreme. The cancellation of the Passion play and the death of their leader threaten these gains. At the end of the film the players themselves, with the exception of Mireille, show themselves ready, naively, to be co-opted by the sly entertainment lawyer who offers to set up a commercial theatre in Daniel's memory and name.

Both the degradation of art and the dislocation of the Church as an institution that fosters true religious and spiritual experience are symbolized in the musical *inclusio* that frames the film as a whole. As the opening credits roll, we are treated to a rehearsal of the second to last movement of Pergolesi's *Stabat Mater*. The rehearsal takes place in the choir loft high in the dome of St. Joseph's Oratory, in which two talented soloists are accompanied by an organist and a professional orchestra. Behind the singers on the balcony are clearly visible the magnificent stained glass windows that adorn the dome. The text reads as follows: "Be to me, O Virgin, nigh/lest in flames I burn and die, /in his awful judgment day. Christ, when Thou shalt call me hence,/be Thy mother my defence,/be Thy cross my victory."

The height is emphasized by the camera, which looks down on Daniel from on high and then assumes Daniel's point of view as he looks up to the performers from the floor of the church. At this stage, Daniel is not yet God incarnate; he is very much a young male actor contemplating a role much larger than himself.

In the final scene immediately before the final credits roll, we encounter these two singers again, singing the final stanza of Pergolesi's *Stabat Mater*. This time they are accompanied not by a professional orchestra but by a tinny ghettoblaster, as they kneel on the platform of a Montreal subway station, a box open for handouts from passers-by. The backdrop this time is not the majestic stained glass of the Oratory but a huge advertisement for "Wild Man perfume," featuring the head of the actor who at the outset of the film heralded Daniel's arrival on the Montreal theater scene.

This is an equivocal ending. On the one hand, it may be viewed as optimistic. After all, these women are now pursuing their music freely, without institutional control. On the other hand, the way in which the two scenes play with height and depth implies a more negative interpretation. These women have gone from the highest place in the city, the dome of the Oratory on top of Mount Royal, to its lowest point far below the city streets. Similarly they have gone from a fully realized rendition of Pergolesi's glorious music, for which they were hired and paid according to union standards, to making do with taped accompaniment and uncertain remuneration. The ambiguity of the scene is underscored by the text they are singing, which is the final movement of the *Stabat Mater*: "While my body here decays,/my soul Thy goodness praise,/safe in paradise with thee. Amen."

There is yet another level of meaning in this contrast. The verses of the *Stabat Mater* are customarily associated with the Stations of the Cross.[27] The verse that is sung during the opening credits is linked to the fourteenth station, when Jesus is laid in his tomb. While this act itself evokes sorrow, it also carries the hope of the resurrection. How fitting, then, that the scene is sung in the dome of the Oratory. By contrast, the verses sung in the subway station speak of decay, in this lowest point in the city. By virtue of the two singers, the subway station has become a cathedral, its lofty ceilings recreating the generous acoustics of the Oratory. This is literally the last station of the cross, the place where Daniel's dream of passionate art is laid to rest as Daniel himself lies at death's door.

Conclusion

The irony of Arcand's *Jesus of Montreal* lies in the juxtaposition of a Passion play that challenges the unique identity of Jesus and the historicity of the Gospel accounts and a frame narrative that closely, if allegorically, follows the contours of Jesus' life as presented in the Gospel accounts. Daniel gathers his disciples, preaches a simple message of honesty and integrity, performs miracles for those who entrust themselves to him and his project, dies as a consequence of the authorities' decision that he must be stopped, then lives on both physically and spiritually in the lives of others. The implication is that it is the story as such, not its historicity, that has the potential to transform people's lives. In ascribing historicity to one particular version of the story and suppressing other constructions, the Catholic Church oppresses the very people whom it claims to serve and debases the glorious artistic achievements that brought beauty to Christian liturgy and expressed profound Christian faith. Scorsese's *Last Temptation*, in focusing on the spiritual struggle of its main character and his ultimate conquest of doubt and weakness, also testifies to Jesus' impact on humankind. As we shall see, this impact is evident most powerfully in the transformation of Judas from Jesus' adversary to his closest disciple.

These two films are the most sophisticated entries in the Jesus film category to date, insofar as they explore the connections among scripture, history, and faith in a nuanced and profound way. Despite or perhaps because of their questioning of these connections, they are powerfully moving in ways that the more pious and literal renditions are not. Yet they, as well as the other films that depart from the form and assumptions of epic biopics, nevertheless remain within the boundaries of the genre as a whole, as their very departures depend upon expectations audiences have developed on the basis of films such as DeMille's *The King of Kings* and the epics of the 1950s and '60s.

The years between 1989 and 2000 saw no new feature-length entries in the Jesus biopic genre, leading to some speculation that the era of the narrative

Jesus movie had passed.[28] Such thoughts were laid to rest by the animated film *The Miracle Maker* (2000) and, even more so, by Saville's *The Gospel of John* (2003) and Gibson's *The Passion of the Christ* (2004). In light of these latter films, both of which return to the reverential norms of the biopic genre, it would seem that Scorsese's and Arcand's movies of the late 1980s were anomalies rather than harbingers of a new iconoclastic trend. Both *The Last Temptation of Christ* and *Jesus of Montreal* depend upon the tendency of Jesus biopics to ascribe historicity to the Gospels and to their own cinematic versions of these Gospels at the same time as they challenge these ascriptions.

PART II

The Subject

3

Jesus of Nazareth

FIGURE 3.1. *Intolerance,* 1916

FIGURE 3.2. *The Miracle Maker,* 2000

FIGURE 3.3. *The Passion of the Christ,* 2004

There are two things we know for certain about Jesus of Nazareth: he was a Jew, and he lived in the early first-century CE when Judea and Galilee were under Roman domination. We know that he was a Jew because of his name, which is a short form of "Yehoshua," meaning Joshua, and because his hometown was Nazareth, a Jewish city in the Galilee. We know that he lived during the lengthy period of Roman rule because of evidence from the Gospels, other first-century sources such as the writings of Josephus, and archaeological remains.

These two facts would seem to be completely straightforward. Yet the Jesus movies display a discomfort with both. Jesus' Jewishness is a conceptual problem because of the central role that he plays in a religion that for sixteen centuries or longer has defined itself over against Judaism.[1] Furthermore, Jesus' particular identity as a Jewish man living in Galilee during the first decades of the first century stands in tension with Christian belief in his identity as the universal savior and messiah who transcends the categories of time, gender, religion, and ethnicity. As Geza Vermes notes, it is still difficult for some Christians and Jews alike to accept, or at least to fully appreciate, that Jesus was a Jew and not a Christian.[2]

The political realities of first-century Palestine pose not so much a theological or religious challenge as a narrative one. The conventions of the biopic genre require that the hero have a positive, transformative, even liberating impact on the broad political context, yet the Gospels are adamant that Jesus' kingdom was not a threat to Roman hegemony in any way. Nor was Jesus implicated in any of the Jewish revolts against Rome, the first of which took place four decades after his death. The Jesus of Nazareth whom we encounter in the biopics is a product of negotiation among these theological and narrative tensions.

Jesus the Jew

In the Gospels

The Gospels unanimously present Jesus as a Jew living and conducting his mission to Jews in first-century Galilee and Judea. Matthew highlights Jesus' Jewishness in the very first verses of his Gospel, in which he gives "an account of the genealogy of Jesus the Messiah, the son of David, the son of Abraham" and includes the three patriarchs to whom first-century Jews traced their lineage: "Abraham was the father of Isaac, and Isaac the father of Jacob, and Jacob the father of Judah and his brothers" (Matthew 1:1–2).[3] Luke tells us that Jesus was circumcised on the eighth day (Luke 2:21), as per God's requirements in

Genesis 17:10–12, and presented at the Temple (Luke 2:22–24), as prescribed in Leviticus 12:6–8.

Jesus' circumcision designates his entry into the covenant community of Israel. As an adult, Jesus lived his life in much the same way as did the rest of his community. He observed the Sabbath (e.g., Mark 1:21–27); he went to Jerusalem for the pilgrimage festivals (John 2:13; 7:2, 10; 12:1); and was present at the Temple at the Feast of Dedication (Hanukkah; John 10:22). In accordance with Jewish practice, Jesus "gave thanks" before distributing the loaves of bread to the multitudes (Matthew 14:19; Mark 6:41, 8:6; John 6:11). The Gospels leave little doubt that even as he challenged aspects of Judaism, Jesus lived within a Jewish world, engaged in Jewish practices, and followed the Jewish calendar.[4]

More controversial is the question of whether Jesus intended his ministry to extend beyond the Jewish population among whom he lived and traveled. While John generally portrays Jesus as universal Savior (John 3:16), the other three canonical Gospels describe him in more parochial terms. Mark 7:24–30 tells of a Syro-Phoenician woman who begged him to cast a demon out of her daughter. Jesus brushes her off with an unkind response: "Let the children be fed first, for it is not fair to take the children's food and throw it to the dogs" (Mark 7:27). He changes his mind only when she retorts: "Sir, even the dogs under the table eat the children's crumbs" (7:28). When Jesus sends his disciples out to preach, he instructs them: "Go nowhere among the Gentiles, and enter no town of the Samaritans, but go rather to the lost sheep of the house of Israel" (Matthew 10:5–6). Even in John, Jesus does not respond to the request of some Greeks who wish to see him (John 12:20–22).[5]

In the most recent phase of historical Jesus research, Jesus' Jewishness is widely acknowledged, yet this aspect of his identity may or not figure prominently in the various constructions of his life. A thoroughly Jewish Jesus appears in the work of Ed Sanders, Geza Vermes, Sean Freyne, and Paula Fredriksen. According to these scholars and others like them, Jesus, like most of those around him in Galilee,[6] observed both the ritual and the ethical requirements of the law,[7] including the laws of Sabbath, purity, sacrifice, and atonement.[8] His teachings were similar to those of the Pharisees,[9] and he subscribed fully to the fundamental Jewish beliefs and practices. Most important to Jesus' mission were eschatology and apocalyptic thinking. Indeed, according to this view, Jesus saw himself as a prophet who foresaw that God would soon step into history to create a radically new world order. Like other prophets before him, he strongly protested against what he perceived as the corruption of true worship in the Temple and hence both spoke and acted against the priests who had authority there.[10]

Other historical Jesus scholars, notably John Dominic Crossan, portray a Mediterranean Jesus. This Jesus is still Jewish, but as a Galilean Jew he is seen as having much in common with other groups in the Mediterranean area. Specifically, Jesus' pithy sayings and aphoristic social critique resemble in form and content the "wit and wisdom of the wandering Cynic sage."[11] Like Gentile Cynics, Jesus and his disciples traveled light, lived on the road, and challenged others to do the same. Jesus' message may have been more communally oriented than that of the Gentile Cynics, and he may have frequented rural regions rather than the urban areas in which the Cynics operated, but otherwise there was little to distinguish them.[12] For Jesus the Jewish Cynic, the kingdom was not to be achieved in a future cataclysmic event but was present now in the quality of people's relations with one another. His willingness to eat with sinners and touch the sick was a direct challenge to the laws, mores, and social boundaries of common Judaism. Jesus' message was symbolized above all in his opposition to the Temple.[13]

The Universal Jesus, sometimes known as the "Anti-Nationalist" Jesus, is even more of an anomaly in his specific cultural and religious context. Among the primary spokesmen for this Jesus are Marcus Borg and N. T. Wright.[14] These scholars argue that Jesus used apocalyptic language metaphorically rather than literally.[15] Jesus was a prophet engaged in radical social criticism expressed through his opposition to the Temple-centered purity-obsessed society and through his practice of inclusive table fellowship. He envisaged an alternative community that sought to live in history under the kingship of God. But the kingdom of God was not assigned to some perfect, future era. Rather, it was expected here on earth in the "time-space" world.[16] In contrast to other leaders within Jewish Palestine who engaged in the politics of purity, Jesus preached and lived the politics of compassion.[17] Jesus called Israel away from the rules of Deuteronomy, which he considered only a temporary phase in the divine plan, and he railed against the Temple, which was the symbol of Judaism's violent nationalism.[18]

All of these scholars acknowledge that Jesus was Jewish, but they differ in the way in which they do or do not take this fact into account when describing Jesus' life and message.

In the Movies

In most films, as in the Gospels, Jesus' Jewishness must be inferred from the setting and context, from his words and deeds, as well as from the way that others speak about him and behave around him. This approach is consistent with the conventions of the biopic genre, which tend to efface their subjects' ethnic, religious, and cultural identities.[19]

A notable exception is Arcand's *Jesus of Montreal*. Because the Passion play that Daniel and his troupe create adopts many of the features of a documentary, it can also explicitly address the issue of Jesus' Jewishness: "Our knowledge of Jesus is so sketchy some claim he never existed. Paradoxically, Jesus wasn't Christian, but Jewish. He was circumcised and observed Jewish law. The destiny of Israel obsessed him."[20]

Many other films, however, also draw attention to Jesus' Jewish surroundings and practices. Zeffirelli's *Jesus of Nazareth* depicts several synagogue scenes, including Sabbath morning services, Jesus' circumcision and bar mitzvah, and the betrothal and wedding ceremonies of Joseph and Mary. The rabbi of the Nazareth synagogue is a prominent and well-developed character, who advises and sustains the young Joseph and Mary and presides over the full range of their life-cycle events. The rabbi's prominent role and many other aspects of the Jewish ceremonies, including the liturgies, resonate with modern Jewish practice at the same time as they strive, through visual elements such as costume and setting, to acknowledge the distance between then and now.

Most Jesus biopics portray the Passover and its ceremonies, both in the Last Supper sequence and also in scenes from Jesus' childhood when, according to Luke, Jesus and his family made a pilgrimage to the Temple. Rossellini's *The Messiah* shows Mary and Joseph setting up a tent in the vicinity of the Temple and preparing for the festival. The camera rests periodically upon a group of young children sitting in a circle and singing "*Hadgadya*" ("One Goat"), an Aramaic song that describes the purchase of a goat for two coins. This song traditionally concludes the Passover seder. Its presence here evokes not only the season but also the sacrifice of Jesus at a future Passover.

Beyond showing these festival and life-cycle scenes, some films make use of Jewish liturgical phrases. In the lively wedding scene in Scorsese's *Last Temptation* the groom recites the usual formula: "You are sacred to me through this ring according to the laws of Moses and Israel." In *Godspell*, one of the least literal renditions of the Jesus story, the clown-faced Jesus sits on the ground surrounded by his disciples, as Jesus may well have done two thousand years earlier, and recites the traditional blessing over the bread and the wine, in well-pronounced Hebrew.

A more ominous scene occurs in Gibson's film. Here Mary wakes up with a start and says in Hebrew: "Listen ... Why is this night different from every other night?" Mary Magdalene responds softly: "Because once we were slaves and now we are slaves no longer." At this moment, John bursts in to tell the women of Jesus' arrest. Their interchange combines two elements from the Passover seder, the traditional home-based service and celebration held on the first day of the Passover festival in Israel (or the first two outside of Israel). The words uttered by Jesus' mother are taken from the first line of the "Four Questions," usually recited by the youngest child at the Seder to encourage children's participation. Mary Magdalene's response is taken from a later part of the Seder that is a remembrance of the Israelite enslavement from which God miraculously freed them. This scene reminds us of the Passover season of Jesus' death, and the salvific context evoked by the reference to the holiday of deliverance from Egypt, at the same time as it calls forth the answer that makes the heart of a mother shudder: this night is different because her son is about to die.

Despite the many hints that the films provide in the course of telling Jesus' story, it is easy to forget that Jesus is Jewish. One reason no doubt is the cinematic Jesus' strident critique of Jewish groups such as the Pharisees or Jewish authority figures such as Caiaphas. But perhaps the main reason that it is so difficult to keep Jesus' Jewishness in mind is the decidedly non-Jewish appearance of the actors who portray him.

In 2001, BBC Worldwide/Reuters published a computer-generated re-construction of the facial appearance of a Jewish male in first-century Judea, using the skull of a man buried in Jerusalem two thousand years ago. This male has a full, square face, dark curly hair, dark eyes and abundant facial hair.[21] The drawing differs considerably from the images of Jesus that typically circulate in western popular culture. The cinematic Jesus is almost always of medium height, with medium brown hair, a short brown beard, and piercing blue eyes.

The only Semitic-looking Jesus on the silver screen is the animated Jesus of *The Miracle Maker*. Otherwise, the biopic Jesus owes his appearance not to assessments of how first-century Judean men really looked, but to Christian popular art such as the biblical illustrations by Gustav Doré and James Tissot. Both artists gave Jesus shoulder-length, curly hair, delicate features, and a strong and well-developed physique that, outside of the baptism scene, remains hidden under voluminous robes.[22] Most influential, however, is the iconic painting by Warner Sallman of 1940 (figure 3.4). In the postwar period of the 1940s and 1950s, this painting was "instantly recognizable by Americans of all races and religions."[23] Stephen Prothero notes that:

> With the possible exception of Leonardo Da Vinci's Last Supper, no
> picture of Jesus is etched so deeply into our imaginations than the
> Head of Christ, painted in 1940 by Warner Sallman. Perhaps this
> is because Sallman's image of Christ has been reproduced in so

FIGURE 3.4. *Head of Christ* by Warner Sallman. © 1941 Warner Press, Anderson, IN. All rights reserved. Used with permission.

many different media; it has been used to illustrate the pages of the Bible, Sunday school literature, calendars, posters, church bulletins, lamps, buttons and even bumper stickers. The *Head of Christ* has been reproduced over 500 million times, making it one of the most popular art works of all time.[24]

Sallman's Jesus was credibly recreated by Robert Powell in *Jesus of Nazareth* and imitated by most American portrayals of Jesus (figure 3.5).

In addition to evoking the images popularized by Sallman, Doré, and Tissot, the light-haired, blue-eyed Jesus of the movies provides an unambiguous visual contrast to Jesus' betrayer, Judas, and the other villains of the

FIGURE 3.5. Robert Powell in *Jesus of Nazareth*.

story—Pharisees and priests—whose roles as Jesus' enemies are accentuated by their sinister appearance, dark clothes, and dark coloring.

Hints of anti-Judaism, if not full-fledged anti-Semitism, are apparent even in films that do not create such obvious differences between Jesus and his Jewish opponents. The prime example is Zeffirelli's *Jesus of Nazareth*. Despite the positive portrayal of Judaism, and the emphasis on Pharisees who clearly admire and approve of Jesus, the film does not escape the taint of super-sessionism. In Zeffirelli's Last Supper scene, Jesus redefines the central ritual symbols of bread and wine.

> Blessed be thou O Lord who has blessed us with thy laws and made bread to issue from the earth. From now on this will no longer be the bread of the passage of our fathers from bondage to freedom. This Passover is for you the passage from the bondage of death to the freedom of life. This is the bread of life. Whoever eats of this bread shall have eternal life. Eat it, for this is my body. Do this in remembrance of me (*pause*). From now on this cup will not only be a memorial and sacrament to the covenant God made with our fathers on Mount Sinai. This is my blood, the blood of the new covenant which is to be poured out for many.

Zeffirelli himself remarked that "the Last Supper was set up according to traditional Jewish ritual and marked the moment when Jesus superseded the ancient rite and gave his disciples and all humanity the Eucharistic mystery."[25] Here, as in his film, Zeffirelli is expressing a straightforward supersessionist theology, implying that the Passover rituals do not retain the meaning they had for Jews once they have been superseded by Jesus' Eucharistic interpretation.

Palestine under Roman Rule

In the Gospels

If the Jesus biopics are ambivalent about Jesus' Jewishness, they have definite ideas about the political situation into which Jesus was born. For the most part they go to great lengths in portraying Roman domination and oppression of the local population. Most of our information about the period leading up to the first Jewish revolt against Rome in 66–70 comes from the treatises of Josephus Flavius, the first-century Jewish historian. Josephus describes in great detail the process that led to the Roman occupation of Judea, the various events of that occupation, and the complex Jewish response. His treatises *The Jewish Wars* and *The Antiquities of the Jews* portray this period as one of tremendous unrest. Judea was bubbling over with apocalyptic and revolutionary fervor that intensified in the decades after Jesus' death and culminated in the first Jewish revolt against Rome in 66–74. The revolt against Rome in 66–70 led to the destruction of the Jerusalem temple and the sacrificial cult, an act that is still mourned in Jewish liturgy and that continues to have an impact in the political arena in Israel.[26]

While the Gospels do not dwell on the details of Roman oppression, they make it clear that the story of Jesus takes place against the background of Roman occupation. Luke's infancy narrative (Luke 1–2) sets the birth of John the Baptist and Jesus at the time of King Herod of Judea (1:1), and assigns John's baptizing mission to the "fifteenth year of the reign of Emperor Tiberius, when Pontius Pilate was governor of Judea, and Herod was ruler of Galilee, and his brother Philip ruler of the region of Ituraea and Trachonitis, and Lysanias ruler of Abilene, during the high priesthood of Annas and Caiaphas" (Luke 3:1–2).

> Joseph and his pregnant wife Mary had to travel to Bethlehem because "In those days a decree went out from Emperor Augustus that all the world should be registered. This was the first registration and was taken while Quirinius was governor of Syria. All went to their own towns to be registered." (Luke 2:1–3)

Roman rule is implied in the references to the denarius as the coin of the realm (Matthew 18:28, 20:2, 22:15–21). The presence of Rome is most evident in the Passion narratives, which ascribe to Pilate, the representative of Rome in Judea, the final say over Jesus' fate.

The Gospel of John hints at the precarious nature of Jewish life in Roman-occupied Judea. In the aftermath of the raising of Lazarus, says John, "the chief priests and the Pharisees called a meeting of the council, and said, 'What are we to do? This man is performing many signs. If we let him go on like this, everyone will believe in him, and the Romans will come and destroy both our holy place and our nation'" (11:47–48).

These statements are more likely to reflect the era in which the Gospels were written (late first-century CE) than Jesus' own time. If the historicity of these statements is doubtful, they are nevertheless available to filmmakers who wish to portray Jesus as the one who provides spiritual freedom for an oppressed people.

The Jewish leadership perforce played a mediating role between the Roman authorities and the Jewish people.[27] This is evident from the Gospels' account of Jesus' arrest and trials, in which Jesus was arrested by a combined Jewish-Roman force. It was the Jewish leaders who made representation to Pilate with regard to the charges against Jesus.

> Now Jesus stood before the governor; and the governor asked him, "Are you the King of the Jews?" Jesus said, "You say so." But when he was accused by the chief priests and elders, he did not answer. Then Pilate said to him, "Do you not hear how many accusations they make against you?" (Matthew 27:11–13)

Whereas Rome ruled Judea directly in the time of Jesus, through the person of the governor Pilate, the Galilee, while a vassal of the Roman empire, was headed by Herod Antipas, the son of Herod the Great. Both of these Herods appear in the Gospel accounts and in the movies based upon them.

Herod the Great makes his most memorable New Testament appearance in Matthew's infancy narrative:

> In the time of King Herod, after Jesus was born in Bethlehem of Judea, wise men from the East came to Jerusalem, asking, "Where is the child who has been born king of the Jews? For we observed his star at its rising, and have come to pay him homage." When King Herod heard this, he was frightened, and all Jerusalem with him; and calling together all the chief priests and scribes of the people, he inquired of them where the Messiah was to be born. They told him,

"In Bethlehem of Judea...." Then Herod secretly called for the wise
men and learned from them the exact time when the star had
appeared. Then he sent them to Bethlehem, saying, "Go and search
diligently for the child; and when you have found him, bring me
word so that I may also go and pay him homage." (2:1–8)

Herod then orders the so-called slaughter of the innocents: "When Herod saw
that he had been tricked by the wise men, he was infuriated, and he sent and
killed all the children in and around Bethlehem who were two years old or under, according to the time that he had learned from the wise men" (2:16–17).

After the death of Herod the Great, his kingdom was divided among his
three sons, each of whom was granted a tetrarchy. The Herod who is mentioned
in the Gospel accounts of Jesus' mission and death is Herod Antipas, one of the
sons of Herod the Great and his wife Malthace. Herod Antipas became the
tetrarch of the Galilee after his father's death (Josephus, *Antiquities* 17.146; *Jewish
War* 1.446). Like his father, Herod Antipas had certain powers when it came to
the internal management of his area.[28] This is evident in his treatment of Jesus:

At that time Herod the ruler heard reports about Jesus; and he said
to his servants, "This is John the Baptist; he has been raised from
the dead, and for this reason these powers are at work in him." For
Herod had arrested John, bound him, and put him in prison on account of Herodias, his brother Philip's wife, because John had been
telling him, "It is not lawful for you to have her." (Matthew 14:1–4)

Although the Gospels do not give a full account of Jewish life under Roman
domination, they hint at the oppressive nature of the regime whether under
direct Roman control as in Judea or indirectly via Herod Antipas as in Galilee.

The Gospel writers also suggest that at least some of Jesus' contemporaries
believed that he had come to free them from Roman rule. In John, the crowds
that enjoyed the meal of bread and fish declared Jesus to be "the prophet who is
to come into the world" (John 6:14). Jesus refuses to accept this role: "When
Jesus realized that they were about to come and take him by force to make him
king, he withdrew again to the mountain by himself" (John 6:15).

In Matthew, Jesus' opponents try to trap him into making a treasonous
statement against Rome:

"Tell us, then, what you think. Is it lawful to pay taxes to the emperor,
or not?" But Jesus, aware of their malice, said, "Why are you put-
ting me to the test, you hypocrites? Show me the coin used for the
tax." And they brought him a denarius. Then he said to them, "Whose
head is this, and whose title?" They answered, "The emperor's." Then

> he said to them, "Give therefore to the emperor the things that are
> the emperor's, and to God the things that are God's." When they
> heard this, they were amazed; and they left him and went away.
> (Matthew 22:17–22)

John's Jesus explicitly disclaims any political aspirations:

> Then Pilate entered the headquarters again, summoned Jesus, and
> asked him, "Are you the King of the Jews?" Jesus answered, "Do
> you ask this on your own, or did others tell you about me?" Pilate re-
> plied, "I am not a Jew, am I? Your own nation and the chief priests have
> handed you over to me. What have you done?" Jesus answered, "My
> kingdom is not from this world. If my kingdom were from this world,
> my followers would be fighting to keep me from being handed over
> to the Jews. But as it is, my kingdom is not from here." Pilate asked
> him, "So you are a king?" Jesus answered, "You say that I am a king.
> For this I was born, and for this I came into the world, to testify to the
> truth. Everyone who belongs to the truth listens to my voice." (John
> 18:33–37)[29]

Jesus of the Gospels has no interest in political power and no intention of
playing a role in overthrowing Roman rule. Not so in the movies.

In the Movies

The Jesus biopics also proclaim Jesus' innocence of the charge of treason
against Rome. At the same time, they assign him a very special role. In their
narratives, the Jews of Judea and the Galilee endured great suffering under Roman domination. Outnumbered and overpowered by the numbers and strength
of the Roman forces, the Jews' only hope was the coming of the Messiah; Jesus,
a fellow Jew, was that messiah.

　　Given that this scenario is absent from our sources, we can only conclude
that this construction of history stems from the conventions of the biopic
genre. Custen notes that studio-era biopics

> were based on a model of history which insisted that change occurred
> not because inequalities or unresolved social or economic unrest cre-
> ated tensions, but rather because uniquely gifted individuals, distrib-
> uted through our history and certain strata of our population, were able
> to see into the future and give us innovative and improved ways to
> live.[30]

If the basic problem of Jesus' society is the oppressive Roman regime, then the logic of the biopic genre requires that Jesus, as a "uniquely gifted individual," somehow offered a solution to Roman oppression, even if this contradicts the Gospels themselves.

Some films rely less upon narrative and character and more upon symbols to convey the oppressiveness of the Roman regime. Scorsese's *Last Temptation* uses shots of a huge Roman statue as a device to remind the viewer of the confrontation between Romans and Jews. *Jesus Christ Superstar* similarly employs the image of a flying eagle, the eagle being the symbol of Rome.

Most biopics, however, establish the broad political context of Roman colonization from the very first frames. *The Gospel of John*, for example, explains at the outset that the Fourth Gospel, and hence the film too is "set in a time when the Roman Empire controlled Jerusalem." But *The Gospel of John* is a model of understatement compared with many of the films that came before it. The silent films and epics elaborate vividly and melodramatically upon the hardships caused by Roman domination. The opening title of the silent film *INRI* identifies its story's setting as Jerusalem, "across whose shoulders the yoke of Rome had lain heavy for almost a hundred years." The silent film *Golgotha* implies the same by beginning its treatment with a reference to "Tiberius Caesar of Palestine," a map of Judea under Roman rule, and a reference to Israel's strong desire to be free. DeMille's *The King of Kings* describes Judea as "groaning under the iron heel of Rome."

In the introduction to the silent movie *Christus*, Caesar himself is drawn into the drama. From the outset, this film situates the Jesus story in the context of Caesar's quest for power. After an intertitle that reads: "His [Caesar's] dream of conquest and a mighty empire," we see Caesar sitting at his desk and dreaming of empire, as visualized in dreamlike clouds that hover in the background of the frame. The next intertitle reads: "Won for him by his legions of warriors," which legions, on horseback, we now see in the background of his dream. The corresponding intertitle identifies the large map in Caesar's "office" as "The itenerary [sic] of Strabone." Caesar examines the map; he casts his arm and hand wide over it, then turns his back and walks away with resolve. He opens a curtain, behind which stands a model of the temple and its precincts. The intertitle reads: "Hail Rome! And the illustrious Caesar—conqueror of the world." He looks at the model with great interest and then orders the census, "the registration of all his subjects, and an accounting of their wealth." Caesar claps his hands to call for his attendant, who comes immediately and hails him with respect. The attendant takes dictation as Caesar issues the order: "Carry my Imperial Command into every city, town and hamlet." The census takers carry out Caesar's command; they ride on horseback into all the villages, ending up in Nazareth, described (mistakenly) as "a poor country town in a northern province of Judea." This sequence of intertitles and filmed scenes attributes the census, and indeed, Israel's suffering, to Caesar's megalomania and greed.

In the biopic tradition, Roman soldiers are invariably violent, vicious, and sadistic. *Ben-Hur* and Zeffirelli's *Jesus of Nazareth* have Roman soldiers raiding small towns in the Galilee and taking whatever strikes their fancy, such as food, or whatever might be of worth, such as livestock.[31] Roman soldiers interrupt Jesus' bar mitzvah celebrations in Nazareth. In Young's *Jesus*, the arrival of Romans on horseback throws the village into turmoil, reminiscent of Hollywood Westerns in which the arrival of outlaws or opponents (as in *Pale Rider*) heralds chaos and danger. This series even builds a narrative around this conventional scene by having a Jewish tax collector (Matthew) accompanied on his rounds by Roman soldiers who, like Tony Soprano's "family," use physical intimidation to collect the money when gentler methods of persuasion fail.

Oppression leading to death is also portrayed in Pasolini's *The Gospel According to Saint Matthew*. This film's version of the slaughter of the innocents is perhaps the most chilling in the entire genre. The camera creates tension by panning slowly over the troops that are arrayed on a mountain ridge waiting for the signal to attack the babies. The tension builds until finally the leader puts two fingers in his mouth, whistles loudly, and the soldiers swoop down on the innocents below. Their uniforms mark them clearly as Roman troops. Matthew's Gospel does not specify which troops were used. It says simply that "When Herod saw that he had been tricked by the wise men, he was infuriated, and he sent and killed all the children in and around Bethlehem who were two years old or under" (Matthew 2:16); in Pasolini's treatment, however, the slaughter was carried out under Roman, not Herodian, auspices.

It is Gibson who takes this theme to its extreme, by lingering for at least twenty minutes upon the spectacle of Roman soldiers whipping and scourging Jesus with sadistic pleasure so obvious and so repulsive that even their officer objects, to say nothing of the poor viewer.

The epics describe Roman oppression in a manner that strongly alludes to Nazi Germany. *Ben-Hur*'s invisible narrator opens with an account of Judean suffering under Roman rule:

In the year of our Lord, Judea for nearly a century had lain under the mastery of Rome. In the seventh year of the reign of Augustus Caesar, an imperial decree ordered every Judean each to return to his place of birth to be counted and taxed. The converging ways of many of them led to the gates of their capital city Jerusalem, the troubled heart of their land. The whole city was dominated by the fortress of Antonia, the seat of Roman power, and by the great golden Temple, the outward sign of an inward and imperishable faith. Even while they obeyed the will of Caesar, the people clung proudly to their ancient heritage, always remembering the promise of their prophets that one day there would be born among them a redeemer to bring them salvation and perfect freedom.

As these words are being intoned, we see Jews obediently lining up to register in Bethlehem under the watchful eyes of Roman soldiers. While not quite as sinister as the film footage of Jews being herded into the ghettoes during the Nazi regime, the sense of powerlessness and oppression are unmistakable.

Even more obvious is Ray's *King of Kings*.[32] This film begins with a lengthy voiceover narration delivered by Orson Welles. Ray's narration is based heavily on Josephus' account. Both the text and the visuals, however, invite us to draw an analogy between the horrors of the first century and those of the twentieth.

Under the eye of General Pompey the holy city trembled; the people were strewn like wheat in harvest time of Rome. While Pompey triumphant dared take the last high place of the still living part of the city: the Temple. Here on this most sacred ground in all Jerusalem now Pompey's horse took its way. Where no pagan had ever set foot in the court of the priests, most irreverent Pompey stood himself down. At last, here was the fruit of the harvest. Here, it was said, lay the treasure house of Jehovah—great statues of gold as bright as the sun in this ancient land. So Pompey, burning for the touch of precious metals, entered the sanctuary. But entering, Pompey found only a scroll of parchment, a covenant with the one God handed down by Moses and venerated through the years. Thus for more than fifty years after Pompey's invasion, the history of Judea would be read by the light of burning towns. If gold was not the harvest, there was a richness of people to be gathered. The battalions of Caesar Augustus brought in the crop. Like sheep, from their own green fields, the Jews went to the slaughter. They went from stone quarries to build Rome's triumphal arches. But Caesar could find no Jew to press Rome's laws onto his fallen land. So Caesar named one Herod the Great, an Arab of the Bedouin tribe, as the new false and maleficent king of the Jews. But from the dust at Herod's feet, rebellions of Jews rose up and Herod, in reply, planted evil seeds from which forests of Roman crosses grew high on Jerusalem's hills. And Herod the Great, passing pleased, made the forests multiply. Yet trapped in this darkness, the Jews survived, by one promise: God would send the messiah to deliver them forth.

The narration now moves from the broad national level to the particularities of Jesus' own story:

> And it came to pass in those days that a decree went out from Caesar Augustus that all the world should be taxed. And all went to be taxed, everyone into his own city. And so it was that Joseph, a carpenter, went up from Galilee unto Bethlehem, to be taxed with his espoused wife Mary who was with Holy Child.

Throughout this recitation, the visual images illustrate the words; the Roman legions marching into Jerusalem, confronting the passive and defenseless priests, many of whom are killed at close quarters. Pompey is extremely dismayed when he raids the Temple treasury and finds only a scroll where he had expected gold. He is sorely tempted to burn the scroll, prospect that recalls the burning of forbidden Jewish books in other eras when Jews were persecuted, and only reluctantly hands the scroll over to the dignified Jewish priest who beseeches him.[33] Meanwhile, the Jews slave for the Romans, are terrorized by Roman soldiers, and killed by the dozens in the Temple precinct.[34] At the end of this lengthy introduction, a quick cut to Jesus' infancy stories implies that here, with this new baby born, their hopes would come to pass.

Despite its reliance on the writings of Josephus, this historical introduction plays fast and loose with the facts. In the first place, Pompey did not precisely invade Judea; he was invited to enter by one of the feuding contenders for the throne of the Hasmonean kingdom, though no doubt some blood was shed.[35] Herod was not an Arab of the Bedouin tribe but an Idumaean.[36]

Most viewers, however, would not be aware of these historical inaccuracies. Instead, they would respond both to the content of the passage and its the mode of delivery. The authoritative voice and the content of the narration, and the formality of the language, recall the cadences of the King James translation of the Bible. The narrator uses "And it came to pass . . . " as a transitional phrase, echoing the King James version of Matthew (7:28, 9:10, 11:1, 13:53, 19:1, 26:1).

The language, including the reference to Jews going like sheep to the slaughter, and the images of the relentless, greedy, and bloodthirsty Pompey all recall Jewish experience under the Nazi regime as much or more than Josephus's account of Galilean and Judean realities under Roman domination.[37] The narrative sequence of Roman imperialism, Jewish suffering, and Jesus' arrival are implicitly compared to parallel to a more modern narrative, namely, the sequence of Nazi imperialism, the Holocaust, and the founding of the State of Israel. The Jews' dream of a messiah in the first decades of the first-century CE is presented as parallel to the Jews' dream of a homeland in the first half of the twentieth century and the appearance of Jesus as God's response to Roman oppression as parallel to the creation of Israel as the world's response to the Holocaust.

If the Jesus biopics agree on anything, then, it is that Rome had an exceedingly oppressive presence in Judea and the Galilee. The Jews were crying out for divine intervention, salvation from the evil forces that desecrated their sacred precincts, killed their children, took their money, and destroyed their morale.

But wait . . . there is a dissenting voice—that of Monty Python. To be fair, *Monty Python's Life of Brian* is not so much dissenting from this opinion as mocking the biopic approach to the topic of Roman occupation. This element comes to the fore in a hilarious scene in which the leader of an anti-Roman revolutionary group lays out the plan for infiltrating Pilate's palace:

FRANCIS   We're getting in through the underground heating system here, up through into the main audience chamber here, and Pilate's wife's bedroom is here. Having grabbed his wife, we inform Pilate that she is in our custody and forthwith issue our demands. Any questions?

COMMANDO XERXES   What exactly are the demands?

REG   We're giving Pilate two days to dismantle the entire apparatus of the Roman Imperialist State, and if he doesn't agree immediately, we execute her.

MATTIAS   Cut her head off?

FRANCIS   Cut all her bits off. Send 'em back on the hour every hour. Show them we're not to be trifled with.

REG   And of course, we point out that they bear full responsibility when we chop her up, and that we shall not submit to blackmail!

COMMANDOS   No blackmail!

REG   They've bled us white, the bastards. They've taken everything we had, and not just from us, from our fathers, and from our fathers' fathers.

LORETTA   And from our fathers' fathers' fathers.

REG   Yeah.

LORETTA   And from our fathers' fathers' fathers' fathers.

REG   Yeah. All right, Stan. Don't labor the point. And what have they ever given us in return?

XERXES   The aqueduct?

REG   What?

XERXES   The aqueduct.

REG   Oh. Yeah, yeah. They did give us that. Uh, that's true. Yeah.

COMMANDO # 3   And the sanitation.

LORETTA   Oh, yeah, the sanitation, Reg. Remember what the city used to be like?

REG   Yeah. All right. I'll grant you the aqueduct and the sanitation are two things that the Romans have done.

MATTHIAS   And the roads.

REG   Well, yeah. Obviously the roads. I mean, the roads go without saying, don't they? But apart from the sanitation, the aqueduct, and the roads—

COMMANDO   Irrigation.

XERXES   Medicine.

COMMANDOS   Huh? Heh? Huh....

COMMANDO # 2   Education.

COMMANDOS   Ohh....

REG   Yeah, yeah. All right. Fair enough.

COMMANDO # 1   And the wine.

COMMANDOS   Oh, yes. Yeah....

FRANCIS   Yeah. Yeah, that's something we'd really miss, Reg, if the Romans left. Huh.

COMMANDO   Public baths.

LORETTA   And it's safe to walk in the streets at night now, Reg.

FRANCIS   Yeah, they certainly know how to keep order. Let's face it. They're the only ones who could in a place like this.

COMMANDOS   Hehh, heh. Heh heh heh heh heh heh heh.

REG   All right, but apart from the sanitation, the medicine, education, wine, public order, irrigation, roads, a fresh water system, and public health, what have the Romans ever done for us?

XERXES   Brought peace.

REG   Oh. Peace? Shut up!^{38}

Humorous as it is, Monty Python did not invent this scenario *ex nihilo*. The Romans' contribution to the quality of material life in Judea is also the subject of a passage in the Babylonian Talmud, Shabbat 33b:

> R. Judah, R. Jose, and R. Simeon were sitting, and Judah, a son of proselytes, was sitting near them. R. Judah commenced by observing, "How fine are the works of these people [the Romans]! They have made streets, they have built bridges, they have erected baths."
> R. Jose was silent. R. Simeon b. Yohai answered and said, "All that they made they made for themselves; they built marketplaces, to set harlots in them; baths, to rejuvenate themselves; bridges, to levy tolls for them." Now, Judah the son of proselytes went and related their talk, which reached the government. They decreed: Judas, who exalted [us], shall be exalted [by always having the privilege of speaking first in any discussion]. Jose, who was silent, shall be exiled to Sepphoris [in the Galilee]; Simeon, who censured, let him be executed.[39]

While the Talmud, written down some five centuries after the time of Jesus, is hardly an accurate historical source for the first century, its picture of Roman infrastructure is supported by the archaeological evidence. Any tourist visiting Israel can see the Roman roads and the magnificent Roman aqueducts that dot the landscape and can visit the grand structures near the Temple mount, at Masada, Herodion, and Caesarea, built by Herod the Great during the period of Roman occupation.[40]

The notion of rebellion is not only implicit in this construction of Roman domination but is also expressed directly by some of the Roman characters in these films. Messala, the fictional Roman tribune of *Ben-Hur*, complains that the Jews refuse to pay their taxes.

SEXTUS   ...don't pay their taxes, an irrational resentment of Rome.

MESSALA   There's nothing new in all that.

SEXTUS   And then there's religion, I tell you, they're drunk with religion. They smash the statues of our gods, even those of the emperor.

MESSALA   Punish them!

SEXTUS   What would that do? We can't even find them.

MESSALA   Find the leaders.

SEXTUS   Oh, you don't know. There's nothing you can put your finger on! I tell you there are strange forces at work here. For instance there's this messiah business.

MESSALA   I know, I know, there was one predicted when I was a boy.

SEXTUS   A King of Jews, who will lead them into some sort of anti-Roman paradise *(scoffs)*. Makes your head spin. Then there's a wild man in the desert named John who drowns people in water. The carpenter's son goes around doing magic tricks. Miracles, they call them.

MESSALA   There's always some sort of rabble-rouser going about stirring up trouble.

SEXTUS   No, no, no. No, no.... This man [Jesus] is different. He teaches that God is near, in every man. It is actually quite profound, some of it.

In *Jesus of Nazareth*, it is Herod who explains the situation:

HEROD   The messiah is a bad dream disguised as a solution to every problem. It's a leveler of scores, a rewarder of righteousness, a scourge for the wrongdoer. It is the dream of everlasting peace.

ROMAN   I understand from what you have said that a messiah is worse than the prophet, from the Roman point of view.

HEROD   Oh, from the Jewish viewpoint too, only you try telling that to the Jews! It's much wiser not to consult them, just wherever the messiah is, crush it underfoot like a young scorpion! No, you can tell great Augustus that he can rest in peace in Rome. There will be no messiahs true or false in Palestine while I am alive.

Conclusion

The cinematic portrayals of Roman domination owe much to other genres, including Westerns, in which the settlers in small towns are victimized by the local "Indian" population or one gang of cowboys victimizes another group, as well as to newsreels, documentaries and feature films about the Second World War. The films' treatment of this theme also expresses a profound belief in personal liberty and in democracy as a political system that is often described as characteristically American.

This strong emphasis on Roman oppression also serves an important narrative purpose. In portraying the situation in Judea and Galilee as unbearably oppressive, the films provide a rationale for three key points in the story: God's decision to intervene on behalf of God's people by sending his son to save them; the people's receptiveness to Jesus and his message; and the Roman and Jewish authorities' alarm at Jesus' activities which threaten their hegemony.

The depiction of Jesus' Jewish context and of the overall political situation of the Jews under Roman rule are the backdrop for Jesus' movie biography, which traces his emergence from an ordinary Jewish family to the role of universal savior. These elements support a back story that establishes the need for political and spiritual redemption and thus describes the fertile ground into which Jesus' person and message were sown. If Jesus of Nazareth does not liberate his people from Roman oppression, perhaps Jesus of Hollywood will.

PART III

The Story

Jesus' Family

4

Mary

FIGURE 4.1. *The King of Kings,* 1927

FIGURE 4.2. *The Gospel According to St. Matthew,* 1964

FIGURE 4.3. *The Last Temptation of Christ,* 1988

Despite the fact that biopics conventionally situate their heroes within their family constellations, mothers play only minor roles in most of these films, to the extent that they are present at all.[1] Mary the virgin mother of Jesus is the notable exception. In almost all biopics, Mary plays the female lead, and indeed is far more present on the screen than she is within the Gospels narratives themselves. Her relatively small, if important, role in the Gospels, far from constraining filmmakers, has allowed them to develop her personality and her relationship with Jesus in many different directions. Mary always, however, retains the cloak of purity and sanctity in which she has been clothed by Christian tradition, theology, art, and popular piety.

The films ask two major questions: what was Mary's role in Jesus' infancy and childhood, and what sort of relationship did Mary and Jesus have in his adulthood? Underlying these questions are assumptions regarding the mother's formative role in the emotional and intellectual development of her children, and the conviction that Mary must have been a part of Jesus' life throughout his ministry.

Mary and the Young Jesus

In the Gospels

Mary makes only brief appearances in the Gospels of Mark and John, which show no interest whatsoever in Jesus' conception, infancy, or childhood. By contrast, she is featured early on in the Gospels of Matthew and Luke, though she plays a rather different role in each. In Matthew, she is the passive, pregnant mother of the Messiah, eclipsed by her husband Joseph. In Luke, she is center stage. Whereas Matthew has an angel appear to the bewildered Joseph to announce Jesus' birth, in Luke it is Mary who receives this announcement. The Lukan Mary is no less startled than the Matthean Joseph: "How can this be, since I am a virgin?" (Luke 1:34). When the angel explains, Mary immediately accepts her fate: "Here am I, the servant of the Lord; let it be with me according to your word" (Luke 1:38). Then she goes off to visit her older cousin Elizabeth, also now pregnant after years of infertility.

Both Matthew and Luke specify Bethlehem as the location of Jesus' birth (Matthew 2:1; Luke 2:7), and give some details about his early years (Matthew 2:13–23; Luke 2:40–51). In other respects their stories differ. The version that has emerged in Christmas pageants, in Christmas carols, and on Christmas cards conflates the infancy narratives of both Gospels, the three magi coming from Matthew's Gospel (Matthew 2:1–12), the shepherds and manger from Luke's account (Luke 2:7–16), and the livestock from common sense (where there is a manger there must be livestock). In Matthew, the details of Jesus' infancy include the family's flight to Egypt after an angel warns that King Herod seeks the child's death (2:13) and their return to Nazareth after Herod's death (2:23). Luke mentions neither Egypt nor Herod's plot. Rather, the Third Gospel describes the typical milestones of Jewish family life in the first century CE: the infant son's circumcision on the eighth day (2:21), travel to the Temple to offer the usual sacrifices after the birth of a son (2:24), and another trip when that son is twelve years old (2:42). This latter trip is the only specific incident in the life of the young Jesus and his family that the Gospels record in any detail:

> And when he was twelve years old, they went up as usual for the festival. When the festival was ended and they started to return, the boy Jesus stayed behind in Jerusalem, but his parents did not know it. Assuming that he was in the group of travelers, they went a day's journey. Then they started to look for him among their relatives and friends. When they did not find him, they returned to Jerusalem to search for him. After three days they found him in the temple, sitting among the teachers, listening to them and asking them questions. And all who heard him were amazed at his understanding and his answers. When his parents saw him they were astonished; and his mother said to him, "Child, why have you treated us like this? Look, your father and I have been searching for you in great anxiety." He said to them, "Why were you searching for me? Did you not know that I must be in my Father's house?" But they did not understand what he said to them. (2:42–50)

Mary does not have a prominent role in these stories, though her presence is acknowledged throughout. The Gospel portrait of Mary is greatly enhanced in the apocryphal texts such as *The Protoevangelium of James (Infancy Gospel of James)*, which recount legends of Mary's infancy and youth, including her betrothal to Joseph at the tender age of twelve.[2]

In the Movies

Almost all films treat Mary with kid gloves. They reverentially highlight her serene beauty, her chastity, and her special relationship with both God and Jesus. Underlying her representation on the screen are centuries of visual art, especially the *Madonna and Child* and *Pietà* motifs as well as traditions that convey the intensity of her love for her son and their intimate relationship in death as in life (figures 4.4, 4.5a–c).

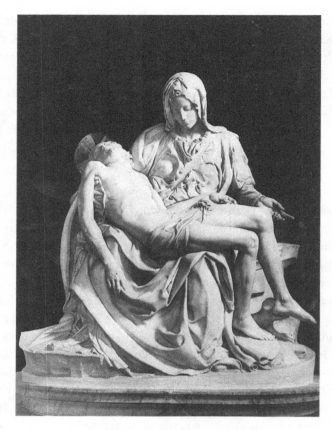

FIGURE 4.4. Michelangelo's *Pietà* (Alinari/Art Resource).

In many films, Mary's garb resembles a nun's habit. Although this outfit is unlikely to have been typical of or even known to Jewish women in first-century Palestine, to contemporary audiences it readily signals Mary's chastity and perpetual virginity.

The most striking cinematic Mary is the young pregnant woman upon whom Pasolini's camera rests long and lovingly at the beginning of his film. This Madonna could as easily belong in any church or art museum, so beautiful and expressive is her face. As she stares out at us, and then at her betrothed husband Joseph, we cannot but believe in her purity and spirituality, and we can well imagine why the divine spirit chose her over all other women.

Films elaborate freely upon the brief hints of Mary's role in Jesus' childhood. Jesus' visit to the Temple in Luke 2:42–50, quoted above, provides a vehicle for establishing Mary's role vis à vis Jesus and in the constellation of

FIGURE 4.5a. Mary and her son in Zeffirelli's *Jesus of Nazereth.*

their small family. *From the Manger to the Cross* is typical. Despite his size and strength, Jesus rides on the donkey as his mother walks along beside him and his father strides ahead. As in the Lukan narrative, Jesus' parents depart Jerusalem after the festivities and are already a day's journey away when they realize that Jesus is not with them. Lest we wonder how it is that they could have not known he was missing for so long, the film portrays a large group traveling together. In such a crowd, Mary and Joseph could easily have assumed that Jesus was walking along with a relative or friend not too far ahead

FIGURE 4.5b. Mary and her son in Young's *Jesus.*

FIGURE 4.5c. Mary and her son in Gibson's *The Passion of the Christ*.

or behind them. When they realize that Jesus is unaccounted for, Mary and Joseph panic. They frantically search for him everywhere, ask everyone, until they finally retrace their steps and come upon him in the Temple teaching the elders. All is well that ends well, and at the end of the day, the Holy Family is united once more. We see the threesome walking away from the Temple, Mary with her arm around her son, Jesus looking up lovingly at her face, and Joseph walking along beside Jesus on the other side.

Rossellini's *The Messiah* expands upon this trip to Jerusalem at great length. Throughout this episode he assigns a major role to Mary. When the family arrives in Jerusalem for the week of the Passover festival, they set up their tent within the large tent colony that provides temporary accommodation in the vicinity of the Temple for the numerous pilgrims coming from outside Jerusalem. Mary then helps her young son get dressed. She tends to him tenderly but briskly, explaining earnestly:

> This is a very important day for you. For the first time in your life you will be allowed into the house of the Eternal, to be blessed in his name. For the first time you will dedicate a sacrifice to Him. Here, this is your *tallith* [prayer shawl]. Do you know what a *tallith* is? A thousand years ago our people were slaves in Egypt until the joyous day Moses our father, blessed be his name forever, liberated them. And for forty years with the rain and the sun beating down our people walked and walked having as their sole protection a white shawl made from sheep's wool. Since then, every man in Israel has his *tallith*.

Throughout this recitation she continues to fuss over his clothing and to speak to him fervently. "As of today you also are a man. And having become a man, with your head covered by your *tallith*, you will be able to speak with doctors and teachers who have studied the Holy Law. Because from now on you belong to the Law, my son, as you know, and the Law belongs to you."

She hugs and kisses him. This is clearly a momentous occasion. Rossellini's Madonna does not treat her child with any particular reverence; she fusses over him in a loving but matter-of-fact way, intent that he learn something about his tradition and not just go through the motions of the ritual.

Aside from the brief notices in Luke 2, the Gospels tell us nothing about Jesus' early life. Jesus biopics generally fill this gap with typical childhood scenes rather than unique events. These scenes allow these films to portray the bonds between mother and son without going too far beyond the familiar contours of the Gospel narrative.

From the Manger to the Cross, like Rossellini's film, portrays Mary as Jesus' tender teacher. The scene is the Holy Family home. Joseph is busy with his carpentry while Mary and a six- or seven-year-old Jesus are looking intently at a scroll together. Mary is seated, with her arm around Jesus. She appears to be reading to him or with him, and explaining as she goes. Jesus nods his head in understanding. Joseph takes a break from his work, leans on his workbench and listens in. Mother and son look fondly and intently at each other. After some time, Joseph turns back to his work. Other films also portray Mary teaching her son to read, a motif that is familiar as well from medieval and renaissance art, such as *Virgin Teaching the Christ Child to Read* by Pinturicchio (1454–1513). The motif provides a vehicle for showing the love of mother for the child, and also for underscoring her seminal role in his early education.

In the 1912 film, the domestic scene is followed by an intertitle: "The child grew strong in wisdom (Luke 2:40)." Jesus, now an adolescent boy strong not only in wisdom but in body as well, carries a big jug out of the house for his mother. Jesus is every mother's dream child: intelligent, attentive, obedient, and helpful.

Recent films often treat Jesus' childhood and adolescence through flashbacks. In Young's *Jesus*, Mary thinks back to the time her son surprised himself by restoring life to a young bird. In Gibson's *Passion*, flashbacks provide respite from the incessant violence. As Mary watches her son stumble under the weight of the cross, she briefly recalls how she would pick up and comfort her young boy when he fell and cried out, and realizes that now too her role is to provide comfort. In the sole light-hearted scene in the entire film, Mary recalls an occasion when she poked fun at her son for building a table so high that people would need chairs in order to sit around it. The playful and affectionate interchange concludes with mother and son splashing each other with water, perhaps an allusion to baptism or perhaps mere sentimental detail. This scene remains reverent even as it highlights the strong bonds between mother and son. Obviously his mother does not see Jesus as perfect. After all, he has just made a strange-looking table. But we the viewing audience know that such tables were what was to come. The scene leaves open the possibility that even in the role of carpenter, Jesus was prophetic of future trends. Or perhaps he was simply following the instructions of a prescient client.

Only Zeffirelli portrays Mary participating in organized Jewish ritual and worship. In this film, Jesus has his coming of age ceremony (bar mitzvah) in the Nazareth synagogue. Jesus' mother, standing at the back of the synagogue, peers at him through the barrier (mehitzah) that separated the women's section from the main part of the sanctuary, reserved for the men. Jesus reads from the Torah and is praised by the rabbi. In his attempt to portray Jesus' Jewishness in an identifiable way, Zeffirelli borrows elements from contemporary orthodox Judaism in which women play a secondary role in public prayer. This aspect of Mary's portrayal coheres well with her role throughout this film. She is present at all stages of Jesus' life, and prominent in the early segments which portray her betrothal, the annunciation, and Jesus' infancy. But at no time does she emerge from the role of the pure and passive spiritual beauty: Mary remains in her place, both literally and figuratively behind the mehitzah that separates men from women in patriarchal societies.

The scriptural gaps easily accommodate both mainstream Christian theology regarding Jesus' origins and basic assumptions of popular psychology regarding the mother's role in the development of her child's psyche and self-esteem, without disrupting traditional family structures that prescribe particular roles for mothers.

The Jesus films portray Mary in two fundamentally different ways. On the one hand, she is intensively involved in her son's early life. She plays an active and positive role in raising him to productive manhood and to this end teaches him some fundamental lessons, from reading to the finer points of Jewish identity. On the other hand, she is the quintessential virgin and spiritual beauty. Her son is the perfect Son of God; her maternal role, as the vessel for the Holy Son, has already been performed with his birth. These two perspectives do not exclude each other completely, but they project an ambivalence about Mary's role in Jesus' early life that may also reflect a tension in Christianity itself.

Mary in Jesus' Adult Life

In the Gospels

In the Gospels, Jesus' relationship with his family during the period of the ministry is even more difficult to discern than during his childhood. For this phase of Jesus' life, filmmakers face not only gaps and silence in the Gospel accounts but also a narrative thread that troubles the idealized waters of the childhood they have imagined for Jesus.

It is plausible or even likely that Jesus had some contact with his birth family during these years. According to Luke 4:16–30, Jesus passed through Nazareth and taught in the Nazareth synagogue (Mark 6:1–6a; Matthew 13:53–58). In the Fourth Gospel Jesus attends a wedding at Cana along with his mother, his disciples (John 2:2), and his siblings (John 2:12) and has a conversation with his siblings before the Feast of Tabernacles (John 7:3–9). Whether Jesus dropped in to see his mother when he was in the neighborhood is left to our imagination.

The Gospels imply some tension and perhaps even a rupture in Holy Family relationships, for which the Holy Son himself is responsible. In his discourses, the Synoptics' Jesus staunchly upholds the fifth commandment to honor father and mother. In Mark 7:10–13, Jesus declares that any action that violates the fifth commandment makes void the word of God:

> For Moses said, "Honor your father and your mother"; and, "Whoever speaks evil of father or mother must surely die." But you say that if anyone tells father or mother, "Whatever support you might have had from me is Corban" (that is, an offering to God)—then you no longer permit doing anything for a father or mother, thus making void the word of God through your tradition that you have handed on. And you do many things like this.

In Mark 10:19, the commandment to honor your father and mother is listed along with several other commandments of the Decalogue, to which Jesus urges obedience:

> You shall not murder;
> You shall not commit adultery;
> You shall not steal;
> You shall not bear false witness;
> You shall not defraud;
> Honor your father and mother.

But Jesus himself violates this commandment when he redefines family relationships in terms of allegiance to God, thus giving expression and priority to the need to honor God above all human relationships. In John's story of the Cana wedding, Jesus responds sharply to his mother's comment that the wine has run out: "Woman, what concern is that to you and to me? My hour has not yet come" (John 2:4). There are numerous ways of explaining (and excusing) this statement, yet at the very least these words imply distance, if not necessarily impertinence and hostility.[3]

Other Gospel stories also are less than positive about Jesus' adult relationship with his family. John 7:3–8 describes a rather hostile conversation between Jesus and his brothers. The brothers urge Jesus to go up to Judea "so that your disciples also may see the works you are doing; for no one who wants to be widely known acts in secret. If you do these things, show yourself to the world." The narrator comments that "not even his brothers believed in him." Jesus responds: "My time has not yet come, but your time is always here. The world cannot hate you, but it hates me because I testify against it that its works are evil. Go to the festival yourselves. I am not going to this festival, for my time has not yet fully come." In this story, Jesus' siblings do not understand or perhaps do not respect Jesus' messianic identity.

The Synoptic Gospels go even further in implying distance and tension within the Holy Family when Jesus apparently denies his familial connections to his mother and siblings. According to Mark 3:31–35:

> His mother and his brothers came; and standing outside, they sent to him and called him. A crowd was sitting around him; and they said to him, "Your mother and your brothers and sisters are outside, asking for you." And he replied, "Who are my mother and my brothers?" And looking at those who sat around him, he said, "Here are my mother and my brothers! Whoever does the will of God is my brother and sister and mother."

Jesus does not sever the connection to his family so much as redefine the notion of family itself. Family ties are no longer to be grounded in biology or genealogy but are to be based on a common relationship with God, that is, "doing the will of God."[4]

Some passages state even more explicitly that anyone who follows Jesus must cut familial ties. According to Matthew 10:35–38, Jesus has come

> to set a man against his father, and a daughter against her mother, and a daughter-in-law against her mother-in-law; and one's foes will be members of one's own household. Whoever loves father or

mother more than me is not worthy of me; and whoever loves son or daughter more than me is not worthy of me; and whoever does not take up the cross and follow me is not worthy of me.

The point is also made in Matthew 19:29, in which Jesus praises those who leave their homes behind: "And everyone who has left houses or brothers or sisters or father or mother or children or fields, for my name's sake, will receive a hundredfold, and will inherit eternal life."

Mark's version of this passage (Mark 10:28–30) contains a more sinister note, that in leaving behind family one also leaves behind safety but inherits eternal life:

Peter began to say to him, "Look, we have left everything and followed you." Jesus said, "Truly I tell you, there is no one who has left house or brothers or sisters or mother or father or children or fields, for my sake and for the sake of the good news, who will not receive a hundred-fold now in this age—houses, brothers and sisters, mothers and children, and fields with persecutions—and in the age to come eternal life."

Luke's Jesus similarly views family dissension as an inevitable product of his ministry:

Do you think that I have come to bring peace to the earth? No, I tell you, but rather division! From now on five in one household will be divided, three against two and two against three; they will be divided: father against son and son against father, mother against daughter and daughter against mother, mother-in-law against her daughter-in-law and daughter-in-law against mother-in-law. (Luke 12:51–53)

Indeed, hatred is required. The Lukan Jesus states categorically that "Whoever comes to me and does not hate father and mother, wife and children, brothers and sisters, yes, and even life itself, cannot be my disciple" (Luke 14:26).

Even if Jesus redefines family anew in light of his own ministry, those around Jesus continue to define *him* by his familial relationships, as in Matthew 13:55 when the crowds in Nazareth ask among themselves, "Is not this the carpenter's son? Is not his mother called Mary? And are not his brothers James and Joseph and Simon and Judas?"

As a human being, Jesus is born into a family and linked socially with them; as a Jewish human being, he owes honor and respect to his parents. As the Messiah and Son of God (cf. John 20:30–31), however, his primary relationship must be with God. This relationship must override his obligations to and connections with his biological family.

In the Movies

Most movies handle Jesus' apparent rejection of his family by ignoring any scriptural threats to family harmony. One exception is Pasolini's *The Gospel According to Saint Matthew*. As in Matthew, Mary and her children come to where Jesus is and ask to see him, but Jesus refuses and turns his back on them. Mary's anguish at her son's denial of family ties is obvious in her facial expression. Later Jesus and his disciples walk past her house; she watches them pass by. Jesus glances back briefly, tears rolling down his cheeks. This scene softens the earlier scene of rejection by displaying Jesus' regret.

Martin Scorsese's *The Last Temptation of Christ* not only portrays Jesus' hurtful words of rejection but lingers on them. As Jesus walks along with his disciples, healing the lame and sick, his mother catches up to him.

MOTHER   Son, come back with me, please.

JESUS (*genuinely puzzled*)   Who are you?

MOTHER (*surprised*)   Your mother.

JESUS   I don't have a mother. I don't have any family. I have a father, in heaven.

MOTHER   Don't say that to me.

JESUS REPEATS   Who are you, I mean really, who are you?

He treats her gently but distantly; he kisses her on the forehead and walks on. She breaks down in tears. Her companion tries to console her:

WOMAN   Mary, why are you crying? Didn't you see them?

MOTHER   What?

WOMAN   When he spoke to you there were thousands of blue wings behind him. I swear to you, Mary, there were armies of angels.

MARY   There were?

WOMAN   Thousands.

MARY   I'd be happier if there weren't.

Is Mary crying because Jesus did not acknowledge her? Does she sense his future with foreboding? Or does she just want him to be an ordinary human being? We do not know. In Jesus' final hours, his memory of his mother returns full force. In an internal dialogue he calls out to her: "Mother, I'm sorry for being a bad son." But she does not hear these words.

Zeffirelli's *Jesus of Nazareth* conscientiously refrains from disrupting traditional stereotypes and values by having Mary, not Jesus, redefine the notion of family. As Mary sits alone, a man comes and says, "Blessed are you among women." He kneels before her, and kisses her hand. "You are his mother." She says: "Anyone who believes in our father in heaven is his brother, his sister, his mother." This displacement deflects the notion that Jesus could have rejected his mother or spoken harshly to her.

Most Jesus biopics simply ignore the problematic aspects of the Gospel accounts and instead portray an ongoing loving relationship between Jesus and his mother. Far from rejecting his mother, Jesus continues to visit her during his adult life, much as adult children today are expected to do. These visits, however, are not simple social occasions. Rather, they are brief interludes in a story of suffering, invariably interrupted by one dire situation or another. These and other scenes allow Mary to express and act upon her concerns for her son's life.

Mary's Knowledge of Her Son's Mission and Fate

In the Gospels

In Luke's Gospel, Simeon prophesies the sorrow that lies ahead for Mary: "This child is destined for the falling and the rising of many in Israel, and to be a sign that will be opposed so that the inner thoughts of many will be revealed—and a sword will pierce your own soul too" (2:34–35). Mary treasures these words, along with all the other extraordinary events of Jesus' childhood, in her heart (2:51). In the course of amplifying Mary's role in Jesus' life the biopics expand upon this motif and present her as having foreknowledge of her son's eventual fate in addition to her faith in his abilities and their divine source.

In the Movies

The Jesus films frequently suggest that Mary understood Jesus' abilities. DeMille's Mary brings a blind girl to Jesus for healing; Young's Madonna orchestrates Jesus' transformation of water into wine at the Cana wedding, minus the distance and faint tension implied in the Johannine source for this episode (John 2:4). In most films, Mary also understands her son's messianic role and anticipated his tragic fate. In *Der Galiläer* Mary sends Jesus off to Jerusalem with the following words: "My son, go your way that God asks of you. He will give the mother-heart strength that it should not break."

Less sanguine is DeMille's Mary. In *The King of Kings*, Mary waits outside the room where the disciples have been having their last supper with Jesus. As the men leave the room, the atmosphere is ominous and solemn. She says, "O my beloved Son, wilt thou not return to Nazareth with me? Here, I fear thine enemies." Mother and son embrace lovingly. As she sadly turns away from him and leaves the room, Jesus also departs along with the other disciples. The camera lingers on the empty room, the laden table, and the wine goblet glowing in the center. A dove, associated early in the film with Mary, flies around the goblet, to the accompaniment of funereal music. In this film too, Mary's belief in Jesus' divinity is taken for granted, but she is not among those that accompany him; she is motivated by a natural fear for the fate that awaits him.

Ray's Mary also understands her son's future role. When a man wants to take Jesus on as his apprentice, saying that there is a big world outside the garden, Jesus' mother refuses the offer: "Someday he will leave me, but someone else will call him . . . my son will know him when he comes."

Scorsese's Mary, on the other hand, is perpetually concerned and upset about her son. She strongly disapproves of his collaboration with the Romans, for whom he builds and sets up crosses for crucifixion. One day she arrives at the crucifixion field where Jesus is aiding in the execution of a fellow Jew and begs him to come back home with her. He refuses. That night he has a terrifying seizure. As he lies writhing on the ground, he moans, "God loves me, I know he loves me, I want him to stop. I can't take the pain, the voices . . . I want to crucify every one of his messiahs. I want him to hate me." At breakfast the next morning his mother confronts him, as, we assume, she has done many times before: "You're sure it's God, you're sure it's not the devil." He responds, "I'm not sure." She continues, "The devil . . . the devil can be cast out." Jesus counters, "But what if it is God? You can't cast out God, can you?" With Mary's help, he packs provisions and leaves for the desert. Unlike the Marys in most of the Jesus films, Scorsese's Mary is not at all certain of her son's divine mission, or even of his sanity.

In *The Greatest Story Ever Told*, as in other epics, Jesus visits his mother when his travels bring him back to Nazareth. In this film, Jesus' visit with his mother ends abruptly when Lazarus, already ill, comes to tell him that "they," his enemies, are seeking him. When Young's Jesus says goodbye to his mother, she, who all along has urged him to follow his divine father's will, challenges his decision and begins to cry; she caresses his hair, and he kisses her hand, and they embrace as he kneels before her.

In other films, Mary drops everything and accompanies Jesus to Jerusalem. This act underscores her devotion to him and also accounts for her presence in Jerusalem at the foot of the cross. In the silent film *INRI*, Mary wanders around in the wilderness in search of her adult son, who has departed for Jerusalem. Late at night, she comes upon a group of shepherds sitting by the fire. She tells them her story and they invite her to sit with them and eat. She says, "I seek Jesus of Nazareth. Know ye aught of him?" They tell her that "he is lodged even now within the city gates." We presume, though we are not told, that the city is Jerusalem. One adds, "He comes from God, he is the messiah." Despite the late hour, and the shepherds' protests, she leaves immediately to continue her search, for she cannot rest until she finds him. Some time later, she does find him in Jerusalem. She stands at the back of the crowd that is watching and listening as he teaches his disciples. Unnoticed, she edges closer, leans against the pillar, watches and listens. The camera cuts back and forth between her and Jesus until he notices her. They exchange glances, she holds out her arms, he rises slowly and walks into her warm embrace. He does not put his arms around her, but leans his head into her breast, as a young child might do. This image is also reminiscent of Luke 11:27, in which "a woman in the crowd raised her voice and said to him, 'Blessed is the womb that bore you, and the breasts that you sucked!' " She clutches his hand and says: "Those who cling to thee now will desert thee in the hour of need. Yet will I be with thee." In this case the mother's devotion is not so much a product of her faith in his messianic identity, which is taken for granted, but her desperate need to be with him in his time of need.

Ray's version of this scene in *King of Kings* begins with a voiceover narration: "For many months Jesus preached in Judea ... he angered the scribes and Pharisees who thought how they might kill him, and numbered his days and knowing the sum thereof, Jesus came to spend time with his mother." Meanwhile we see Mary joyfully rushing toward him with her water jug. Lovingly, the two greet and kiss each other. He takes the jug from her and follows her into the house. She seems rather agitated, however. As Jesus sets about fixing a chair, she paces the room and nervously winds wool onto a skein. The music contributes to the mood of anxious anticipation. Enter Peter and John, who inform Jesus, "We have done all that you asked. It is time we leave for Jerusalem." Jesus tells her, "The chair will have to wait until I return." She replies, "The chair will never be mended." An intense look passes between them. Mary walks purposefully, sets down the skein, and declares, "I am going with you." Here Mary's faith combines with maternal love and the desire to protect her son.

In adulthood, then, the movie Madonna and Child maintain a perfectly harmonious, loving relationship, even in the face of the Gospel evidence to the contrary. Theologically speaking, it could not be otherwise for the perfect son and his divinely selected mother, but they also exemplify the need for families to support one another in adversity, and for mothers to remain eternally devoted to their children.

Mary at the Foot of the Cross

In the Gospels

The biopic Mary's worst fears are realized when Jesus is sentenced to crucifixion. Tradition places Mary, along with Mary Magdalene and John the Evangelist (the traditional identification of the Beloved Disciple), at the foot of the cross. This picture is based on John 19:25–27:

> Meanwhile, standing near the cross of Jesus were his mother, and his mother's sister, Mary the wife of Clopas, and Mary Magdalene. When Jesus saw his mother and the disciple whom he loved standing beside her, he said to his mother, "Woman, here is your son." Then he said to the disciple, "Here is your mother." And from that hour the disciple took her into his own home.

A number of Marys also appear at the foot of the cross in the Synoptics, but it is not explicitly mentioned that Jesus' mother was among them (Matthew 27:67; Mark 15:40; and Luke 24:10).

In the Movies

The Jesus movies exploit Mary's presence at her son's crucifixion for all of its dramatic potential and emotional impact (figures 4.5 a–c). In Gibson's version, Mary and her companions, Mary Magdalene and John the Beloved Disciple, are so close to the cross that they are showered—baptized?—with blood and water when the Roman soldier pierces Jesus' side (John 19:35). Rossellini's film implies that not only Jesus was sacrificed on the cross but also his mother. This film omits the conventional procession of Jesus with the cross, during which he stumbles, and instead focuses on Mary as she runs through the streets of Jerusalem, following the cross to Golgotha, and stumbling twice. In this way, Rossellini implies, Mary truly and fully participates in the mission and death of her son, just as she participated actively and equally in Jesus' preaching and teaching activities throughout the ministry.

Even more striking is Rossellini's *Pietà* scene. The camera dwells on her suffering face as she watches him die on the cross, and then on the *Pietà* scene in which she cradles the dead Jesus in her arms after he is removed from the cross. Rossellini lingers on this image, in what has been described as the "most stunning iconographic aspect" of this film. Brunette has argued that the shot is blatantly sexual, an effect heightened by the slow zoom of the camera through the icon onto the men watching behind the cross, hence drawing attention not only to the mother–son couple but also the prurient gaze of the nearby men.[5]

Mary as Believer and Disciple

In the Gospels

Rossellini's sexualized Madonna hints at the fluidity and ambiguity of Mary's relationship to her adult son and to the fledgling Christian movement after his death. Acts 1:14 includes Mary as well as Jesus' brothers among the group, including the disciples in the "upper room," at the time of Jesus' resurrection: "All these were constantly devoting themselves to prayer, together with certain women, including Mary the mother of Jesus, as well as his brothers." Aside from this passage, the New Testament firmly consigns Mary to her maternal role.

In the Movies

Not so the biopics. A number of Jesus movies portray Mary not only as cognizant of her son's identity and fate, but as a follower, disciple and even fellow teacher. In Young's Jesus, Mary travels around with Jesus and his disciples and is present in many scenes from his ministry. In Rossellini's The Messiah, Mary's role is even more prominent. Indeed, this film portrays Mary as Jesus' closest associate and partner. This partnership begins when Jesus is chased out of the Nazareth synagogue, an event implied in Matthew 13:57. She catches up with him; they walk along together. From that moment on she almost never leaves his side. At the seashore where they live and work, Mary teaches children and the other disciples about the kingdom of God. "When everyone remembers to love, this will be the kingdom of God and fulfillment of the Law."

This representation echoes central elements of Catholic Mariology, in which Mary is seen as having a vital role as an instrument in redemption, as "Advocate, Auxiliatrix, Adjutrix, and Mediatrix."[6] This Mary is the disciple par excellence, elevated above all other disciples.

Mary's role as disciple has the effect of complicating the hierarchical relationship that naturally exists between mother and son. The cinematic representations of Mary as co-teacher call to mind the traditions that depict Mary as Jesus' consort, in her role as the Queen of Heaven. In this role she may have absorbed mythological elements from ancient Near Eastern goddess worship as well as from Revelation 12, which describes a "woman clothed with the sun, with the moon under her feet, and on her head a crown of twelve stars; she was with child and she cried out in her pangs of birth, in anguish for delivery" (12:1–2).[7]

Not only is Mary sometimes Jesus' peer, but she is also sometimes considered, paradoxically, to be the "daughter of her Son."[8] As Rosemary Ruether notes, "Since Mary is the historical mother of Jesus and the church is the daughter-bride of Christ and the mother of reborn Christians, the identification of Mary with the church creates a confusion of symbolic sexual relations that is typical of Mariology ever since."[9] The Renaissance art tradition, in particular the Pietà sculptures and paintings, develops this motif. In Michelangelo's famous *Pietà*, for example, Mary looks even younger than Jesus, and there is a faintly erotic element to their posture, even as the sculpture also emphasizes her sorrow at his death. This tradition is evident in the films of Zeffirelli and Rossellini, in which Mary remains young even as her son becomes an adult. These films do not emphasize Mary's other roles, but they hint that the dynamics of age and of hierarchy that govern our human familial relationships were modified, perhaps even suspended, in the case of the Holy Family.

Most filmmakers, however, are rather uncomfortable with the blurring of hierarchical role distinctions. In most films, Mary's role remains maternal throughout. If she follows her son, it is in order to watch over him as she did when he was a child (*INRI; The Passion of the Christ*) or to support him in his life's work as mothers are expected to do (Young's *Jesus*). In these films, Jesus' mother ages naturally, whether through the artistry of the makeup crew and camerawork, as in Young's *Jesus*, or through the use of a different actor (as in Pasolini's film).

The tradition of portraying Mary as perpetually young is spoofed in Luis Buñuel's *The Milky Way*. Indeed, this is the only film that even attempts to poke fun at Jesus' mother (in *Life of Brian* it is not Jesus' mother but Brian's that is the object of some derision). Buñuel's film implies that there was something vaguely unhealthy, if not downright unholy, in the relationship between Mary and Jesus, or, more precisely, in Mary's feelings about her son. In one scene, we come across Buñuel's Mary as a young, frivolous woman who admires her son the carpenter because of his handsome beard, just as a young bride might admire her attractive and manly husband. In another scene, we see Jesus running energetically down a path in the forest. One of his disciples stops him and reports: "Master, the guests have arrived. Your mother and brothers await you." Jesus answers, "Here is my mother and brother. . . ." This leads us to expect that, as in the Synoptic Gospels, he will now redefine his notion of family. But no, after a brief interlude, we return to the scene of an outdoor wedding feast set up in a clearing. Jesus is seated at the table, eating, drinking, talking, and laughing. At a neighboring table, his mother regales those around her with stories of Jesus' birth. When the angel announced that she was pregnant by the Holy Spirit, she reveals, "At first I didn't believe, then I was very happy." This Mary never ages either physically or emotionally; she remains an adolescent mother enamored of and awestruck by the famous son to whom she gave birth. Buñuel's targets here are not Mary and Jesus as such, but the clichés and conventions of the art and film tradition as well as Catholic Mariology.

Conclusion

The Gospels' silences allow considerable scope for filmmakers to expand upon Mary's relationship with her son throughout his childhood into adulthood. Mary's relationship with Jesus also shifts from his youth to his adulthood, but in films in which she continues to have a prominent role, as in the biopics by Rossellini, Scorsese, and Young, the shift is confusing. As in any family, the mother-child hierarchy becomes less pronounced as the child matures, but in the Jesus movies, the hierarchy is either reversed, as when Mary becomes Jesus' disciple, or equalized entirely. The latter is more problematic than the former, for an equal relationship potentially carries erotic connotations left unexpressed except in the Queen of Heaven Mariology that is hinted at in a small number of these movies.[10] On the whole, however, the Jesus biopics uphold the theological status quo. Many factors contribute to this theological conservatism, including the filmmakers' frequently expressed wish to affirm the faith of their presumed Christian audience, or, at least, not to offend them.

In addition to artistic and theological influences, Mary's cinematic portrayal is affected by the conventional psychological assumptions of modern western society: the connection between childhood experiences and adult identity, and the notion that one of the marks of a mature adult is the quality of her or his relationship with parents and other family members. As a perfect being, Jesus must have had a happy childhood and he must have retained a lifelong loving relationship with his mother.

Surely one factor in the cinema's interest in Mary is her prominent role in Catholicism. But on the whole, her film presence serves a christological purpose, insofar as it helps to flesh out (so to speak) Jesus' personality and experiences, and to transform him simultaneously into a role model and a focus of faith. In doing so, these films attempt to keep Mary in the picture while acknowledging the priority of Jesus' relationship with God.

Finally, these films emphasize the absolute devotion of mother to son. While this no doubt reflects somewhat on theological notions of the relationship between Mary and Jesus, it also portrays an ideal that downplays the possibility or importance of mothers having roles in the world separate from their children.

Viewing Mary as Jesus' partner in God's plan for redemption may be highly empowering for women.[11] Yet she has this role by virtue of having given birth to a male child, not through her own activities. Mary is thus an equivocal figure, at the same time attainable and unattainable, and representing a model of behavior and relationship with God that can be both inspiring and limiting.

5

Joseph

FIGURE 5.1. *The Gospel According to St. Matthew,* 1964

FIGURE 5.2. *Jesus of Nazareth,* 1977

FIGURE 5.3. *Jesus,* 1999

Despite the many differences between their infancy accounts, the Gospels of Matthew and Luke struggle with the same embarrassing point: Mary is pregnant with Jesus out of wedlock. How could this be? Did Joseph and Mary have sexual relations before their marriage? Or did Mary have relations with someone else while she was betrothed to Joseph? The Gospels of course have their own answer: Mary was impregnated by the Holy Spirit, with God's child. If so, however, where is Joseph in this picture?

The Question of Joseph

In the Gospels

Except for the opening chapters of Matthew and Luke, the Gospels virtually ignore Joseph. The Gospel of Mark makes no reference to Joseph, and John refers to him only in identifying Jesus: in John 1:45, Philip tells Nathanael: "We have found him about whom Moses in the law and also the prophets wrote, Jesus son of Joseph from Nazareth," and in John 6:42 some of those who heard Jesus speak after distributing the miraculous meal of loaves and fishes marvel: "Is not this Jesus, the son of Joseph, whose father and mother we know? How can he now say, 'I have come down from heaven'?" (cf. Luke 4:22).

In Luke's infancy narrative Joseph is present but not center stage; his presence is indicated in the references to him as Mary's husband (1:27), as being from Bethlehem, as descended from David (2:4), and as Jesus' putative father (3:23). Luke 2:27 refers to the child's parents, thereby including Joseph as well as Mary.

By contrast, Matthew's infancy story centers around Joseph, at least until the child is born. Whereas Luke's narrative focuses primarily on Mary, Matthew's story is told from Joseph's point of view; it describes his surprise at finding Mary pregnant, his resolve to divorce her quietly, and his role as the recipient of the angel's prophecies.

> Now the birth of Jesus the Messiah took place in this way. When his mother Mary had been engaged to Joseph, but before they lived together, she was found to be with child from the Holy Spirit. Her husband Joseph, being a righteous man and unwilling to expose her to public disgrace, planned to dismiss her quietly. But just when he had resolved to do this, an angel of the Lord appeared to him in a dream and said, "Joseph, son of David, do not be afraid to take Mary as your wife, for the child conceived in her is from the Holy Spirit.

She will bear a son, and you are to name him Jesus, for he will save his people from their sins." (Matthew 1:18–21)

The Gospels provide no other information. But ancient fascination with him is evident in the apocryphal gospels, which are rich in legendary material, most and perhaps all of it fictional. In *The Protoevangelium of James* 9:1–2, Joseph is a widower who is chosen by lot to be Mary's husband. Joseph is not particularly pleased to be so chosen, and indeed he initially refuses to take her as his wife: "I have children, and I am an old man, and she is a young girl. I am afraid lest I become a laughing-stock to the sons of Israel." But the priest threatens him with death: "Fear the Lord thy God, and remember what the Lord did to Dathan, and Abiram, and Korah; how the earth opened, and they were swallowed up on account of their contradiction. And now fear, O Joseph, lest the same things happen in thy house." The fear of God in him now, Joseph takes her into his keeping.

But instead of staying home to look after her, he leaves her on her own while he tends to his business. Upon his return, he finds her in advanced pregnancy and immediately panics. His first thought is that, due to his negligence, she has been unfaithful, or even "defiled." When he confronts Mary, however, she denies any wrongdoing. All would have been well had not Annas, a scribe, seen Mary and immediately reported her pregnancy to the priest. The priest promptly calls both Mary and Joseph in for interrogation. To his mind, the most logical explanation of Mary's condition is that Joseph himself has "defiled" her. When the priest insists that Joseph give her up, however, Joseph bursts into tears. Relenting, the priest then tries them by ordeal and learns that indeed they had been telling the truth. The priest dismisses them, saying, "If the Lord God has not made manifest your sins, neither do I judge you."[1]

The relationship between Joseph and Jesus is evident in a series of vignettes in *The Gospel of Pseudo-Matthew* (8th–9th century) and *The Infancy Gospel of Thomas* (140–170), in which the young Jesus exercises his miraculous powers, with disastrous results for some of his playmates. Inevitably the parents of the young children complain to Joseph and demand that he deal with his son's behavior. Occasionally he asks Mary to discipline the child, as we see in *The Gospel of Pseudo-Matthew* 26: "I dare not speak to Him; but do thou admonish Him, and say: 'Why hast Thou raised against us the hatred of the people; and why must the troublesome hatred of men be borne by us?'" On other occasions, Joseph does admonish Jesus directly, as in chapter 29: "And Joseph came up to Jesus, and admonished Him, saying: 'Why doest thou such things? For already many are in grief and against thee, and hate us on thy account, and we endure the reproaches of men because of thee.'"

In these apocryphal texts Joseph takes his role as Jesus' father seriously. Jesus, in turn, is devoted to his father, and helps him out when possible:

> Now Joseph was a carpenter, and used to make nothing else of wood but ox-yokes, and ploughs, and implements of husbandry, and wooden beds. And it came to pass that a certain young man ordered him to make for him a couch six cubits long. And Joseph commanded his servant to cut the wood with an iron saw, according to the measure which he had sent. But he did not keep to the prescribed measure, but made one piece of wood shorter than the other. And Joseph was in perplexity, and began to consider what he was to do about this. And when Jesus saw him in this state of cogitation, seeing that it was a matter of impossibility to him, He addressed him with words of comfort, saying: "Come, let us take hold of the ends of the pieces of wood, and let us put them together, end to end, and let us fit them exactly to each other, and draw to us, for we shall be able to make them equal." Then Joseph did what he was bid, for he knew that He could do whatever He wished. And Joseph took hold of the ends of the pieces of wood, and brought them together against the wall next to himself, and Jesus took hold of the other ends of the pieces of wood, and drew the shorter piece to Him, and made it of the same length as the longer one. And He said to Joseph: "Go and work, and do what thou hast promised to do. And Joseph did what he had promised." (*Pseudo-Matthew* 37:1–4)[2]

The most poignant text about the relationship between Joseph and Jesus is the *History of Joseph the Carpenter*.[3] Ostensibly written by Jesus, this book is a long meditation upon the life and death of Joseph, who lived to the ripe old age of 111. It expands upon Joseph's lengthy prayer before his death, a long deathbed scene, and the miraculous happenings thereafter. What comes through most clearly, however, is the intense love that "Jesus" expresses toward his father. These apocryphal texts testify to the fact that at least some Christians were attentive to the relationship between Joseph and Jesus and took care to portray it as a loving one.

In the Movies

Some films handle the Joseph quandary in the same way the Gospels of Mark and John do: they omit him completely. Joseph is absent from those films that depart the most from the Gospel accounts, such as *Last Temptation* and *Jesus of Montreal*, as well as from the musicals of the 1970s. He is also absent from the cinematic version of *The Gospel of John*, for the simple reason that he is absent from its scriptural source. In most films, however, Joseph assumes the role of Jesus' father. The biopics show little interest in Joseph as a character in his own right, but only as a minor member of Jesus' nuclear family in his infancy and childhood. By the time Jesus has grown up and started out on his ministry, his father has faded out quietly.

From the Manger to the Cross is typical in showing Joseph as the one who takes care of Mary and Jesus during Jesus' early years. In the series of scenes entitled "The Period of his Youth," the small family is contented, a "Happy Holy Family." Mary and Joseph are focused solely and entirely on Jesus' well-being. He rewards their devotion with his own. Within this loving threesome, however, the relationships are not entirely symmetrical. The mise-en-scène (framing of the scene) almost invariably has Mary and Jesus in closer proximity to each other than the other two possible pairings. Mary and Joseph rarely occupy the same frame alone together after Jesus' birth, and Joseph is always just a bit more distant physically from Jesus than Mary is. This is apparent in the scene in which Joseph and Mary find Jesus teaching the elders in the Temple. As they walk down the Temple stairs and head home, Jesus is positioned between Mary and Joseph but closer to his mother than to Joseph; he gazes up intently at Mary and she at him while Joseph looks fondly upon them both.

Similarly, in Zeffirelli's film more than sixty years later, there is visibly a closer bond between Jesus and his mother than between Jesus and Joseph, though Joseph cares deeply for Jesus. In one scene, we see the three praying together early in the morning in Nazareth after their return from Egypt. Joseph prays: "Hear O Israel, the eternal our God the eternal is one" (Deuteronomy 6:4) and they all bow. Mary has her hand on the child's shoulder, while Joseph stands ever so slightly off to the side.

Rossellini is much more interested in Mary than in her husband. Nevertheless, he gives Joseph an important role in his version of the Temple scene. After Mary has instructed Jesus in the significance of the occasion, Joseph arrives and takes the child off to buy a lamb for the Passover sacrifice. Joseph places his arm around Jesus' shoulder and explains how to choose the right lamb. We see a close-up of Jesus' face as they prepare to offer the sacrifice. Mere mortals might avert their eyes from the graphic images, but Jesus watches intently as the lamb is slaughtered, hung up, and disemboweled. The entire scene foreshadows Jesus' sacrifice of his own life at a future Passover feast. Whatever the dire implications of this scene, however, these segments also convey the love that bonds the Holy Family and the thoughtful way that Joseph and Mary raised Jesus to adulthood.[4]

While Joseph has only a minor role in most Jesus movies, there are three which pay him considerable attention: those of Pasolini, Zeffirelli, and Young.

THE GOSPEL ACCORDING TO ST. MATTHEW. In most Jesus films, Joseph is portrayed primarily in relationship to Jesus. The most striking exception is Pasolini's film, which from the outset focuses attention on Joseph's relationship with Mary.

The film opens with a lengthy extreme close-up of the young Mary, who perfectly captures the mystery and beauty of the Madonna of Byzantine iconography and Renaissance art. Our focus then shifts to Joseph as he stares intently at Mary. We soon see why he looks both surprised and upset: Mary is great with child.

The camera cuts back and forth between their two faces. Mary's face remains still and impassive, but we can sense that she is beseeching Joseph to stay with her. Joseph's face conveys love and hurt. They continue to stare at each other, until Joseph leaves, walking down the long path away from Mary as she stares after him. There is no dialogue, as this exchange is not present in Matthew, nor is there any perceptible soundtrack until Joseph walks away from Mary along a path to a village. There he watches children at play until he himself sits down to rest and soon falls asleep. Suddenly he is awakened by the angel Gabriel, who announces that Mary is with child by the Holy Spirit. The joyous African folk mass *Missa Luba* (1963) is now heard in the background, as Joseph hurries back to Mary. She walks out of her house to await him, and as he enters the courtyard she smiles beatifically.

That their happiness continued after the child was born is evident in a scene that is unparalleled in any film, nor in any text of which I am aware. The Holy Family, returning from Egypt, takes a break at a rocky beach. Joseph surveys the beach as Mary spreads a blanket on the sand. He stares at her beautiful, earnest, and loving face and eyes. She smiles slowly. The camera cuts back to Joseph. He meets her gaze and smiles back. The camera then turns to a small child of perhaps two years of age as he walks cheerfully away from a group of playing children. The boy—Jesus, of course—continues toward the camera and then breaks into a run. Joseph holds out his hands to the child and the boy runs toward him. Joseph picks him up tenderly. The camerawork as well as the facial expressions and gestures of the three characters implies their family connection as mother, father, and son. The soundtrack is a soothing symphonic score; there is no dialogue, given that this scene is absent from Pasolini's source.

The scene is an everyday one that conveys the strength of the family's love for one another and their enjoyment of one another's company. Particularly moving is the image of the child basking in the warmth of his family, the sun, and the beach. The son's tiny toga, worn over a pair of short pants and (one assumes) diapers, is the only sign that the sequence may be set in the distant past. Otherwise the scene is a timeless tribute to familial love and devotion.

The power of Pasolini's presentation is in the camerawork, which takes us into Joseph's point of view—his love for Mary, his shock at her pregnancy, his ready acceptance of the angel's announcement, and his love for Jesus, all with almost no words on his part. But then...he disappears.

JESUS OF NAZARETH. Zeffirelli's film also spotlights Joseph in its early segments. Joseph is a dutiful, righteous young man. His marriage to Mary had apparently been arranged by their parents. Events unfold as in the Gospels of Matthew and Luke. Joseph is an exemplary young husband and takes care of the infant Jesus as if he were his own. He instructs Jesus and a pack of other young boys in his carpentry shop. Along with his practical advice he also imparts some life lessons:

> Our work has a second meaning in God's eyes...As we use a ruler to make straight lines, God gave us rules to keep our lives straight.... God gives the wood and man with his skill and invention that God gave him is always finding new uses, sometimes wonderful uses for it.

The young Jesus—startlingly blond and blue-eyed—looks on with interest as Joseph explains: "A ladder can sometimes reach from earth to heaven." Joseph may have Jacob's ladder in mind (Genesis 28:12) but Jesus, like any other young child, takes him quite literally and climbs up a tall ladder nearby while his father's back is turned. We see the beauty of the land that the child surveys, and watch as his father's eyes, catching him on his way up the ladder, express first panic and then joy.

As in Rossellini's film, Zeffirelli's Joseph teaches Jesus how to choose a lamb that is suitable for the Passover sacrifice. As they proceed up to Jerusalem, Joseph tells Jesus to look at the city, and the camera provides us with an extreme close-up of his intent gaze, as if to imply that he knows what will happen to him in this place in the future. Later, Joseph places a pure white lamb on Jesus' shoulders, kneels down to tell him, "This is a lamb without blemish," and smiles at him meaningfully. This brief moment not only reflects the joy at Jesus' coming of age but also foreshadows his Passion, when he himself will be the sacrificial lamb.

In his lengthy deathbed scene, the dying Joseph is tended by his loving wife. They are alone in a simply furnished room. A light shines intensely through the window, reminiscent of the light that accompanied the angel's annunciation to Mary of Jesus' conception. Joseph has aged considerably, but Mary only slightly.

> JOSEPH FRETS   Mary... you will be left alone. They [*he looks at a group of young men, perhaps his sons*] will run the shop. But Jesus... We have always known it was not for us that Jesus came to earth... If only I could have stayed a little longer.
>
> [*Mary, with her gaze, implores him to stay.*]
>
> JOSEPH   God's will be done.
>
> MARY   Be at peace, Joseph.
>
> JOSEPH (*looking at the light shining through the window*)   Into thy hand I commend my spirit. [Luke 23:46]

We then hear the rabbi in voiceover as he conducts the funeral service.

ROBERT YOUNG'S JESUS. We find the most fully formed Joseph in Young's *Jesus*. Joseph and Jesus work and travel together as itinerant carpenters. They have a close, good-humored, and loving relationship. Joseph is much older than Mary, in keeping with the legends recounted in the apocrypha and his depictions in art. His Eastern European accent evokes the European Jewish community that was decimated by the Holocaust, as well as the Eastern European Jewish immigrants to the Lower East Side of New York, many of whom, like Joseph, worked as itinerant laborers. His son is not just an American Jesus, but a first-generation, American, Jewish Jesus, the repository of his immigrant father's hopes and dreams.[5]

Like many fathers, Young's Joseph has definite plans for his son. These emerge when Jesus confesses his love for Mary of Bethany. Normally such an announcement would have been met with a father's approval; after all, Mary is beautiful, pious, and from a good family. But Joseph intimates to Jesus that he has a higher calling that precludes marriage. It is never clear, at least to this viewer, why this higher calling should rule out the ordinary domestic pleasures of marriage and children, but Young, unlike Scorsese, is no iconoclast.

Jesus' attachment to Joseph is evident throughout, but most poignantly when his father dies. In the course of an argument over how Jews should respond to the bullying tactics of Roman soldiers and tax officials, Jesus stalks out of the room to sulk alone on the stairs of their house (which bears an uncanny resemblance to a two-story suburban American home). His mother comes out to talk to him. Jesus, upset, tells her: "I know what Father wants. I know he thinks I should. . . ." His mother interrupts, perhaps used to running interference between father and son: "He thinks you should do what your heart tells you. Come back inside, please."

They go back in to find Joseph collapsed on the floor, dying. They rush to him. As he breathes his last, Joseph murmurs: "Jesus, Jesus I love you, I love you as my own." The camera cuts abruptly to the funeral the next day and lingers on the faces of Jesus and Mary. Jesus then enters the tomb. He is very upset and angry at Joseph for leaving him, and even angrier with God: "Father this is too heavy. . . . You shouldn't ask this of me." Jesus is very vulnerable, like any human being in grief. He looks up and says, in an almost hopeful and yet challenging way: "You can give him back to me! You can do it now! Give him back to me! Now! (*escalating desperation*). Give him to me, I am in need! I cannot walk this road alone! Raise him! Raise him up into my arms! Let it be your will, Father. I cannot do this alone! RAISE HIM!"

God's silence is deafening. Jesus collapses in tears on his father's body. The camera cuts to Jesus working in the carpentry shop. His project is not going very well.

JESUS, FRUSTRATED   I am not as talented as he was.

MARY   Jesus, he loved you.

JESUS   I disappointed him.

MARY   He thought he had disappointed you.

JESUS (*incredulous*)   How?

MARY   He knew you had a father in heaven.

JESUS   Joseph was my father.

Mary now tells him the story of the annunciation, thirty-one years before. She carries her own burden of guilt, remembering how upset Joseph was at her pregnancy. Jesus reassures her: "He loved you with all his heart." She counters: "He loved you, as if you were his own."

Long after Mary has shifted her focus to God's will for his son, Jesus himself still longs for Joseph, and thinks of his mission not so much as doing the will of his heavenly father but as following the path for which Joseph had prepared him. As Jesus tells John the Baptist, Joseph would have wanted Jesus to move on, to serve God as John does. For Jesus, Joseph was and always will be his father, even as he comes to accept that he is also the son of God.

Conclusion

The Jesus movies present an asymmetrical relationship within the family unit. In the Happy Holy Family, the bonds between mother and son are almost always more intense and emotional than those between father and son, or, at least, the former are more easily expressed. The notable exception to this pattern is Young's *Jesus*, which elevates the role of Joseph and focuses attention on his relationship with Jesus, perhaps as a reflection of psychological theories regarding the importance of the male figure to their sons.[6] Also in evidence are definitive gender roles whereby the father is the breadwinner and the one who represents the family in the community and the woman is active in the domestic sphere and as the primary caregiver for her children. Even films in which Mary plays a prominent and active role, and in which Joseph is portrayed as a nurturing and highly involved father stay well within the boundaries of traditional theology and conservative family values.[7]

The creation of a full picture of Jesus' family life reflects two main sets of intersecting concerns. On a theological level, the Jesus biopics' treatment of Jesus' family reflects the tension between the human and divine aspects of Jesus' nature. Generally the problem is solved chronologically: in his youth the human side predominates, and in his adulthood, the divine. The barometer is the role allocated to Joseph; Jesus' divine side comes to the fore as Joseph fades out of the picture. On the psychological level, the films that treat the relationship between Jesus and Joseph testify to our society's emphasis on the role of the father in the healthy development of the child.

The emotional and psychological aspects of the Happy Holy Family of Mary, Joseph, and Jesus are consistent with the Christological elements in their emphasis on the nuclear family and the belief that the well-being of the adult is grounded in his or her childhood experiences in the bosom of the family.

The portrayal of the Happy Holy Family thus plays upon competing notions: the perfection of the Holy Family into which the Savior was born and spent his early years, and the contemporary idealization of the family as the social unit that shapes each of us. The former image is a static one in which this family differs from all others in its completeness of love, devotion, and divinely mandated purpose. The latter is one that we viewers can more readily identify with. It too is characterized by love, but small tensions are permitted, and the powerful role of the parents, both mother and father, in shaping their child's life, personality, and fate, are acknowledged. In this idealized family, each parent knows her or his role and lives it out for the sake of the child.

6

God

FIGURE 6.1. *The King of Kings,* 1927

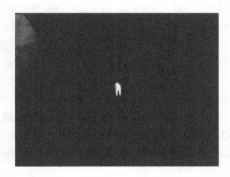

FIGURE 6.2. *The Greatest Story Ever Told,* 1961

FIGURE 6.3. *Jesus Christ Superstar,* 1973

Jesus stands out among his fellow biopic heroes for one salient reason: God is his father. The Gospel writers devised various ways of persuading their audiences of the truth of their audacious claim regarding Jesus' divine origins. They did so in various ways: by describing the angel's annunciation of Jesus' miraculous conception; calling upon the testimony of reliable witnesses such as John the Baptist, Jesus' followers, and God; recounting Jesus' miraculous deeds; and, finally, portraying his resurrection, or, more precisely, his post-resurrection appearances to his followers.

But how to illustrate this extraordinary paternity on the silver screen? The visual representation of Jesus' divine identity presents a unique and almost insurmountable challenge. The reason for this is theological: for Christianity, as well as for the other monotheistic religions, God is not visible. For Christians, it is Jesus who brings corporeality to the divine, as the Word made flesh (John 1:14). God's presence in the narrative and his role as Jesus' father can be shown only indirectly.

Miraculous Birth

In the Gospels

The Gospels of Matthew and Luke both have annunciation narratives in which the angel, God's reliable mouthpiece, announces that Mary has conceived through the Holy Spirit, but they stop short of describing how this miraculous event actually took place. In Matthew, the announcement is made after the fact, as the angel tells Joseph in 1:20: "Joseph, son of David, do not be afraid to take Mary as your wife, for the child conceived in her is from the Holy Spirit." In Luke, the angel forewarns Mary before she is pregnant: "The Holy Spirit will come upon you, and the power of the Most High will overshadow you; therefore the child to be born will be holy; he will be called Son of God."

Despite their reluctance to bring us into the bedroom, the evangelists do not see God's paternity of Jesus as mere metaphor. It is a reality outside of the realm of the purely human and biological. Even in the first century, in which many of the evangelists' original readers, particularly Gentiles, would have been aware of and even perhaps believed in the possibility of divine-human coupling or the elevation of human beings such as kings or pharaohs into the divine realm, the claim that Jesus was the Son of God was astonishing.[1]

In the Movies

On screen as in scripture, the Holy Family differs from all other families in two important ways: The Son is fathered not by the male human being who cares for and supports him but by God through the Holy Spirit, and he is born to a virgin. With a few notable exceptions, most movies do not cast doubt on either of these points.

The challenge is how to portray Jesus' unusual conception cinematically. Some films just ignore the annunciation or relegate it to a brief flashback. Others portray it more or less literally. Silent movies such as *Christus* and *INRI* replicate the mise-en-scène of Renaissance painting in which a life-size angel, a human form with large wings, approaches an understandably frightened young Mary to announce her pregnancy by the Holy Spirit.[2]

Pasolini provides a variation on this artistic theme. His angel is a young, androgynous, and wingless figure, dressed simply in white, with shoulder-length black hair. This representation coheres with his later realistic portrayal of Satan. In giving completely human form to these supernatural figures, Pasolini implies that the forces of good and evil are not supernatural forces but elements integral to the everyday world in which Jesus, and all of us, live out our lives.

An exception among the silent films is *From the Manger to the Cross*, which uses light to evoke the presence of the angel. This image implies the divine origin of the angel's message and of Mary's impending pregnancy. Mary is awoken from sleep by a bright light that shines on her; she stares at it, reaches out her hand as if to beckon to someone off screen, and then speaks. The intertitle in this section quotes Luke 1:28: "And the angel came unto her/Hail, thou that art highly favoured, the Lord is with thee: blessed art thou among women."

Some six decades later, Zeffirelli's *Jesus of Nazareth* also uses light to symbolize divine revelation. Mary is awoken from her slumber by a bright shaft of light from the window. She obviously hears words inaudible to the movie audience, for she speaks to the light as if responding to someone. Mary's startled response wakes up her mother Anna. Initially incredulous, the two women come to believe the divine message of Mary's impending, miraculous pregnancy.

The annunciation scene is absent from films that focus primarily on the Passion, such as *Jesus Christ Superstar* and *The Passion of the Christ*, or on the ministry, as in *Godspell*. And not all films toe the standard theological line that takes Mary's virginal conception of Jesus literally. Not surprisingly, two of the most iconoclastic Jesus biopics, *Monty Python's Life of Brian* and Denys Arcand's *Jesus of Montreal*, assert that their hero's father was anything but divine. Monty Python's Brian is a proud if somewhat unlucky anti-Roman revolutionary. One day he returns home to find his mother preparing to "entertain" a

Roman soldier. Brian is naturally very upset. His response forces his mother to reveal the secret of his paternity.

> MOTHER   Your father isn't Mr. Cohen...He was a Roman, Brian, he was a centurion in the Roman army. Nautius Maximus...The next time you go on about the bloody Romans, don't forget you're one of them!
>
> BRIAN   I'm not a Roman, I never will be! I'm a kike, a yid, a heebie, a hook-nose, I'm kosher, mum, I'm a Red Sea pedestrian and proud of it. *He stalks off.*

This scene is not to be taken as a direct challenge to Jesus' own divine paternity. It derives its humor in great measure from Brian's emphatic assertion of his Jewish identity by using every anti-Semitic epithet in the book. Of course, the hero of *Monty Python's Life of Brian* is Brian, not Jesus, but this is merely a pretext for the irreverent, humorous view that the movie takes of some aspects of Christian piety. As we have seen, a similar theory of Jesus' paternity is presented, with more gravity, in *Jesus of Montreal.*

Both *Life of Brian* and *Jesus of Montreal* draw on ancient Jewish sources that describe Jesus as the illegitimate son of Mary and a Roman soldier.

> He who cuts upon the flesh. It is tradition that Rabbi Eliezer said to the Wise, "Did not Ben Stada bring spells from Egypt in a cut which was upon his flesh?" They said to him, "He was a fool, and they do not bring a proof from a fool." [Ben Stada is Ben Pandira.] Rav Hisda said, "The husband was Stada, the paramour was Pandira." The husband was Pappos ben Jehudah, the mother was Stada. The mother was Miriam the dresser of women's hair, as we say in Pumbeditha, "Such a one has been false to her husband."[3]

The notion that the Jews believed Jesus' father to have been Panthera also appears in early Christian sources. According to the apocryphal *Acts of Pilate* 2.3–6, Jesus' ignominious birth is a factor in the Jewish elders' desire to destroy him:

> And Pilate, having summoned Jesus, says to Him: What do these witness against thee? Sayest thou nothing? And Jesus said: Unless they had the power, they would say nothing; for every one has the power of his own mouth to speak both good and evil. They shall see to it.
>
> And the elders of the Jews answered, and said to Jesus: What shall we see? first, that thou wast born of fornication; secondly, that thy birth in Bethlehem was the cause of the murder of the infants; thirdly, that thy father Joseph and thy mother Mary fled into Egypt because they had no confidence in the people.[4]

Similarly, Celsus's Jew, in Origen's treatise *Against Celsus*, book 1, chap. xxviii, accuses Jesus of having "invented his birth from a virgin" and upbraids Him with being "born in a certain Jewish village, of a poor woman of the country, who gained her subsistence by spinning, and who was turned out of doors by her husband, a carpenter by trade, because she was convicted of adultery."[5] Interestingly enough, despite their debunking of the notion of Jesus' divine paternity, neither *Life of Brian* nor *Jesus of Montreal* has any role for an earthly father, not even an adoptive one.

Witnesses to Jesus' Identity as the Son of God

In the Gospels

The Gospel writers were well aware that at least some members of their audiences required persuasion that Jesus is indeed the Son of God. To this end, the Gospel of John draws upon a forensic motif and calls upon a series of witnesses to Jesus' identity: himself, John the Baptist, the works that he can do, God the Father, and the Hebrew Scriptures.

> If I testify about myself, my testimony is not true. There is another
> who testifies on my behalf, and I know that his testimony to me is true.
> You sent messengers to John, and he testified to the truth. Not that
> I accept such human testimony, but I say these things so that you may
> be saved. He was a burning and shining lamp, and you were will-
> ing to rejoice for a while in his light. But I have a testimony greater than
> John's. The works that the Father has given me to complete, the very
> works that I am doing, testify on my behalf that the Father has sent me.
> And the Father who sent me has himself testified on my behalf. You
> have never heard his voice or seen his form, and you do not have his
> word abiding in you, because you do not believe him whom he has sent.
> You search the scriptures because you think that in them you have
> eternal life; and it is they that testify on my behalf. Yet you refuse to come
> to me to have life. (John 5:31–40)

In the Movies

Taking their cue from the Gospels, the biopics also call upon human witnesses to Jesus' identity as God's son. In *Ben-Hur* an older man named Balthazar points to Jesus and tells Judah, "The child has become a man, and the man, oh I know it now, is the Son of God." In Young's *Jesus*, Joseph is a primary witness to Jesus' divine sonship. Early in the movie, the Romans come through Nazareth on their way to Jerusalem. The camera focuses in on Joseph at work in his carpentry shop, as he converses with a customer.

MAN   You are not watching the soldiers, Joseph.

JOSEPH   (*with resignation*) We have seen Romans before.

MAN   Yes, and we will see them again. Jesus neglects his work.

JOSEPH   (*defending Jesus, quotes Jesus' words to the man*) "I must be about my father's business."

Both Jesus and Joseph acknowledge God as Jesus' father, even if others are as yet unaware of the truth.

The biopic Jesus himself, like his scriptural counterpart, testifies before Caiaphas that he is indeed the Son of God. Matthew's account (Matthew 26:63–66) is the basis for the slowest-moving scene in Zeffirelli's seemingly interminable epic. The camera lingers in extreme close-up on Jesus' face for longer than most viewers' patience can endure, as he struggles to utter the words "I am" in response to Caiaphas' question: "Are you the son of God?" Jesus' tendency to look up at the sky, as if communicating with his divine father, also reminds us of his connection to the divine.

Such human witnesses are well within the capabilities of cinema. More challenging are the superhuman witnesses. We have already seen how the movies cope with the annunciation stories. Films frequently fall back on visual and aural devices to denote the divine witnesses to Jesus' identity. In DeMille's *The King of Kings*, the chalice on the table where Jesus and his disciples have shared their last supper glows and attracts a fluttering dove after all the diners have left the room. In Young's *Jesus*, light shines on Jesus and glows when John baptizes Jesus and then says, "Behold the Lamb of God." [6]

In addition to these effects, films make use of objects or elements associated with the divine, or, more precisely, with Jesus as Son of God. One is the star that, according to Matthew, guided the three magi to Jesus: "When they had heard the king, they set out; and there, ahead of them, went the star that they had seen at its rising, until it stopped over the place where the child was. When they saw that the star had stopped, they were overwhelmed with joy" (Matthew 2:9–10). The moving star has become a cliché in the Jesus film genre, appearing in epics such as *Ben-Hur* and *The Greatest Story Ever Told,* as we see the three magi on their camels silhouetted against the night sky, and, in precisely the same mode, in *Monty Python's Life of Brian,* where the magi mistakenly pay a visit to Brian's manger before they realize their mistake.

The Miracles

In the Gospels

For the Gospel writers, the most graphic evidence that Jesus is divine is his ability to perform miracles. As Jesus says in the Gospel of John, "The works that the Father has given me to complete, the very works that I am doing, testify on my behalf that the Father has sent me" (John 5:36). In the Fourth Gospel, Jesus' miracles are called "signs" and they reveal Jesus' glory (2:11) to those who witness them and who comprehend the truth behind them. In the Synoptics, Jesus accomplishes numerous healings and exorcisms, though it is not always clear that the beneficiaries and witnesses truly understand what these acts signify about Jesus' identity.

Thus, before he raises Lazarus from the dead, Jesus prays to God: "Father, I thank you for having heard me. I know that you always hear me, but I have said this for the sake of the crowd standing here, so that they may believe that you sent me" (John 11:41–42).

But this evidence is not persuasive to everyone. In fact, the main cause of Jesus' falling out with the Jewish authorities is his repeated claims to divine sonship. When the Jewish authorities object to Jesus' healing of a lame man on the Sabbath, Jesus responds: "My Father is still working, and I also am working" (John 5:17). The narrator explains that "[f]or this reason the Jews were seeking all the more to kill him, because he was not only breaking the Sabbath, but was also calling God his own Father, thereby making himself equal to God" (John 5:18). According to Matthew 26:63–66, it is this "blasphemy" that precipitates Jesus' trial before Pilate, his condemnation and his death. Jesus is silent when questioned by the high priest after his arrest, until he is put under oath:

> Then the high priest said to him, "I put you under oath before the living God, tell us if you are the Messiah, the Son of God." Jesus said to him, "You have said so. But I tell you, from now on you will see the Son of Man seated at the right hand of Power and coming on the clouds of heaven." Then the high priest tore his clothes and said, "He has blasphemed! Why do we still need witnesses? You have now heard his blasphemy. What is your verdict?" They answered, "He deserves death."[7]

For those who do not believe Jesus to be the son of God, Jesus' sayings and acts constitute blasphemy; for those who do, they testify that Jesus shares his

Father's divine nature. Throughout their narration, the Gospels aim to transform the readers too into witnesses to Jesus' identity as Messiah and Son of God.

In the Movies

MIRACLES. In the movies, as in the Gospels, Jesus' miracles and exorcisms testify to his identity; in portraying these miraculous acts, the films also provide an opportunity for viewers to become witnesses. But whereas the ancient audiences of the Gospels may not have questioned the credibility of the miracles, many contemporary viewers certainly do. The role of science and rationality in our culture raises an important issue for many filmmakers: do they omit Jesus' miracles or include them? And if they do include them, do they portray the miracles literally or in some other fashion?

The films adopt a variety of approaches. Some portray Jesus' miracles on screen and take them literally as physical healings and exorcisms; others may take them literally but only talk about them rather than portray them visually. A number of films suggest that the physical miracles are metaphors for the spiritual response or healing that people experienced in their encounters with Jesus. This metaphorical interpretation may either substitute for or accompany a more literal interpretation. In many films, characters express skepticism about Jesus' abilities to perform miracles, and one or two deny these abilities entirely.

The early silent movies adopt a rather literal representation. *Der Galiläer* presents a highly stylized version of the healing of a blind man. As Jesus makes his way through a huge crowd, a blind man approaches him: "Lord, give light to the blind! That I can see and implore your holy eyes! I believe, I believe in you." Jesus, in close-up, closes the man's eyes, and looks up to heaven. He then opens the man's eyes: "And because you believe, God almighty will help you. I will it, be seeing!" The man immediately exclaims: "Merciful God, I can see!" The formerly blind man and all who witnessed the miracle bow down to worship Jesus. In a similarly unrestrained manner, *From the Manger to the Cross* devotes an entire section to "The Beginning of Miracles." This section covers the highlights of Jesus' miracle-making career: the healing of the man on the pallet (Mark 2:1–12), the wedding at Cana (John 2:1–11), the walking on water, and the raising of Lazarus.

The literal approach is by no means limited to early silent films. The 2003 film *The Gospel of John* depicts the Johannine "signs" in a straightforward manner.[8] And while Young's *Jesus* focuses primarily on Jesus' human side, it too depicts a number of miracles, such as turning water into wine at the Cana wedding. In this film, the miracles serve to persuade Jesus' skeptical friends, the viewing audience and Jesus himself that he is more than an ordinary man.[9]

Scorsese's *Last Temptation* portrays miracles that do not appear in the Gospels, most memorably Jesus tearing his own "sacred heart" from his body and offering it, dripping with his blood, to the disciples, who understandably recoil from this gift.[10]

The raising of Lazarus (John 11) is the most dramatic of Jesus' miracles. Films such as Young's *Jesus* and *Last Temptation* portray it poetically by using excellent camerawork to show us the inside of the tomb and Lazarus' point of view as he is called out of the grave. Again this may be intended to bring the viewer to identify with Lazarus and to see the possibility of resurrection through heeding Jesus' word just as Lazarus does.

If a literal interpretation is not limited to older films, neither is a metaphorical approach limited to the more recent contributions to the Jesus biopic genre. Perhaps the most thoroughgoing metaphorical explanations are found in DeMille's silent *The King of Kings*. The healing of a blind girl, for example, is closely tied to the spiritual sight that characterizes faith. Jesus prefaces the healing by declaring, "I am come a light into the world that whosoever believeth in me shall not abide in darkness" (cf. John 12:46). As he heals the girl, a light comes over her and then the camera assumes her point of view as she begins to see Jesus' face emerge from the blur. This is the viewer's first glimpse of Jesus too; we come to sight, that is, we are healed from our own blindness, at the same moment as she is. Similarly, the exorcism of Mary Magdalene's seven demons is interpreted metaphorically as her repentance of the seven deadly sins that had possessed her until her dramatic and transformative encounter with Jesus. That healing is to be seen primarily in a spiritual sense is emphasized in a humorous scene, in which a little girl asks Jesus to fix her doll's leg. Whereas she, and perhaps the audience, was expecting a miracle, Jesus repairs the doll quite simply by sewing the leg back on with needle and thread.

The Jesus epics affirm Jesus' ability to perform miracles at the same time as they portray the skepticism of some characters about this ability. *The Greatest Story Ever Told* presents a dramatic rendition of the healing of a lame man in the Nazareth synagogue where Jesus has been preaching.

JESUS   In the scriptures it is written, I desire mercy and not sacrifice [Hosea 6:6]. Only through faith is there salvation.... In the eyes of God, no man is crippled, except in his soul.

DISABLED MAN   It is simple for you to say. I cannot walk.

JESUS   Rise, and you shall walk.

THE MAN   Are you mocking me? I tell you, I cannot walk.

JESUS   You have not tried, because your faith is weaker than your legs.

MAN   I worship God and my faith is strong.

JESUS   Then rise and walk.

The man gets up slowly and gradually, hesitantly, begins to walk toward Jesus.

MAN   Look at me, I'm walking. You, you're Jesus of Nazareth. You have made me walk!

JESUS   No, it is your faith that has made you well. There are many who cannot walk. There are many more who can but will not.

The physical healing is framed and hence placed in the context of the deeper spiritual message.

Report of this event reaches the ears of Caiaphas, who is already worried about Jesus.

CAIAPHAS   Tell me, how can we know that this man was really crippled?

MAN WHO REPORTED THE MIRACLE   I have known the man for years. This is the first time I have seen him walk.

COURTIER   Ridiculous, tales of children, sorcery.

Caiaphas orders the courtier to go to Galilee to investigate this matter.

COURTIER (*sighing*)   Of course. Only a child would believe such a story.

NICODEMUS (*who offers to accompany the courtier to Capernaum*)   I have always been fond of children's stories. Children's stories always have a central truth.

In this sequence, the film makes the connection between healing and faith and also affirms the literal reality of the miracle itself. The courtier who mocks the miracle perhaps expresses the view of many moviegoers who may not literally believe in the possibility of miracles. Nicodemus, while not quite committing himself to such belief, gives voice to what may well be the central message of this section: that while we may not know whether the Gospels' miracle stories are true in a literal sense, they, like other stories, have an undeniable message that is available to us if we are open to hearing it.

In many films, the role of the skeptic is played by Herod Antipas, in keeping with his role in the Gospel of Luke:

When Herod saw Jesus, he was very glad, for he had been wanting to see him for a long time, because he had heard about him and

was hoping to see him perform some sign. He questioned him at
some length, but Jesus gave him no answer. The chief priests and
the scribes stood by, vehemently accusing him. Even Herod with
his soldiers treated him with contempt and mocked him; then
he put an elegant robe on him, and sent him back to Pilate.
(Luke 23:8–11)

Many films play up this scene for all it is worth, depicting Herod as a foppish,
foolish man in contrast to the dignified Jesus. In *The Greatest Story Ever Told*,
for example, a drunken Herod asks Jesus to perform a miracle: "I am told you
do all manner of marvels. Things which defy reason. I do not believe you can
do any of these things. Let me see one of these miracles." The crowd laughs;
Jesus remains silent. "Imposter!" continues Herod. "You cannot. But I can. Do
you know that I, the Fox, can raise one finger and a man will lose his head?"

In Ray's *King of Kings*, Jesus does not perform many miracles, but Lucius,
Pilate's right-hand man reports on them to Pilate and his entourage.

LUCIUS   Noble Pilate, the day before the Ides of April, a man, Jesus, left
Jerusalem accompanied by five of his disciples, Peter, Andrew, John,
Philip, and Nathanael. Outside the walls of the city, they were joined by a
sixth disciple, a man called Judas Iscariot. They traveled north. The
fourth day after the Nones of May, the man Jesus and his disciples
entered the town of Capernaum. There, Jesus lay hands on a madman
and cast out the demon in him. The same evening the man Jesus brought
a dying child back to health. Two miracles in one day.

CLAUDIA   Lucius...these...things, can they really be true?

LUCIUS   I do not know my Lady, I myself have never seen a miracle.

PILATE   There are no such things as miracles, only fools who believe in
them. Continue.

Lucius continues his report on Jesus' activities: the gathering of the disciples, his acquaintance with Mary Magdalene, and his stroll across the water.
Pilate tears the pages from Lucius' hands, but Lucius continues by memory to
recount the stilling of the storm. Pilate tosses the report into the water and
stalks out. Pilate's wife fishes the report out of the water. Lucius' report informs
not only Pilate but also the viewer, who then has a choice either to reject the
information, like the arrogant Pilate, or be open to it, or, at least, intrigued by it,
like Lucius and Pilate's wife.

Ray's and Stevens's epics mildly endorse the belief in Jesus' miracles, even
as they acknowledge that some may find such stories ludicrous. A stronger

point of view is expressed in the Passion play within *Jesus of Montreal*, which describes the belief in miracles as characteristic of ancient society:

> Today we cannot imagine how people lived and thought a century ago. This story is 2000 years old. Back then people thought the earth was flat . . . that stars were lamps hung on the firmament. They believed in evil spirits, demons, miraculous cures, resurrection of the dead. The East swarmed with prophets, charlatans, magicians . . . Jesus was also a magician. He was said to have grown up in Egypt, the cradle of magic. His miracles were more popular than his sermons.

Whereas Jesus' ability to do miracles is explained away in the Passion play, Daniel's ability to work wonders is described in more realistic yet still awe-inspiring terms, as when his heart and corneas are transplanted into other human beings to give one a new life and the other new sight.

Not surprisingly, the belief in Jesus' ability to perform miracles provides comedic material for Monty Python's *Life of Brian*, in which a healed leper complains to Brian that now that he is well he has lost his means of livelihood, namely, begging. Other supernatural elements of the story are evoked by a sudden shift into animated mock science fiction mode, as Brian is shown riding on a space ship that crashes into the Temple area. Witnesses call Brian a "lucky bastard" for surviving the crash.

Buñuel's *The Milky Way* provides the most caustic critique of the belief in miracles. As Jesus and his disciples walk along, they encounter two blind men.

JESUS   What can I do for you?

MEN   Have pity on us, Son of David.

JESUS   Do you think it is in my power to do what you ask? Your faith shall make it happen.

Jesus lifts them up by the hand. One of the disciples brings some sand. Jesus spits on it and rubs their eyes.

ONE MAN (*in wonder*)   I see people like trees walking.

OTHER MAN   A miracle, Lord. I see grass, trees. A miracle, Lord. I can see thee.

JESUS   Be careful. No one must find out.

ANOTHER MAN   Why hide that thou hast healed them? . . . Sometimes I wonder why we have to keep the miracles hidden. At Capharnaum, thou hadst performed so many in public. And multiplied the loaves and fishes in the presence of thousands.

JESUS Do not believe that I am here to bring peace unto earth. I am here not to bring peace but the sword.

FORMERLY BLIND MAN Lord, a bird has just passed. I recognized it by the sound of its wings.

But as the scene goes on, we realize that in fact the blind men are still blind, for they stumble and fall so frequently that it is obvious that they cannot see two steps in front of them. Finally they fall in the ditch.

The Resurrection

In the Gospels

The most dramatic proof that Jesus was the Son of God is of course the resurrection. None of the Gospels describes the physical resurrection of Jesus, just as they do not describe his conception. Rather, they provide accounts of the discovery of the empty tomb, and the disciples' subsequent encounter with the risen Lord. The versions of this story differ. Mark's Gospel originally ended with just a brief notice of the discovery of the empty tomb:

> When the sabbath was over, Mary Magdalene, and Mary the mother
> of James, and Salome bought spices, so that they might go and
> anoint him. And very early on the first day of the week, when the
> sun had risen, they went to the tomb. They had been saying to one
> another, "Who will roll away the stone for us from the entrance
> to the tomb?" When they looked up, they saw that the stone, which
> was very large, had already been rolled back. As they entered the
> tomb, they saw a young man, dressed in a white robe, sitting on the
> right side; and they were alarmed. But he said to them, "Do not
> be alarmed; you are looking for Jesus of Nazareth, who was cruci-
> fied. He has been raised; he is not here. Look, there is the place
> they laid him. But go, tell his disciples and Peter that he is going
> ahead of you to Galilee; there you will see him, just as he told you."
> So they went out and fled from the tomb, for terror and amaze-
> ment had seized them; and they said nothing to anyone, for they
> were afraid. (Mark 16:1–8)

Realizing, perhaps, that the women's failure to report Jesus' resurrection created a credibility gap for this version of the story, those responsible for the transmission of Mark's Gospel added to the narrative, stating that the women did after all tell Peter what had happened (16:8b) and describing Jesus' subsequent appearances to Mary Magdalene and other disciples, and his ascension.

Matthew's version also places women at the empty tomb; it recounts the story of the angel reporting Jesus' absence and the women's meeting with Jesus. According to Matthew, the guards had a somewhat different understanding of Jesus' disappearance than did the angels or the disciples:

> While they were going, some of the guards went into the city and told the chief priests everything that had happened. After the priests had assembled with the elders, they devised a plan to give a large sum of money to the soldiers, telling them, "You must say, 'His disciples came by night and stole him away while we were asleep.' If this comes to the governor's ears, we will satisfy him and keep you out of trouble." So they took the money and did as they were directed. And this story is still told among the Jews to this day. (Matthew 28:11–15)

Matthew does not comment on this report, but the continuation of the story clearly shows that he does not take it very seriously. Jesus reveals himself to the disciples and then commissions them to spread his message to the world:

> And Jesus came and said to them, "All authority in heaven and on earth has been given to me. Go therefore and make disciples of all nations, baptizing them in the name of the Father and of the Son and of the Holy Spirit, and teaching them to obey everything that I have commanded you. And remember, I am with you always, to the end of the age." (Matthew 28:18–20)

Luke's version does include a report by the guards, but it adds Jesus' encounter with his disciples in Emmaus:

> Then he said to them, "These are my words that I spoke to you while I was still with you—that everything written about me in the law of Moses, the prophets, and the psalms must be fulfilled." Then he opened their minds to understand the scriptures, and he said to them, "Thus it is written, that the Messiah is to suffer and to rise from the dead on the third day, and that repentance and forgiveness of sins is to be proclaimed in his name to all nations, beginning from Jerusalem. You are witnesses of these things. And see, I am sending upon you what my Father promised; so stay here in the city until you have been clothed with power from on high." (Luke 24:44–49)

Finally, in John's version, Mary Magdalene visits the tomb alone, then reports her discovery to the disciples. She echoes the concern that "they" have taken the body away. Peter and the Beloved Disciple race to the tomb, find it empty, and depart. But Mary stays on to weep at the tomb. She then encounters Jesus, who commissions her to go and tell the disciples. Later Jesus appears to the disciples and says to them:

> "Peace be with you. As the Father has sent me, so I send you."
> When he had said this, he breathed on them and said to them,
> "Receive the Holy Spirit. If you forgive the sins of any, they are
> forgiven them; if you retain the sins of any, they are retained."
> (John 20:21–23)

Thomas, who was absent when Jesus came, refused to believe until he has seen Jesus for himself and placed his hand in his side. Jesus returns and offers Thomas tangible proof, but also chastises him mildly:

> A week later his disciples were again in the house, and Thomas
> was with them. Although the doors were shut, Jesus came and stood
> among them and said, "Peace be with you." Then he said to Thomas,
> "Put your finger here and see my hands. Reach out your hand and
> put it in my side. Do not doubt but believe." Thomas answered him,
> "My Lord and my God!" Jesus said to him, "Have you believed be-
> cause you have seen me? Blessed are those who have not seen and yet
> have come to believe." (John 20:26–29)

Despite their differences, these accounts all testify to the disciples' belief in Jesus' resurrection, their conviction, as a result, that Jesus was truly God's son, and their understanding of the important role they had to play in the transmission of Jesus' message now that Jesus had ascended to be with his Father. The resurrection not only demonstrated Jesus' divine sonship but also guaranteed salvation for his believers, as John's Jesus insists: "In my Father's house there are many dwelling-places. If it were not so, would I have told you that I go to prepare a place for you?" (John 14:2).

In the Movies

The Gospels do not describe Jesus' resurrection as such. Similarly, many Jesus biopics avoid showing Jesus' physical resurrection. At the most, we see an image of the resurrected Jesus, as in Gibson's *The Passion of the Christ,* which shows us a perfectly whole and healthy Jesus, exactly as he must have been before his ordeal, with the exception of the nail holes in his hands and feet.

Usually, however, the focus is on the impact of the resurrected Jesus on those around him.

The Greatest Story Ever Told follows the outline of Matthew's account closely, including the alarm of the guards and the belief that the Jews have stolen the body, adding an ironic comment on the part of one individual that the entire incident will blow over within a week. But while these events are going on, we hear the loud and joyous strains of the Hallelujah Chorus from Handel's oratorio *The Messiah*. This is a message to the viewer that the action taking place on the screen—the disciples' anguish, fear, uncertainty, and joy, the Jews' and Romans' incredulousness—is insignificant when compared with the truth of the resurrection and its transformative impact on the lives of subsequent believers, including the movie viewers themselves. In the end, Max von Sydow ascends into the heavens, to resume his place in the dome of the Byzantine church from which he had descended in the opening frames of the film.

On the other end of the spectrum is Arcand's Jesus. The Passion play suggests that Jesus' resurrection was a figment of his disciples' imaginations. So vivid did he remain for them, and so bereft were they in their grief, that they saw him everywhere and soon came to believe that he had indeed risen from the dead. The frame narrative does, however, provide a resurrection of sorts. There is no doubt that Daniel Coloumbe, whose name means "Dove" in French, dies of his injuries, for his followers, and, with them, we viewers, witness his cremation. But his death brings new life, not just figuratively for the lives of his followers, but literally, for those who receive his corneas and heart.

Skepticism and Denial

In the Gospel

The Gospel writers are fully aware that their claims about Jesus' identity were difficult for some people to accept, let alone understand. John's Gospel recounts the disbelief of some Jews gathered in Jerusalem for a festival: "And there was considerable complaining about him among the crowds. While some were saying, 'He is a good man,' others were saying, 'No, he is deceiving the crowd'" (John 7:12). Later others marvel: "And here he is, speaking openly, but they say nothing to him! Can it be that the authorities really know that this is the Messiah? Yet we know where this man is from; but when the Messiah comes, no one will know where he is from" (John 7:26–27).

Jesus himself, however, is certain of his identity. He reveals it directly to the Samaritan woman whom he meets at the well: "The woman said to him, 'I know that Messiah is coming' (who is called Christ). 'When he comes, he will proclaim all things to us.' Jesus said to her, 'I am he, the one who is speaking to you' " (John 4:25–26). He is less direct at his own trials, but the message is nevertheless clear. At his trial before Caiaphas, "They said, 'If you are the Messiah, tell us.' He replied, 'If I tell you, you will not believe; and if I question you, you will not answer. But from now on the Son of Man will be seated at the right hand of the power of God.' All of them asked, 'Are you, then, the Son of God?' He said to them, 'You say that I am' " (Luke 22:67–70). And when Pilate asks Jesus, "So you are a king?" Jesus responded, "You say that I am a king. For this I was born, and for this I came into the world, to testify to the truth. Everyone who belongs to the truth listens to my voice" (John 18:37). But in both cases Jesus' words are taken as a declaration that he is God's son.

The evangelists also firmly believe in Jesus' messianic identity. The Fourth Evangelist declares at the end of his Gospel that "This [the Beloved Disciple] is the disciple who is testifying to these things and has written them, and we know that his testimony is true" (John 21:24). Their Gospels can be seen as elaborate efforts to bring their readers to the same certainty.

In the Movies

A small number of Jesus biopics share this same motivation, notably Heyman's *Jesus*, which was made for evangelistic purposes. Most, however, apparently assume that their target audience is already convinced, or as convinced as they need to be. The major epics, as well as DeMille's silent classic before them and Zeffirelli's *Jesus of Nazareth* and the majority of other major feature films simply present Jesus as the Son of God and Messiah. While they may follow the Gospels in portraying the skepticism of some characters in the story, they reassuringly leave little room for doubt about either Jesus or their own viewpoint.

But it is the exceptions to this overall trend that provide the most interesting portrayals of Jesus. As we have already seen, *Jesus of Montreal* explicitly denies Jesus' divinity and instead presents him as a human being, if a special person with the power to transform the lives of others. A number of other films explore in a more nuanced way the tension between Jesus' human and divine natures, and the uncertainties that might plague him, or the viewer, about his true identity.

JESUS CHRIST SUPERSTAR. The Jesus of *Superstar* is a self-centered, angry man obsessed with his superstardom and seemingly oblivious to the obligations inherent in his special status as God's son. Of all his disciples only Judas perceives the problem. Judas laments Jesus' delusions of grandeur and views Jesus' increasing sense of self-importance, fueled by the adulation of Mary Magdalene and the other disciples, not only as inappropriate but also as dangerous. Judas is convinced that Jesus is no more than human, a factor that by no means diminishes his love for Jesus.

Jesus' behavior throughout the film only confirms Judas' point of view. If most films treat the celluloid savior in an overly reverential manner, *Jesus Christ Superstar* shows him as anything but dignified. Jesus is impatient, self-absorbed, and chronically irritated by the demands of those around him. As the lame and needy clamor for his attention, he tries to retreat: "Don't push me ... there's too little of me. Don't crowd me. Leave me alone."

The Superstar's main worry is that his disciples will forget him. He lacks any sense of divinely given purpose; he is preoccupied with his own person and posterity. His disappointment in his followers emerges clearly as they drink the wine served at the last supper; Superstar manages to turn the institution of the Eucharist (Matthew 26:27–28) into a farce: "For all you care this could be my blood."

This representation of Jesus is completely inconsistent with the Gospel accounts. But then again, the main goal of the musical is not so much to convey the Gospel message in a contemporary way but to comment on the cult of celebrity: concern for genuine art is eclipsed by an egocentrism that allows stars to view themselves as "crucified" by a world that fails to love and honor them as they believe they deserve.

THE LAST TEMPTATION OF CHRIST. Scorsese's stated purpose is to portray the eternal struggle between the spirit and the flesh. In contrast to almost all other Jesus movies, and following the lead of Kazantzakis' novel, Scorsese's rendition enters into (the fictional) Jesus' own consciousness and point of view. What emerges is a Jesus who differs considerably from the stereotypical Christ figure of the biblical epics. His Jesus is obsessed with his profound uncertainty about his own identity. Is he the Son of God or not? He is tormented by voices, subject to hallucinations, and surprised by the words that come out of his own mouth.

In a powerful scene early in the film, Jesus writhes on the ground as he describes in voice-over what he is experiencing at that moment:

> The feeling begins. Very tender. Very loving. Then the pain starts.
> Claws slip underneath the skin and tear their way up. Just before
> they reach my eyes they dig in and I remember.... First I fasted for
> 3 months. I even whipped myself before I went to sleep. At first it

worked, then the pain came back, and the voices. They call me by
name, Jesus . . . Who is it, where are you, why are you following me?

The door bursts open and Judas is framed in the doorway. Given Judas' very
human identity—he is interested primarily in the physical rather than the
spiritual—his appearance at this juncture appears to be only coincidental. But
upon subsequent viewings, that is, once Judas has played out his full and complex role in Jesus' life, the sequence is both ironic and deeply meaningful.

Later we see Jesus writhing again: "God loves me, I know he loves me.
I want him to stop, I can't take the pain. The voices and the pain. I want him to
hate me. I fight him and make crosses so he'll hate me. I want him to find
somebody else. I want to crucify every one of his messiahs."

Others seem to know Jesus better than he knows himself. In the desert
immediately after he leaves Mary Magdalene's boudoir, Jesus encounters a hermit who tells him, "I know who you are." Later, we learn that the hermit had
already died at the time of this encounter. In conversation with the dead hermit's
disciple, Jesus bares his soul. He tells the disciple:

> I only came here to know God. All my life I have wanted to hear
> God's voice, I dedicated my life to him. . . . You think it is a blessing to
> know what God wants? I'll tell you what God wants. He wants to
> push me over. Can't you see what's inside of me? All my sins. I'm a
> liar, a hypocrite, afraid of everything, I don't ever tell the truth, I don't
> have the courage. When I see a woman I blush and look away. I want
> to but I don't take her, for God, and that makes me proud. And my
> pride ruins Magdalene. I don't steal, I don't fight, I don't kill, not
> because I don't want to, but because I'm afraid . . . you want to know
> who my mother and father are, you want to know who my God is,
> fear. You look inside me and that's all you'll find . . . Lucifer is in-
> side of me. He says to me, "You're not the son of King David, you're
> not a man, you're the son of Man. You're the son of God, and more,
> God." You want to ask me anything else?

This speech complicates the straightforward dichotomy inherent in the rivalry
between God and Satan that one can read between the lines of the Gospel
narratives. Scorsese's Jesus is deeply suspicious of the voice that tells him that
he is the Son of God, for he sees it as a level of hubris that could only be attributed to Satan.

The final struggle between spirit and flesh, the divine and the human,
occurs on the cross. At this point, the camerawork and soundtrack draw us into
Jesus' point of view. The clamor of the onlookers, shouting and wailing on the

crucifixion field, is suddenly muted, and the colors brighten unrealistically. A young, red-haired girl approaches and to Jesus' astonishment takes him down from the cross.

> I'm the angel who guards you. Your father is the God of mercy, not punishment. He saw you and said, "Aren't you his guardian angel? Well, go down and save him, he's suffered enough." Remember when he told Abraham to sacrifice his son? Abraham was just about to kill the boy with his knife when God stopped him. So if he saved Abraham's son, don't you think he'd want to save his own? He's tested you and he's happy with you. He doesn't want your blood. He said, "Let him die in a dream, but let him live his life."

> JESUS   All the pain, that was real?

> SHE   Yes, but there won't be any more. You've done enough.

> *She removes the crown of thorns from his head. As she removes the nails from his hands and feet, he asks:* "I don't have to be sacrificed?"

> SHE   No, no you don't.

> JESUS   I'm not the messiah?

> SHE   No, no you're not.

> *Jesus sighs, with a mixture of relief and regret.*

Jesus enters into domestic life with alacrity, and for four decades he lives like a man, with wives, children, and gainful employment. But during the Roman siege of Jerusalem in the year 70 of the Common Era, he finds himself back on the cross. There he dies in triumph and bliss, all doubts—about himself, about God—now resolved. The domestic Jesus was a figment of Jesus' own imagination, the longest and most extravagant hallucination of all. Both comforting and disturbing, this reverie allows him finally to resolve the question that has tormented him his entire life.

Young's Jesus

Young's Jesus also struggles with the paradox of his human and divine identitiy, but in a more conventional way. Jesus is not plagued with doubts and torments; he lives the life of an ordinary young man. He works at his trade and spends time with his beautiful young cousin, Mary of Bethany. He loves his parents, but is particularly close to his father Joseph, whom he admires greatly. It is Joseph who teaches him that his true father is God, and what that must mean for his own destiny. Jesus accepts these teachings only reluctantly, and then only out of love and devotion to Joseph's memory.

This Jesus displays the full range of emotions, particularly in his adolescence. He sulks and acts out when things do not go his way; after arguing with his parents he storms upstairs (his first-century Galilean home bears an uncanny resemblance to a suburban split-level house) and slams the door very hard. Even as he matures, accepts his destiny, gathers disciples and goes forth, Jesus retains his childhood capacity for joy. At the wedding at Cana, Jesus dances with abandon. The disciples complain to his mother that Jesus is wasting his time when there is so much work to do against Rome. His mother does not seem perturbed; he is a man, she says. This does not satisfy his disciples, who wonder why they are following Jesus around when they should be fishing with their brothers in Galilee. Andrew expresses their perspective: "I will dance when Israel is free and men are honest."

JESUS   It will be a very slow dance.

ANDREW   It won't come at all if we wait for you. I thought when I found John the Baptist, he said you were the one. And you spend your time drinking wine and dancing!

Andrew is disappointed in Jesus. This is not how a political savior should behave. At this point, Jesus' mother points out that the wine has run out (obviously Jesus is not the only one enjoying himself, though no doubt he too has drunk his fill). Jesus proceeds to turn water into wine as Andrew looks on in surprise. Jesus' ability to perform miracles overcomes Andrew's skepticism. Later on, we see Jesus and his disciples running into town, refreshing themselves at the town well, and splashing each other with water. This scene echoes the musical *Godspell*, in which Jesus' followers also splash around in a water fountain in New York. In both cases the playful bantering evokes baptism and the abundance that Jesus is thought to provide.

This television series gives us a Jesus who endures the inevitable identity struggles and explorations of adolescence and emerges as the Son of God. In doing so, it provides an equivocal model. In most respects Jesus was just an ordinary young man, who battled with the same issues and problems as do all adolescents, except for one fact: he was the Son of God. This leaves the film with a tepid message: be the best you can, just as Jesus was, and rise to the challenges that come your way, as Jesus did.

THE MILKY WAY. Rivaling *Jesus of Montreal* as an explicit exploration of the man/God paradox is Buñuel's *The Milky Way* (*La Voie Lactée*). On their way to

Santiago de Compostella, the pilgrims come upon an exclusive restaurant where the staff is preparing for the dinner hour. As they set the tables, the maitre d'hôtel responds to theological questions raised by his waitstaff on the topic of Jesus' humanity and divinity. Martha, one of the staff, begins the discussion:

> MARTHA   Monsieur Richard, one thing I have trouble understanding is how Christ could be a man and God at the same time.

Here she recalls her namesake, Martha of Bethany, who also engaged in some theological discussion with Jesus, according to Luke 10:28–32 and John 11, at the same time as she waits on tables (John 12).

> RICHARD   Yes, Martha, it is difficult. Look, when the devil takes the form of a wolf, for instance, well, he's a wolf and he's still the devil. It's almost the same with Christ.
>
> *Martha starts asking another question.*
>
> RICHARD   (*dismissively*)   Would you mind helping in the cloakroom? Do you know what time it is?
>
> MARTHA   Right away, sir.
>
> WAITER   But if Jesus was God, how could he be born and die?
>
> RICHARD   A very good question. If Jesus was God, how could He be born and die? If you only knew how many heretics talked about that! Some said that Christ was only God. That his human form was a fantasy, an illusion.
>
> WAITER   So he didn't eat?
>
> RICHARD   They said he didn't. He pretended to. And of course, he didn't suffer, he didn't die, etc. That was the opinion of Marcion and the Monophysites.
>
> OTHER WAITER   And Nestorius too?
>
> RICHARD   That's right, and they even said that Christ witnessed his own crucifixion, Simon having assumed His appearance. The other heretics said the opposite, that Christ obviously wasn't God but a man. Just a man. Get rid of this pear. It's over-ripe.
>
> OTHER WAITER   But he could laugh, couldn't He? And cough? They always show Him to be so dignified and solemn, walking slowly, with His hands like that [raises them]. After all, he must have walked like everyone else.

The scene cuts abruptly to the time of Jesus. We see Jesus, dressed in his "usual" outfit of blue and red robes, jogging up to the disciples, who have been waiting for him impatiently.

DISCIPLES We're late.

JESUS What time is it?

DISCIPLES Almost the sixth hour.

JESUS I'm hungry.

At this point, one comes running up: Master!

JESUS What?

OTHERS The guests have all arrived. Your mother and brethren also.

JESUS Behold my mother and my brethren! [*motions to the disciples*]. For whoever shall follow the will of my Father, in heaven, he is my brother, my sister, and my mother!

He goes off, and the camera now returns to the waiter, who asks, "If He was a man, He must have been like any other man?"

The camera then cuts back quickly to the first-century dinner. During the course of the meal, one of Jesus' disciples reminds him: "They are all awaiting your words." Jesus then begins a long rambling tale that is extraordinarily difficult to follow but that he himself, more than a little tipsy, finds very humorous indeed. The story is a parody of the canonical parables:

JESUS There was a rich man who had a steward and (*Jesus laughing*) the same was accused by him that he had wasted his goods. And he called him and said, "Why do I hear this of thee? Account for thy steward-ship for thou mayest be no longer my steward." Then the steward said within himself: "What shall I do? For my master taketh away from me my stewardship?" To dig I have no strength, to beg I am ashamed. Ah, I know what I will do, that when I am put out of the stewardship they will receive me in their houses.... The wedding couple then asks: And then?

JESUS Just a minute (*as he is drinking; then tips over the cup to show that it is empty and laughs*). So he called every one of his master's debtors unto him and said unto the first, "How much owest thou to my master?" "One hundred measures of oil," he answered. And he said to them, "Take thy bill and sit down quickly and write fifty." Then he said to another, "And what owest thou?" "One hundred measures of wheat," he an-swered. The steward said, "Write down eighty." And the master praised his unjust steward because he had done wisely. For the children of this world are in their generation wiser than the children of light.

The guests burst into appreciative laughter.

At this stage the disciples comment to Mary that the bottle is empty; she informs her son, as Mary does in John 2:

MARY   Come! (*to her son*). They have no more wine.

JESUS   Woman, what concern is that to you and me? My hour has not yet come!

MARY   Do whatever he tells you.

JESUS   Fill all these vases with water, and serve them. They shall have wine.

The camera provides a close-up of Jesus, then cuts away to the hotel.

RICHARD   So he was just like any other man! In the fourth century, after the Council of Nicaea, many Christians fought and even died to find out whether Christ was like the Father, or consubstantial.

The maître d' breaks off the discussion to welcome the dinner guests who have begun to fill the dining room.

This scene cleverly calls into question the conventions and stereotypes not so much of the Jesus films but of the well-known Renaissance representations of Jesus. In doing so, it also challenges the notion that Jesus was different from any ordinary man. Note that in contrast to Young's *Jesus*, in which Jesus' ability to provide wine is pivotal to his fledgling mission, here the camera cuts away just before the miracle does—or does not—occur. The inevitable conclusion, as the maître d' noted, is that Jesus was just like any other man: he is occasionally or perhaps chronically late for dinner; he rambles incoherently when he has had too much to drink; he runs around in the woods when opportunity arises; he is surrounded by people who not only tolerate but love him. In this scene it is the maître d' who has the dignity and the respectful following that a priest, or maybe Jesus himself might have commanded. Unlike Jesus, who is only a guest at the wedding dinner and a rather unruly one at that, the maître d' is the one who teaches his staff and provides a place at the table for all who enter his establishment.

THE PASSION OF THE CHRIST. If the silents and epics portray a Jesus who has numerous witnesses to his powers and messianic identity, Jesus Christ Superstar, Young's Jesus, and the films of Scorsese, Buñuel as well as Arcand, entertain the possibility of doubt, whether in the mind of Jesus, the mind of the viewer, or in the mind of the filmmaker. In a class of its own, however, is Gibson's opus. This film presents a paradoxical situation. On the one hand, its story presents flat characters who are either all good (Jesus, his mother, Mary Magdalene, Claudia, the disciples) or all evil (the Romans and the Jewish authorities). Obviously Gibson himself believes in Jesus' divinity, and expects that the reader will do the same.

But for some viewers, the film has the opposite effect. Far from perceiving Jesus' identity as the Son of God through his ability to endure the extreme suffering inflicted upon him, some viewers may fail even to perceive his humanity. The reason is simple: the relentless, numbing violence. For most of the film Jesus does not resemble a man so much as a hunk of raw meat. By reducing Jesus to an oozing pulp, Gibson has also demoted him from a human-divine being to a subhuman one. If Gibson intended to show Jesus' superhuman forbearance, he also made it almost impossible to feel compassion or concern as the relentless beating and bleeding prevent us from seeing Jesus as anything more than the broken body that becomes his own. It is no wonder that some scholars and reviewers have referred to this film as religious pornography.[11] Not only is Jesus' divine identity erased but his human identity is too.

Conclusion

The challenge to filmmakers is to make both Jesus' human and divine aspects evident to their viewers. Audiences who bring a prior knowledge of and even belief in Jesus as the son of God will easily see this view reflected in the films and overlook any potential credibility gap. Other audiences, however, may be mystified at the claim and may also fail to see the divine component in these silver-screen saviors.

None of these films fully overcomes the modern era's faith in science and the consequent skepticism about the miraculous. To the extent that movies simply expect us to accept Jesus' divine identity and God's divine paternity, they also fail to provide us with a Jesus who is believable in both his human and divine aspects. For such viewers, the most appealing Jesus may well be the very human Daniel/Jesus of Arcand's opus. Otherwise, the most successful— meaning, interesting—Jesus figures to secular audiences are those that struggle with their own identities. The genial Jesus of Young's miniseries, who has allegiance to two fathers, may be the most believable, as he views Joseph as his "real" father, and only gradually, and perhaps grudgingly, comes to acknowledge that God has a stake in him as well. Scorsese's Jesus is less believable but more emotionally compelling. His struggle is not between earthly and heavenly father but between God and Satan as the one who is guiding his path. We see him visibly struggling in a way that makes us feel some empathy or perhaps impatience. Fundamentally, however, this theme cuts to the core of the Jesus movies as a category within the biopic genre. From one point of view, these films tell the life story of an individual who has a profound crisis of identity, but from another point of view they do no less than recount a foundational moment in the divine biography itself.

PART IV

The Story

Jesus' Friends

7

Mary Magdalene

FIGURE 7.1. *The King of Kings,* 1927

FIGURE 7.2. *Jesus Christ Superstar,* 1973

FIGURE 7.3. *The Passion of the Christ,* 2004

What would a biopic be without romance? But how to inject romance into the story of the celibate son of God? Very few movies about Jesus dare to involve him in affairs of the heart or the body; those that try are roundly chastised for their audacity. But this restriction does not prevent Jesus films from the silent era to the present from exploiting the aura of sexuality that has long surrounded one of Jesus' most famous followers, Mary Magdalene.[1]

The Gospels provide scant details of Mary's association with Jesus. The fact that Jesus exorcised her demons (Luke 8:2; cf. Mark 16:9) suggests a profound transformation on her part.[2] Her presence at the foot of the cross along with Jesus' mother Mary implies a long-standing and close association with the family. The most detailed, and suggestive, passage in the Gospel literature is John 20:1–18, in which she goes to the tomb early on Sunday morning, finds it empty, and then encounters the Risen Lord. Mary is the first witness of the resurrected Lord and serves as an "apostle to the apostles."

These brief but tantalizing references provide filmmakers with the raw materials for a full-fledged romantic character. Their treatments address four questions: What was Mary's life like before meeting up with Jesus? How did she meet Jesus and come to travel with him? What was her status among and relationship with the disciples? And, most intriguing, what was her relationship to Jesus?

Mary's Life before Jesus

In the Gospels

The Gospels provide almost no information about Mary Magdalene's life before she appears among Jesus' entourage. Luke refers to Mary briefly (Luke 8:1–3):

> Soon afterwards he went on through cities and villages, proclaiming and bringing the good news of the kingdom of God. The twelve were with him, as well as some women who had been cured of evil spirits and infirmities: Mary, called Magdalene, from whom seven demons had gone out, and Joanna, the wife of Herod's steward Chuza, and Susanna, and many others, who provided for them out of their resources.

From this passage we may surmise that Mary had resources with which to support Jesus and his disciples, and that she had been possessed by seven demons until Jesus exorcised them.

The hypothesis that the historical Mary Magdalene was a wealthy busi-
nesswoman is developed in detail by Marianne Sawicki. Sawicki argues that
Mary's identification with the town of Migdal, which was also called Migdal
Nunya, meaning "fish tower," implies her involvement in the salt fish export
business. If so, we might posit international commercial and political connections.[3] Others make the contrary assessment. Luise Schottroff, for example,
cautions us against seeing her, as Luke does, as "a relatively wealthy city-
dweller far away from Palestine. . . . She belonged to the apparently very broad
class of the poor among the Jewish population at that time."[4]

The matter of Mary Magdalene's demons is even more difficult to evaluate.
Sawicki suggests that she may have suffered from a serious illness that had
abated and then returned in a more virulent form. The return and intensifi-
cation of the illness were implied by the multiplicity of demons. The relapse
was so serious that Mary showed signs of psychological affliction. When Jesus
healed her, he not only alleviated her bodily ailments but also allowed her to
rejoin her kinship group and her community.[5] Carla Ricci too suggests that the
demons were indicative of a psychological disorder. She suggests that Mary
Magdalene "may have been a woman of strong sensibilities, whose equilibrium
had not withstood the impact of the painful problems life can bring, particularly
those special problems a woman faced in the Palestine of Jesus' time."[6] All of
the theories remain pure speculation. In fact, our sources do not allow us to
discern anything about Mary Magdalene's physical or emotional health.

By far the most persistent element in Mary Magdalene's public image is
sexual promiscuity. Yet the Gospels provide no evidence about her sexual life,
let alone for promiscuity or prostitution. Rather, Mary Magdalene's reputation
for sexual immorality arose in the early centuries of the Church, and came
about as she was conflated with two unnamed women in the Gospel tradition.
One is the anonymous "sinner" who anoints Jesus' feet on the occasion of a
dinner party at the home of Simon the Pharisee:

> One of the Pharisees asked Jesus to eat with him, and he went into
> the Pharisee's house and took his place at the table. And a woman
> in the city, who was a sinner, having learned that he was eating in
> the Pharisee's house, brought an alabaster jar of ointment. She stood
> behind him at his feet, weeping, and began to bathe his feet with
> her tears and to dry them with her hair. Then she continued kiss-
> ing his feet and anointing them with the ointment. Now when the
> Pharisee who had invited him saw it, he said to himself, "If this
> man were a prophet, he would have known who and what kind of

woman this is who is touching him—that she is a sinner." (Luke
7:36–39)

The second is the anonymous woman caught in adultery (John 7:53–8:11):[7]

> Early in the morning he came again to the temple. All the people
> came to him and he sat down and began to teach them. The scribes
> and the Pharisees brought a woman who had been caught in adul-
> tery; and making her stand before all of them, they said to him,
> "Teacher, this woman was caught in the very act of committing
> adultery. Now in the law Moses commanded us to stone such
> women. Now what do you say?" They said this to test him, so that
> they might have some charge to bring against him. Jesus bent down
> and wrote with his finger on the ground. When they kept on ques-
> tioning him, he straightened up and said to them, "Let anyone among
> you who is without sin be the first to throw a stone at her." And
> once again he bent down and wrote on the ground. When they heard
> it, they went away, one by one, beginning with the elders; and Jesus
> was left alone with the woman standing before him. Jesus straight-
> ened up and said to her, "Woman, where are they? Has no one
> condemned you?" She said, "No one, sir." And Jesus said, "Neither
> do I condemn you. Go your way, and from now on do not sin again."

In addition, Mary was identified with Eve, who, as the woman who is thought
to have brought sexuality into the world through her disobedience of the divine
command.[8] In identifying Mary Magdalene with these three biblical women,
the tradition transformed her into an enduring object of prurient interest.

Mary Magdalene, however, is also associated with other women. One such
was Mary of Bethany (Luke 10:28–32; John 11; John 12), who, to our knowledge,
was pure as the driven snow. More surprisingly, she is also on occasion identified with Mary, Jesus' mother. In a vision of Cyril of Jerusalem (fourth-century
CE), Mary Magdalene declares: "I am Mary Magdalene because the name of the
village wherein I was born was Magdalia. My name is Mary of Cleopa. I am
Mary of James son of Joseph the Carpenter."[9] A similar identification occurs in
the Gospel of Bartholomew and Bartholomew's Book of the Resurrection.[10]

Mary has even been identified with goddess figures from outside biblical
tradition, such as Ishtar, Venus, Aphrodite, and Lady Wisdom. Malvern sum-
marizes these accretions:

> During the turbulent centuries of Christianity's beginnings, the Mag-
> dalene sketched in the canonical Gospels undergoes complex
> metamorphoses. Bits and pieces of goddesses not quite dead cluster

around the Mary Magdalene pictures in the Gospel of John as the woman who, lamenting the dead Christ, seeks him, and finding him resurrected, rejoices. She becomes a prostitute through identification of her with Luke's anonymous "sinner" who anointed the Christ. She absorbs the identity of the woman of Bethany who also, according to the canonical Gospels, anointed Jesus and thus becomes *the* anointer of the Anointed. Through her acquisition of a sister, Martha, and a brother, Lazarus, she is moved into closer relationships with Jesus. And her closeness to the Christ is further augmented in the Apocrypha where she is shown as the woman whom Jesus loved more than any other, Jesus' companion, 'the inheritor of the Light,' Christ's feminine counterpart, the Christian goddess of wisdom.[11]

In the Movies

In Christian tradition, Mary Magdalene has many faces, only one of which is that of a repentant adulteress or prostitute. Yet it is this element that has dominated, both in the popular imagination and in the conventions governing the Jesus biopic genre. One reason for this persistence may well be its usefulness. The view that Mary Magdalene was sexually immoral serves both to spice up the Jesus story, and to make it fit for moral instruction. Jesus biopics of all eras were as eager as other film genres to satisfy the public's appetite for the sexually suggestive. Mary Magdalene provides the only opportunity for a female sexual and love interest within the otherwise chaste story of Jesus of Nazareth.

The silent Jesus biopics combine Mary's presumed wealth and her alleged promiscuity in a stock scene that portrays her as a wealthy, beautiful courtesan. In *INRI*, a descriptive intertitle introduces Mary to the viewer: "Now there dwelt in the town a certain woman who had forgotten the teachings of her people." Mary, dressed in a white dress with "flapper" beads on the bodice is in the house that she shares with other courtesans. The other women are singing and playing instruments; Mary, meanwhile, is surrounded by men who fawn over her with offerings of flowers. Mary accepts their adoration but her manner is aloof, even stern.

Enter Jesus. Sizing him up as yet another admirer, Mary approaches him with a practiced smile. Her smile fades, however, as they stare at each other. The camera cuts back and forth between their faces. She tries to look away, then raises her arm across her eyes to avoid meeting his gaze. She, and the viewer, become aware of her immodest appearance. She hugs herself as if chilled and, in anguish, lets down her long hair so that it covers her body. She kneels down before Jesus and bends her head to his feet. The camera then cuts to Jesus, who looks up, and holds up his hand, to the amazement of the crowd. Mary raises her head and holds out her arms in a gesture of acceptance. He looks down and speaks to her. A restless crowd is now preparing to stone her with huge rocks. After Jesus intervenes on her behalf, she collapses by her bed.

Had the man been anyone other than Jesus, the voluptuous setting, Jesus' approach, and the intensity of the gaze between them would have heralded the beginning of a torrid romance.[12] As it is, the scene entertains and titillates but it nevertheless asks us to accept that the power of redemption and not the power of sexuality is at work.

Wealth and promiscuity also go hand in hand in the parallel scene in *Christus*. Like *INRI*, this silent film portrays Mary Magdalene as a beautiful courtesan in luxurious surroundings. She gazes at Jesus from the window above as she absent-mindedly plays with a bouquet of flowers. An intertitle describes her state of mind: "As she fondles the flowers—emblems of purity and chastity—her troubled conscience cries out against her iniquity." Now agitated, Mary drops the flowers from her hands, clasps her hands to her breasts, covers herself with a robe of white, and leaves her home to go out into the street searching for Jesus. She asks a child where he might be found. The camera cuts to Jesus in the house of the Pharisee; Mary comes in, removes her veil, and wipes Jesus' feet with her flowing hair. Jesus says: "Her sins, which are many, are forgiven, for she has loved much." He lifts up her head and speaks with her. She stands up and walks backwards and out of his presence as the Pharisees look on.

The scene builds upon Mary's customary conflation with the anonymous woman of Luke 7:36–39. While the movie is coy about her profession, her sexual promiscuity is implied; still, she is portrayed sympathetically as someone ripe for salvation. As in *INRI*, Mary's transformation is wrought by Jesus' intense gaze, and symbolized by a change to modest garb.

The feistiest and most flamboyant of all silent Magdalenes is DeMille's, who is center stage in the film's lengthy and amusing opening scene. As in the earlier silent movies, Mary is portrayed as "a beautiful courtesan," who entertains men in her decadently wealthy home. This Mary, however, is neither coy nor conflicted; rather, she "laughed alike at God and Man." Scantily dressed, she is surrounded by foppish men dressed in what was likely the 1920s image of "Oriental" (Middle-Eastern) men. Like her own pet leopard, Mary is imperious and wild. Her theme music is sensuous and slinky, evoking the supposed exoticism and decadence of the Orient as construed in film during the first third of the twentieth century.

As the scene opens, Mary is furious with her lover, Judas, who has vanished without a word. But one of her suitors knows Judas' whereabouts. Mary gasps—"a Woman! Her name—tell me, old Frog, or I choke thee"—and attacks him. Sputtering, he reveals: "Nay, 'twas no woman I saw him with—but a band of beggars, led by a carpenter from Nazareth."

Confident that she will not only reclaim her lover but also turn the head of this carpenter, she prepares to go to Nazareth immediately. "Go fetch my richest perfumes! Harness my zebras—gift of the Nubian King! This carpenter shall learn that He cannot hold a man from Mary Magdalene!" One suitor cautions: "Mary, I wager this purse of gold, thou canst not take Judas from Him! He hath some magic power—I, myself, beheld Him *heal the blind!*" Mary laughs this off confidently. "I take thy wager—I have blinded more men than He hath ever healed!" The suitor persists, however: "Cleopatra's ring against thy boast! Thou hast no chance with magic such as His—'tis said this Man hath *raised the dead!*" Before she can continue the dispute, her zebra-drawn chariot arrives, led by a young and virile charioteer. Mary cries: "Farewell—we go to call upon a carpenter!" The film then cuts to Nazareth, and, with a certain amount of narrative fanfare, finally introduces the viewers to Jesus. The Mary Magdalene subplot then resumes with Mary Magdalene's encounter with Jesus and the exorcism of her seven demons. *The King of Kings* is one of the very few films to portray this scene, but DeMille exploits its potential as metaphor to underscore Mary's sinfulness and hence the moral distance she travels when she repents.[13]

The scene begins with Mary's entry into Nazareth, as she searches for her lover Judas. "Where is this vagabond carpenter?" She demands. After someone points her in Jesus' direction, she struts over to Jesus and fixes her sultry gaze upon him. Then he looks at her and she cowers suddenly unsure of herself. She looks away, then stares back at him again. Jesus stands up and they stare at each other. She makes as if to leave, but turns back to him and then walks backwards as if she has been blinded; the audience gets its last good look at her attractive and scantily clad figure as Jesus continues to stare at her, and then pronounces: "Be thou clean!" As in the earlier silent movies, Jesus' gaze initially makes Mary highly uncomfortable, but then exercises its transformative power.

One by one, all of her demons depart, though not without a battle. For DeMille, the seven demons are the seven deadly sins: Lust, Greed, Pride, Gluttony, Indolence, Envy, and Anger. As soon as the last one departs, Mary Magdalene is suddenly fully dressed; she has robed herself, covered her hair, and assumed a facial expression of reverence and modesty. The camera cuts from Mary Magdalene to Mary, the mother of Jesus, then back to the Magdalene as she bends before Jesus and kisses the hem of his robe. Jesus puts his hand upon her hair and says: "Blessed are the pure in heart for they shall see God." Lust and her associates are banished, replaced by piety, purity, and chastity.

Mary's revealing outfit, her insolence, indolence, and hedonism, are meant to entertain and to titillate, important aspects of the moviegoing experience in the silent era.[14] The scene, however, does not fundamentally challenge the lofty aims articulated in the introductory titles: to convey the story of Jesus in a reverent manner that can lay some small claim to carrying out the mission to which Jesus called his disciples.

In the epics of the 1960s Mary is no longer a wealthy, self-assured courtesan. She has become a troubled woman who lacks self-respect or social support until she meets Jesus, his family, and his disciples. In Ray's *King of Kings*, she comes from Jerusalem to Nazareth to see where Jesus lives. To Mary, Jesus' mother, she describes herself as "a woman of sin" who has done much evil. She asks Mary to speak to her son on her behalf. Mary comforts her, invites her in for a meal, and tells her: "You would not have sought out this house if God had not wanted you to." In *The Greatest Story Ever Told* she is the woman caught in adultery, clothed in scarlet, with long flowing hair. This image is "quoted" in Gibson's film, which flashes back briefly to show us Mary, clad in red, as she lies in the sand clutching Jesus' ankle. The scene is not amplified; only viewers who bring prior knowledge of the Gospel passage, as well as of the tradition that identifies the woman caught in adultery as Mary Magdalene, will understand its significance here. Both films emphasize Mary Magdalene's transformation, symbolized by her change in wardrobe from a red robe to white modest garments, her long loose hair the only reminder of her disreputable past.

In Zeffirelli's *Jesus of Nazareth*, Mary Magdalene is identified with the woman who anoints Jesus' feet at Simon's house (Luke 8). The scene is dramatic. Jesus has been invited to dine in the home of a Pharisee, where a large crowd welcomes him warily. Their polite discussion is interrupted by Mary Magdalene who enters the room, wearing red and bearing a vial of oil. The atmosphere in the room is charged as the Pharisees object strenuously to the presence of this sinful woman, but Jesus welcomes her.[15]

PHARISEE   What's the matter?

OTHERS   Yes, yes. Whore! Yes it's her.

PHARISEE   What is she doing?

Mary bends down to kiss Jesus' feet.

BACKGROUND   She's defiling him.

SIMON   This is no place for you, woman. Leave quickly.

JESUS   Simon, sit down.

SIMON   But Rabbi, you know what kind of a woman this is.

JESUS   Simon, please.

Mary kisses Jesus' feet.

JESUS   Simon, when I came into your house, you didn't pour water over my feet or kiss me in greeting or anoint my head with oil. She has washed my feet with her tears and dried them with her hair and anointed them. Daughter, your sins, and I know they are many, are forgiven you, because of the greatness of your love.

BACKGROUND   Only God can forgive sins. No man!

JESUS   Your faith has saved you. Go, and sin no more.... Daughter, take this ointment and keep it till my burial. Go in peace.

The Pharisees watch her leave in silence.

Although Zeffirelli does not identify Mary as the adulterous woman of John 7:53–8:11, the Pharisees' response to her presence in their midst establishes Mary's sinful past and reminds us of the great moral distance she has traveled. The main point, however, is to contrast Jesus with the Pharisees. The Pharisees' commitment to the law is here shown to be rigid and elitist. By contrast, Jesus has compassion for everyone regardless of their social status.

Of the more recent films, it is Scorsese's *Last Temptation* that places the most emphasis on Mary Magdalene's reputation as a "sinful" woman. In Scorsese's film, Mary is a prostitute who services men from morning to night and is also identified as the woman caught in adultery. In this latter scene, Jesus interferes just as the crowd prepares to stone her, and secures her release by threatening a leader, Zebedee, with a bit of blackmail.

JESUS *(belligerently)*   Who has never sinned? Who? Which one of you people has never sinned? Whoever that is, come up here! And throw these!

ZEBEDEE   I have nothing to hide.

JESUS   Be careful, Zebedee, there is a God. He has seen you cheat your workers, he has seen you with that widow, what's her name?

SOMEONE FROM THE CROWD   Judith!

JESUS REPEATS   Judith....

Zebedee drops the stone, caught in his own hypocrisy. Jesus lifts up the terrified Mary Magdalene, who has been silent throughout. They cling to each other and walk away. Disciples follow behind, subdued. To himself, Jesus mutters: "God does so many miracles. What if I say the wrong thing? What if I say the right thing?" Jesus sits Mary down beside him, and asks the disciples to come closer. From this point on, Mary Magdalene is included among Jesus' disciples but, apart from the final dream sequence, the emotional and sexual tension between them has dissipated.

Jesus Christ Superstar too portrays Mary Magdalene as an integral part of Jesus' inner circle. But within this group her role is unique: to care for Jesus' physical needs. Mary Magdalene ensures that Jesus eats, drinks, and rests, to the extent that this is possible for a fugitive. Judas, however, bears an animosity toward her and criticizes Jesus for associating so closely with a woman "of her kind." In one scene, the camera takes us through a marketplace in which women are the most prominent commodity. While Mary Magdalene is not pictured among them, the implication is that Jesus has saved Mary, and can save other women, from this degradation.

In Young's less controversial film, Mary is not the woman who is caught in adultery, but her appearance—heavy make-up, cheap and showy clothing— evokes the stereotype of twentieth-century prostitutes as portrayed in the media.[16] The camera-work implies her sympathy for and identification with the woman as it cuts from Mary's pained facial expression to the helpless woman. After Jesus rescues the woman, Mary stares at him until he acknowledges her. He invites her to join him and his troupe.

JESUS   Do you want to come with us?

MARY (*warily*)   Where?

JESUS   Does it matter?

MARY   Yes. I go where I want, I'm free.

JESUS (*gently*)   You're not free, but you could be, if you come with us.

MARY   You treated her [the woman caught in adultery] like... like she was worth something.

JESUS   She is, and so are you.

Here Jesus articulates the view that an individual's worth is intrinsic rather than dependent on one's social roles, activities, or appearance. Freedom does not mean the absence of familial or other constraints; the freedom that Jesus offers is a spiritual state that includes freedom from negative judgments based on appearance or sexual behavior.

A film that studiously avoids associating Mary Magdalene with sexuality or promiscuity is the children's animated movie, *The Miracle Maker*. The film explains Mary's "possession" as mental illness. The narrator, the young girl Tamar (Jairus's daughter), witnesses Jesus' compassionate treatment of the woman who is suffering a fit of "madness," which heightens Tamar's interest in Jesus both because of her own compassionate nature and also because she too, like Mary, suffers from an apparently incurable illness. In avoiding the theme of sexual promiscuity, the film was not primarily catering to its young audience, but rather aiming for greater consistency with the Gospel of Luke, its primary source.[17]

Films after 1980 place less emphasis on Mary's promiscuous past. Nevertheless, Mary does not lose her reputation as a wanton woman. Even if they do not overemphasize her sinfulness, her clothing, hair, and makeup all allude to her promiscuity. This change may reflect the broader societal openness toward sex and sexuality that accompanied the widespread availability of birth control, and the loosening of strictures on the way that sexuality is portrayed on screen. Yet the admonitions from the Production Code era still linger. Even now, Mary's behavior remains unacceptable. In our era, however, her "demons" are not the seven deadly sins but the legacy of her troubled past and the symptom of an unstable personality. Magdalene still needs redemption.

Mary among the Apostles

In the Gospels

The Gospels of Luke and John indicate that Mary was well-known to the disciples and may even have been a regular member of their group.[18] In Luke, as we have noted, Mary and other women travel with Jesus and the disciples and provide financial support for them (Luke 8:3); in John 20, she runs to the disciples with the news of the empty tomb and later, with the message that the risen Jesus has ordered her to convey.

Three of the Gospels explicitly place Mary Magdalene at the scene of the crucifixion, whether from a distance (Synoptics) or immediately nearby (John). Matthew 27:56 specifies that Mary Magdalene, Mary the mother of James and Joseph, and the mother of the sons of Zebedee were present at the foot of the cross while Mark 15:40 comments that Mary Magdalene, Mary the mother of James the younger and of Joses, and Salome were among those looking on at a distance. Luke 24 refers to women from Galilee who witnessed the crucifixion and then saw where Jesus' body was laid. Luke 24:10 refers to Mary Magdalene, Joanna, and Mary the mother of James who, among other women, told the apostles of the empty tomb. This note may also imply that these three women were present at the crucifixion. John 19:25 comments that "standing near the cross of Jesus were his mother, and his mother's sister, Mary the wife of Clopas, and Mary Magdalene."

The theme of Mary Magdalene as disciple and apostle is not unique to our own era, in which feminist biblical criticism has paid attention to the possibilities for women's leadership in the Jesus movement as a model for contemporary Christian life.[19] In fact, there is a medieval legend that Mary Magdalene evangelized southern Gaul, in conjunction with her double apostolate as prophet and preacher, and that she also engaged in baptism.[20]

In the Movies

With the exception of *Jesus Christ Superstar*, in which Mary is Jesus' personal attendant, the cinematic Magdalene does not provide support of any sort for the disciples. Rather, she is the one who receives (emotional) support from Jesus. In ignoring Luke's brief note (Luke 8:3), the films imply that Jesus did not depend upon anyone but was supported by God alone. As in the gospels, she is often portrayed as traveling along with Jesus and his followers, indeed, as a member of his inner circle.

In the epic tradition, Mary Magdalene is a regular and familiar face in the crowds of disciples and followers who walk with Jesus, witness his miracles and listen to his speeches. Like most of the other characters, she has little to say on these occasions, but she is often present on the screen. In Zeffirelli's version of the multiplication of the loaves and fishes, the camera pans the "audience," that is, those who partook of the miracle and hence witnessed it. The camera lingers on Mary as she grasps the meaning of what she has just seen. Mary is overcome by emotion, tears of joy streaming down her face. In this way, she exemplifies the believer who witnesses the miracles and comes to a gradual and full understanding of Jesus' true identity. In some films, such as *Last Temptation*, Young's *Jesus*, and *The Gospel of John* she is present as a participant at the Last Supper. These films exploit the silence of the Gospels on the matter, while others, particularly those whose Last Supper scenes mirror Leonardo Da Vinci's famous painting, do not include any female disciples.[21] For their account of the crucifixion, the biopics most often rely upon the Fourth Gospel and portray Mary at the foot of the cross along with Jesus' mother and a young male disciple, John son of Zebedee.[22] Mary Magdalene's presence at the climax of Jesus' life implies her close relationship with Mary the mother of Jesus, and, of course, Jesus himself.

One striking element of the biopic treatment of Mary Magdalene is the attention paid to her relationship to another Mary, Jesus' mother. This theme is present throughout the genre, beginning with the epics and continuing through Gibson's film. In *The Greatest Story Ever Told*, as well as in Young's *Jesus*, Jesus' mother takes the younger Mary under her wing and offers her hospitality and a maternal shoulder to cry on. In Young's *Jesus*, they are almost always in each other's company as the action moves relentlessly toward the

Passion. Once the trials begin, they comfort each other as they await news. Mary Magdalene weeps: "I can't watch them murder him." Mary, grieving but calm, responds: "Pray for my son, you will stand by him with me." The two embrace. Similarly in Gibson's movie, the two women are inseparable. On occasion they are joined by a third woman, Claudia, Pilate's wife. Claudia is highly sympathetic to them but due to her husband's role she must keep her distance. Claudia's affinity for the two women emerges in the scene in which Claudia gives them clean white linens to wipe the copious amounts of Jesus' blood up from the pavement upon which he has been tortured and scourged.

Zeffirelli's film even has Mary, mother of Jesus, acknowledge Mary Magdalene as one of the family. The women are stopped by the guards as they rush together to the crucifixion field. Mary must make a choice between in-cluding Mary Magdalene in their family or leaving her behind.

GUARD   Hey, hey, hey, hey, hey, who are you?

MARY   Jesus' mother.

GUARD   How can you prove it?

GUARD 2   Hey! She *is* his mother. Go. (*stops MM*)

MM   Please, I'm one of the family.

GUARD 2   Is that right?

MARY (*hesitating only slightly*)   Yes, she is one of the family.

Whatever mild distaste Jesus' mother may have felt at including Mary in the family has dissipated by the third day. Early in the morning, the three women in black walk toward the tomb.

GUARD   Hey, stop! Who are you? Where are you going?

MARY   We are the family of Jesus of Nazareth, who lies here.

GUARD   What do you want?

MARY   To enter the tomb.

GUARD   Why?

MARY   To anoint the body, to bring fresh linen, herbs, spices. It is our custom.

GUARD   Why didn't you do that when you brought him here?

MARY   The Sabbath began, we could not buy them.

GUARD   What do you think? (*to other guard*).

OTHER GUARD   They're only three women, let them go.

The close association of Mary Magdalene with Mary, Jesus' mother, serves to domesticate Mary, by bringing her into the family, and at the same time defusing the potential of a romantic or sexual entanglement with Jesus or anyone else in the "family."

Between the silents, epics and post-70s dramas, the attitude of the filmmakers toward Mary has changed, from fascination with and exploitation of her sexuality in the silent films, to the pious moralization evident in her treatment in the epics, to a sympathetic and respectful treatment in the later films. This shift is expressed not only in dialogue, camera-work, and other visual elements but also in the choice of which Gospel scenes to emphasize. Whereas the silent and epic treatments focus on the adulterous woman and female "sinner" scenes, usually identifying Mary with both of these unnamed women, the later films emphasize her role as apostle to the apostles and ascribe to her a close relationship with Mary, mother of Jesus.

If we did not "know" that Mary is neither Jesus' sister nor his wife or lover, we might even think that the two Marys were related as mother-daughter, or mother-in-law/daughter-in-law. In Young and Gibson in particular, they are each other's mainstay in time of crisis, turning to each other for support and comfort, bound by their love for Jesus, their fear for his life, and their sorrow at his fate.

Apostle to the Apostles

In the Gospels

Mary's big movie scene occurs at the empty tomb. In all four Gospels, Mary comes to Jesus' tomb on Sunday morning (Matthew 28:1; Mark 16:1; Luke 24:10; John 20:1). But it is John 20 that provides the most detailed and poignant account and that is the source for her reputation as "apostle to the apostles." When Jesus reveals himself to Mary in the garden, he bids her to "go to my brothers and say to them, 'I am ascending to my Father and your Father, to my God and your God.' Mary Magdalene went and announced to the disciples, 'I have seen the Lord'; and she told them that he had said these things to her" (John 20:17–18).

The response of the disciples is not stated; we do not know whether they accepted or dismissed her comments. The biopic treatments of this gap reveal not only their response to this specific question but also imply their answers to the question of whether Jesus had female disciples. This question remains pertinent to the contemporary discussion of whether women are or should be included among the church leadership.[23] It is noteworthy, however, that John

20 contrasts her favorably with Doubting Thomas. Whereas Mary Magdalene believes without touching Jesus, Thomas refuses to believe "Unless I see the mark of the nails in his hands, and put my finger in the mark of the nails and my hand in his side, I will not believe" (20:25).

In the Movies

The Jesus biopics follow the Gospel of John in their portrayal not only of the crucifixion scene but also of Jesus' resurrection appearances. For this reason, many depict Mary Magdalene's emotional encounter with Jesus at the empty tomb. But at this point, most fall short of declaring her to be the "apostle to the apostles." As Jane Schaberg points out, Zeffirelli's Mary Magdalene is displaced by other characters: Jesus' mother, at the foot of the cross, and the disciples, especially Peter, after the resurrection. In the latter scene, the disciples do not believe Mary; they are evasive, almost embarrassed by her certainty. At the end of the film, Jesus appears to the disciples; they gather and then are sent out to make more disciples. For Schaberg, "the power of the Magdalene's last scene and the empty door . . . has drained all power from these all-male scenes that follow it. . . . In spite of Peter's attempt to pull us in, the resistant viewer has been long gone, out the door with the Magdalene."[24]

But in Young's *Jesus* Mary's testimony is taken seriously by everyone, including the disciples. When Mary Magdalene sees the tomb is open she runs back to the disciples:

MARY MAGDALENE   They've stolen his body!

DISCIPLE   What?

MARY MAGDALENE   The stone was rolled away! They've taken his body!

PETER   Taken?

MARY (*Jesus' mother*)   They've taken his body?

All the disciples get up. John and Peter run out.

DISCIPLE   John, Peter, no! It's not safe!

John and Peter run to the tomb and discover it empty.

PETER   John!

JOHN   He is risen!

PETER   Risen? No, the body's stolen!

JOHN   He said "After three days, I will rise again!"

PETER   Risen?

JOHN   He's alive!

They both smile and laugh and run out of the tomb, and bump into Mary Magdalene.

JOHN   Mary, he's alive!

PETER   He said he would rise after three days, he's alive!

JOHN   Come on! We must tell the others! Come on!

Mary Magdalene walks toward the tomb and starts to cry.

JESUS   Woman! Why are you weeping?

MARY MAGDALENE   They carried my Lord away. Tell me where you bring him, please!

JESUS   Mary.

Mary Magdalene embraces Jesus, sobbing.

JESUS   Mary, you must let me go now, so I may ascend to my father. Now go to the others and tell them I'm alive. Mary, you go and tell them for me.

Mary appears before the disciples.

DISCIPLES   What do you mean you think you've seen him? It's been three days, he's dead.

MARY MAGDALENE   I've seen him.

MARY   Is it true, Mary?

MARY MAGDALENE   Yes, it's true. I've seen him. I talked to him.

THOMAS   This is ridiculous, we saw him crucified, we buried him ourselves. How could he be alive?

PETER   How could Lazarus be alive?

JOHN   How could blind men see?

THOMAS   I'm sorry, but I don't believe that death is conquered that easily. There are too many other possibilities.

DISCIPLE   He is the son of God!

THOMAS   Jesus himself said there would be false prophets. We have to be careful! This could be a trick!

MARY   Thomas, you must believe.

THOMAS   I want to, believe me Mary, I want to, but my mind won't let me, I'd have to see for myself.

MARY MAGDALENE   Thomas, I saw him.

THOMAS   Are you sure it was him?

Mary Magdalene smiles.

THOMAS   Did you see the wounds in his wrists?

Mary Magdalene is silent.

THOMAS   See? She can't be sure. Something else is going on here. Unless I see the mark of the nails, no, unless I put my finger in the mark of the nails, I will not believe.

JESUS   Peace be with you.

All the disciples turn around.

Less conventional is the Passion play that is at the core of *Jesus of Montreal*. This play adopts the perspective of Doubting Thomas by suggesting that the desire of the disciples to encounter their dead master again was so strong that it caused them to see him everywhere. The vision of the Risen Lord was born of love and desperation, not reliable sensory perception.

CONSTANCE   He'd been long dead. Five years, perhaps ten. His disciples had scattered . . . disappointed . . . bitter . . . and desperate.

RENÉ   To die, to sleep, no more. To end the heartache and the thousand shocks that flesh is heir to. That is the deliverance we long for. To die, to sleep, perchance to dream. . . . Who would fardels bear to grunt and sweat under a weary life, but that the dread of something after death, the undiscover'd country whence no traveler returns, makes us rather bear those ills we have, than fly to others that we know not of.[25]

CONSTANCE   No traveler but one, him.

Mireille opens a gate and runs to Martin.

MIREILLE   I saw him!

MARTIN   Who?

MIREILLE   Him.

MARTIN   Come on.

MIREILLE   I swear. At first I wasn't sure. He's different. Suddenly I knew it was him speaking to me. (*Martin scoffs and walks away.*) He was right there. I swear. Believe me.

DANIEL (*as Jesus*)   You two seem sad.

CONSTANCE   We were recalling a lost friend.

MARTIN   A great prophet.

DANIEL (*as Jesus*)   Take this (*breaks bread*).

CONSTANCE   Lord. It's you! It's you!

MIREILLE (*as narrator*)   Slowly people were convinced. He had changed. No one recognized him at first. But they all came to believe he was there.

Mary and Jesus

In the Gospels

John 20:1–18 not only presents Mary as the "apostle to the apostles," but it also intimates that Mary enjoyed a special relationship with Jesus that was quite different from that enjoyed by the other disciples. Indeed, when read carefully, sexual allusions abound. The most obvious reference is Jesus' admonition in 20:17: "Do not hold on to me, because I have not yet ascended to the Father." The warning is ambiguous: is Mary already touching him, in which case Jesus is asking that she cease and desist, is she reaching up to touch him, a touch which Jesus wishes to avoid, or is Jesus simply anticipating that in her joy at finding him alive she is likely to throw herself at him?[26] On any of these readings, however, both the romantic potential and Jesus' rejection of Mary's touch emerge clearly.

But the sexual allusions go beyond this verse. Ancient audiences familiar with either the Greek or Hebrew versions of the Song of Songs would have noticed some striking similarities in wording between this biblical love song and John 20:1–18. These parallels are not meant to suggest that Jesus and Mary were physical lovers but that their reunion after Jesus' death consummates the spiritual love affair between Jesus (God) and his followers (believers), an interpretation entirely in keeping with the ways in which the Song of Songs was read by ancient Jews and, later, by Christians.[27]

In the Movies

As we have seen, the silent films linger on the smoldering stares between Jesus and Mary that in any other type of film would have them locked in a passionate embrace before the next intertitle. Other elements of these films, however, do not allow us to view the passion in these gazes as anything but piety and repentance. The epics of the 1960s and 1970s, while no longer governed by the need to adhere to the Production Code, nevertheless protect Jesus' virtue by steering him away from compromising situations.

Later films, however, occasionally step, tentatively or boldly, over the line to imply or explicitly to portray Jesus and Mary as lovers in the romantic and sexual sense. Young's *Jesus* presents an intimate evening conversation. In another film, with another hero, an encounter like this, on a sultry summer evening, would have led to romance. Here, it leads only to the spiritual devotion implied in John 20.

JESUS   My father taught me how to get the best wood from a tree like this.

MARY   Were you a good carpenter?

JESUS   It's good I started preaching.

Mary laughs.

JESUS   See, Joseph used to say that everyone's hands were educated, but it wasn't true He was the wisest man I've known, wise and generous, he would give his last crust to a stranger.

MARY   Even to a Gentile?

JESUS   You question me too, Mary?

MARY   No, never, I would never question you.

JESUS   But you question yourself?

MARY   I just don't understand how you can believe in someone like me.

JESUS   God forgives you, Mary.

MARY   If I were a man, I would be your most loyal disciple.

JESUS   Those who speak for me are my disciples.

Here Mary expresses her devotion to Jesus and her gratitude to him for accepting her as she is. The feminist struggle for participation in Christian community leadership is implicitly evoked in her initial assumption that she is excluded from discipleship by her gender, an assumption that Jesus challenges.

Even the visual aspects of this film discourage us from viewing Jesus and Mary as a potential couple. In the first place, their appearance suggests a discrepancy in their age; Mary Magdalene looks considerably older than Jesus, though somewhat younger than his mother. Second, their clothing suggests a discrepancy in social status. Jesus is dressed in the loose flowing clothing that is a nod both to the bathrobe and sandals costuming of the epics and to the hippie or youth styles of the 1960s and later. Mary, by contrast, is overdressed

and wears heavy makeup. These differences show that for Young's *Jesus* Mary
would not have been the right love interest for Jesus even if he were not the Son
of God. In fact, the film offers a much more suitable candidate in the figure of
the young, demure Mary of Bethany, whose age and fashion style coheres
much better with those of Jesus. Mary is very much in love with Jesus, and he
with her. It takes him some time to accept that his divine identity and mission
must keep him from marrying her. She understands this fully only when he
returns to Bethany and raises her brother Lazarus from the dead.

Jesus Christ Superstar and the films of Arcand and Scorsese explore the
erotic potential of the relationship between Jesus and Mary in greater depth. In
Jesus Christ Superstar, Mary Magdalene is almost always in close physical
proximity to Jesus as she cares for his physical needs—food, drink, rest, and,
perhaps, more. They frequently embrace, with a fervor that steps beyond the
bounds of platonic or spiritual friendship. Mary sings at length of her love for
Jesus, in the famous solo: "I Don't Know How to Love Him." Judas, of course,
disapproves:

> Yes, I can understand that she amuses,
> But to let her kiss you, stroke your hair,
> That's hardly in your line.
> It's not that I object to her profession,
> But she doesn't fit in well,
> With what you teach and say.
> It doesn't help us if you're inconsistent,
> They only need an excuse to come after us, to put us all away.

Jesus responds with anger:

> Who are you to criticise her,
> Who are you to despise her,
> Leave her leave her, let her be now,
> Leave her leave her, she's with me now,
> If your slate is clean then you can throw stones,
> If your slate is not then leave her alone!
> I'm amazed that men like you,
> can be so shallow thick and slow,
> there is not a man among you,
> who knows or cares if I come or go.

Here Jesus may simply be coming to Mary's defense, as his scriptural counterpart does for the anonymous adulteress in John 7:53–8:11. But Mary's behavior implies a far greater intimacy, as she caresses him and coos:

Try not to get worried,
Try not to turn on to
Problems that upset,
Don't you know everything's all right now, everything's fine.
I want you to sleep well tonight.

Mary loves Jesus and expresses her love physically. Jesus accepts her love and her physical attentions, and even seeks them out. At one point, she offers: "Let me try to cool down your face a bit." She anoints him, and Jesus purrs: "Mary, that is good . . ." Were it not for his exalted identity, viewers would not question that they were sexually involved. As it stands, the jury is out.

Arcand's film is even more ambiguous. The Mary Magdalene figure in *Jesus of Montreal* is Mireille, who comes to the acting troupe led by Daniel/Jesus after a career of "selling her body" in television advertisements. There are two scenes that imply physical intimacy. In one scene, she sits beside him and lathers him up as he bathes. The easy intimacy implies an ongoing sexual relationship. The scene alludes to the various anointing scenes in the Gospels, including the one involving the anonymous woman who, as we have noted, is often conflated with Mary Magdalene. The second scene occurs after the "cleansing" of the Temple, in which Daniel has vigorously and violently chased the advertising tycoons out of the theater in which they are holding auditions for a beer commercial. What prompted Daniel's burst of anger was the director's demand that Mireille remove her sweatshirt as part of her audition. Afterwards, outside the theater, Mireille grabs Daniel's shirt and runs her hands down his chest as they gaze into each other's eyes. She says, "I love you, you crazy nut," and kisses him on the cheek. Does this imply a sexual relationship or not? Daniel is ascetic in appearance and refined and reasonable in his behavior. He is loving toward Mireille, but also toward the others who are bound to him in the Passion play project. Mireille clearly loves him, but whether this love is consummated sexually is never made explicit.[28] Arcand's point surely is that Daniel, unlike the hypocritical Father LeClerc, has not taken a vow of celibacy. Whether he and Mireille have a sexual relationship is irrelevant to Jesus' salvific role.

Most notorious, however, is Scorsese's film. That Mary and Jesus had a past fraught with sexual and romantic tension is clear in the early scenes of the film. Jesus waits in the entryway to the boudoir where she is "entertaining" men the whole day through. After all her clients have left, he enters the room where she is lying naked with her back to him. She turns and sees him, and immediately pulls the sheets over herself, recalling the response that the silent Magdalenes had to Jesus' penetrating gaze. But this Mary clearly has a long and complicated prior relationship with this Jesus. When she catches sight of him, she gasps in surprise: "What are you doing here?"

JESUS   I want you to forgive me. I've done too many bad things. I'm going to the desert and I need you to forgive me before I go. Please.

MARY MAGDALENE   Oh, I see. You sit out there all day with the others, and then you come in here with your head down saying "Forgive me?" Forgive me . . . It's not that easy. Just because you need forgiveness don't ask me to do it.

JESUS   I'm sorry.

MARY MAGDALENE   No, get out, go away! I just . . . I just . . .

JESUS   Look, Mary, look at this. God can change this. God can save your soul.

MARY MAGDALENE   He already broke my heart, he took you away from me and I hate both of you.

JESUS   Hate me, blame me, it's all my fault, but not God's. Don't say that about God.

MARY MAGDALENE   Who made me feel this way about God?

JESUS   I know, that's why I'm here. That's why I want you to forgive me. I'll pay my debt. I know the worst things that I've done and to you.

MARY MAGDALENE   Pay it and go away.

JESUS   Mary? Don't you remember?

MARY MAGDALENE   No, I don't remember, why should I? Nothing's changed. Say the truth. You want to save my soul. This is where you'll find it. You know that. You're the same as all the others only you can't admit it. You're pitiful. I hate you. Here's my body, save it. Save it.

She takes his hand and puts it on her stomach. Jesus turns away and tears his hand away.

MARY MAGDALENE   Is that the way you're sure you're a man? Turn away, don't look at me. You don't have the courage to be a man, don't look at me! You weren't hanging on to your mother, you were hanging on to me, now you're hanging on to God. You're going into the desert to hide because you're scared. Now go, whenever I see you my heart breaks. *She touches his cheek and mouth and chin and knee.*

MARY MAGDALENE: I do remember when we were children. Never have I felt so much tenderness toward anyone as I felt toward you then. All I ever wanted was you, nothing else.

JESUS: What do you think I wanted?

MARY MAGDALENE: Please, stay. Is it so bad sharing a prostitute's room? I won't touch you, I promise, you'll still be a virgin for the desert.

JESUS: Mary, I'm sorry, I can't stay.

He gets up to go off to the desert.

The scene implies sexual longing on both parts but emphasizes Jesus' refusal to consummate the relationship. At this early stage we do not know whether to read his refusal as strength, weakness, or fear. The dialogue reverses the usual dynamic attributed to this relationship. Whereas in Young and other films, Mary seeks forgiveness from Jesus for her sexual misdemeanors, here it is Jesus who seeks Mary's forgiveness for having driven her away from God and the conventional life of marriage and family.

Later on in the film, Jesus rescues Mary Magdalene from those who would stone her for adultery. From that point on she accompanies him as a follower or disciple, the sexual tensions dissipate, and she does not take on a distinct role in the narrative. But in a final fantasy scene, the dynamic changes completely. Jesus steps down from the cross and walks across a bright meadow to wed Mary Magdalene. Mary is wearing virginal white; their sexual union is joyful and uncomplicated by guilt. She becomes pregnant, but dies before the child is born. Jesus then cohabits with both Mary and Martha of Bethany, with whom he has a number of children. *The Last Temptation* is about domesticity, of which sexuality is an important part but not an end in itself.

Conclusion

The Gospel account of Mary Magdalene leaves gaps with regard to her life before she joined up with Jesus' group, her role among the apostles, and her relationship with Jesus. Filmmakers are by no means the first to fill these gaps. Mary has held an enduring allure for theologians, writers, artists, and many others, male and female, who have used their imaginations to fill out this character in ways that reflect their own interests and concerns.

Until the 1980s, Jesus biopics played up Mary's promiscuous past; the later films, including Gibson's, do not necessarily ignore this traditional view of Mary as repentant whore but neither do they emphasize it nor do they pass moral judgment upon her to the same extent as do the earlier films. In the silent movies, and more subtly, in recent ones as well, Mary fills the requirement for sexual titillation, though she is tamed by her transformation to a modest and pious woman.

A similar change over time can be seen in the cinematic treatments of Mary Magdalene's relationship to the disciples. The Gospels are silent on the question of whether Mary or other women were among the closest disciples, leaving it to filmmakers to make up their own minds. The early films, including the silents and the epics, omit her, but some include her and Jesus' mother.[29] This development reflects the influence of the women's movement and changes in the hierarchies of some Christian communities to include women on an equal basis with men.

The third and perhaps trickiest issue is the relationship between Mary and Jesus. Most biopics show this relationship as asymmetrical, as is Jesus' relationship with all of the disciples. Jesus takes care of Mary spiritually; although she reciprocates somewhat in her anointing of him and her devotion, the hierarchy is clear. Hanging in the air is the aura of sexuality that is rarely developed fully either in the Gospels or in the biopics. The reasons for the Gospels' silence on the matter are not possible to discern, but at the very least reflects their lack of interest in Jesus' personal life that is also in evidence in the brevity of their accounts of his childhood. On the part of the filmmakers one may speculate that a number of factors are at work: the remnants of the Production Code which prohibited irreverential treatments of religious figures; concerns that portraying a sexually active Jesus may offend their target audiences (a concern that *The Da Vinci Code* may well have dispelled) and perhaps genuine attempts to uphold a conservative "family values" agenda that disapproves of extramarital sex, on the part of Jesus or any other character.[30]

But theology, specifically Christology, is also at stake. The movies offer offer three different portrayals of Jesus. One is an asexual Jesus whose human nature did not extend to or include sexually intimate relationships. Rather, his love is impersonal, offered equally to all of humankind. The modern film that comes closest to representing this is Arcand's *Jesus of Montreal*, in which Daniel/Jesus loves all of his friends (his "disciples").

Then there is the conflicted Jesus, who, being human, has sexual feelings and desires, upon which he does not or cannot act due to his higher mission. This is the case in Young's *Jesus* and Scorsese's *Last Temptation*. In both of these films, but particularly the latter, Jesus is shown as struggling against his human nature and sexual desire for women. This dynamic is in itself evidence of the profound impact of Christian theology on our culture's understanding of Jesus' personhood. Nowhere in the Gospels does it say that Jesus had to be celibate, and indeed we do not know that he was (or was not), as the Gospels, in contrast to Paul (1 Corinthians 7) are not at all interested in this question.

Finally there is the sexual Jesus. This Jesus comes to the fore in the fantasy portion of *Last Temptation*, and, perhaps more openly, in *Jesus Christ Superstar*, where the focus is on Jesus as a celebrity whose divinity is by no means clear even to his followers.

It would be tempting to suggest that the varied portrayals of Mary Magdalene, particularly in her relationship with Jesus, represent our society's relatively recent preoccupation with sexuality in general, and the ongoing questions regarding Jesus' fundamental humanity, of which sexuality, at least in theory, would be a part. But in fact the history of Christian tradition, theology, literature, and art have been preoccupied with this issue, and with Mary Magdalene's role in Jesus' life, for close to two millennia.[31] The runaway commercial success of Dan Brown's novel *The Da Vinci Code*, which claims that Jesus and Mary married and had a child whose line continues to this very day, also testifies to an ongoing fascination with Mary not only in Christian circles but in our culture more generally.

8

Judas

FIGURE 8.1. *Jesus Christ Superstar,* 1973

FIGURE 8.2. *Jesus of Nazareth,* 1977

FIGURE 8.3. *The Last Temptation of Christ,* 1988

Jesus may be the hero of the Jesus biopics, but Judas—the disciple who betrays Jesus unto death—is their most compelling figure. Whereas the cinematic Jesus is usually static, entirely good, and therefore predictable, Judas is volatile, dramatic, intense, and surprising. As one of the few Gospel characters who undergoes emotional development—from devotion to betrayal to remorse to suicide—Judas holds great promise for filmmakers seeking to inject passion and drama into their Jesus biopics. No wonder, then, that he carries the dramatic weight of many of these films.

Judas is also a potent figure from a theological perspective. This disciple raises in a stark way the possibility that basking in Jesus' presence guarantees neither faith nor morality. Further, Judas is the subject of an equivocal theology. On the one hand, he must surely be held accountable for handing Jesus over to the authorities. On the other hand, is not Jesus' Passion essential for the fulfillment of the divine plan of salvation? Were it not for the crucifixion, there would be no sacrifice and no resurrection. Finally, in the history of interpretation and cultural appropriation, Judas plays a central role as a character around whom the issue of anti-Judaism and anti-Semitism coalesce.[1]

The New Testament portrait of Judas leaves numerous gaps. Indeed, Judas is barely mentioned before the events leading up to the Passion. Most pressing, however, is the question of motivation: Why did Judas betray Jesus? Underlying this issue is an even more tantalizing question: What was the nature of Judas's personal relationship with Jesus?[2]

The Betrayal

In the Gospels

The Gospels assume that readers are already familiar with Judas' role in Jesus' final hours. This may be one reason for their lack of emphasis on Judas' motivations for betraying Jesus. They do, however, provide some indirect hints that later interpreters, including biopic filmmakers, developed at greater length.

The Gospel of Matthew sees greed as one motivating factor. Matthew describes how Judas Iscariot "went to the chief priests and said, 'What will you give me if I betray him to you?' They paid him thirty pieces of silver. And from that moment he began to look for an opportunity to betray him" (Matthew 26:14–16).

Whether he was greedy or not, Judas' act set in motion a series of events that, however tragic, were also essential to Jesus' mission of salvation, according to the New Testament as well as later Christian theology. If so, Judas' action, though repugnant, was also a divinely ordained necessity.[3] As Jesus teaches his disciples, "the Son of Man must undergo great suffering, and be rejected by the elders, the chief priests, and the scribes, and be killed, and after three days rise again" (Mark 8:31). The Gospel of John develops this point at length:

> No one has ascended into heaven except the one who descended from heaven, the Son of Man. And just as Moses lifted up the serpent in the wilderness, so must the Son of Man be lifted up, that whoever believes in him may have eternal life. For God so loved the world that he gave his only Son, so that everyone who believes in him may not perish but may have eternal life. (3:13–16)

This theological concept, however, is difficult to render in cinematic terms.

Despite the fact that Jesus' death is part of the divine plan, Judas's role in the matter is still seen as shameful.[4] Indeed, Luke blames Satan for Judas's act of betrayal:

> Now the festival of Unleavened Bread, which is called the Passover, was near. The chief priests and the scribes were looking for a way to put Jesus to death, for they were afraid of the people. Then Satan entered into Judas called Iscariot, who was one of the twelve; he went away and conferred with the chief priests and officers of the temple police about how he might betray him to them. They were greatly pleased and agreed to give him money. So he consented and began to look for an opportunity to betray him to them when no crowd was present. (Luke 22:1–5)

John too hands over a measure of responsibility to Satan. By the time the disciples gather for their meal, John says, "The devil had already put it into the heart of Judas son of Simon Iscariot to betray him" (John 13:2). The motif becomes even more elaborate during the final meal itself:

> After saying this Jesus was troubled in spirit, and declared, "Very truly, I tell you, one of you will betray me." The disciples looked at one another, uncertain of whom he was speaking. One of his disciples— the one whom Jesus loved—was reclining next to him; Simon Peter therefore motioned to him to ask Jesus of whom he was speaking. So while reclining next to Jesus, he asked him, "Lord, who is it?" Jesus answered, "It is the one to whom I give this piece of bread when I have dipped it in the dish." So when he had dipped the piece of bread, he gave it to Judas son of Simon Iscariot. After he received the piece of bread, Satan entered into him. Jesus said to him, "Do quickly what you are going to do." Now no one at the table knew why he said this to

him. Some thought that, because Judas had the common purse, Jesus was telling him, "Buy what we need for the festival"; or, that he should give something to the poor. So, after receiving the piece of bread, he immediately went out. And it was night. (John 13:21–30)

This passage holds in tension the role of Satan and the requirements of the divine plan. Jesus is not only aware, in a prophetic sense, of what Judas is about to do and why, but he also triggers the betrayal himself when he commands, "Do quickly what you are going to do" (John 13:27).

More concrete, and hence easier to depict, are the potential political angles to Judas's behavior.[5] Was Judas one of those who expected Jesus to liberate Israel from the yoke of Roman rule? If so, then two possibilities come to mind: that Judas wanted to engineer a "face off" between Jesus and the authorities that was essential in order to start the revolution,[6] or that Judas became disillusioned when he realized that Jesus was not a political savior after all.

As to what exactly Judas betrayed—Jesus' identity? His whereabouts? His putative anti-Roman activities?—the Gospels are not very clear. According to Schweitzer, Judas revealed that Jesus believed himself to be the messiah; according to Sanders, Judas told the Romans that Jesus claimed to be a king; according to Chilton, Judas revealed the ideology of the meals, that is, Judas betrayed what he had experienced with the disciples in the farewell dinner with Jesus. Brown argues that Judas' intention was to show the Jewish authorities how they could arrest Jesus without public disturbance.[7]

In the Movies

With the exception of the early silent films and Gibson's *Passion*, the Jesus biopics attempt to show cause-and-effect with regard to the major events in Jesus' life. Even so, a handful of films do not supply Judas with a motivation for betraying Jesus. In *The Greatest Story Ever Told*, Judas is highly distressed but we are not told why. Throughout his meeting with the Jewish authorities he is distraught and even confused (as is the viewer).

JUDAS (*weeping*) I will give him to you, if you promise that no harm will come to him.

JEWISH AUTHORITIES If you are willing to give him to us, why do you care what happens to him?

JUDAS Jesus is the purest, and kindest man I have ever known. I have never seen him do anything but good. His heart is gentle, old people worship him. Children adore him. I love him.

JEWISH AUTHORITIES   Very well. We will do our best to see that no harm comes to the man. Where do we find him?

JUDAS   You cannot.

JEWISH AUTHORITIES (*impatiently*)   Just tell us and we will send the guards.

JUDAS   I will lead you to him tonight. I must be there. I'm not so much a coward that I cannot face him when I stab him.

JEWISH AUTHORITIES   We shall be waiting.

In *Jesus of Montreal*, on the other hand, Judas does not appear at all in the portions of the Passion play that are presented to the movie viewers, though he may well have had a role in the full version that was seen by the play's audience on Montreal's Mount Royal. Within the frame narrative, however, there are a number of candidates. One is the security guard at St. Joseph's Oratory, who alerts the priest, Father Leclerc, that the actors are on the premises and plan to stage a final performance of the Passion play despite Leclerc's explicit orders to the contrary.[8] But this is a passing moment, related to the comic role that the guard plays elsewhere in the film. Father Leclerc himself betrays Daniel when he shuts down the Passion play because it challenges the authority of the Church. Even some members of Daniel's acting troupe are prepared to betray him, that is, his artistic vision, by negotiating with "Satan," the lawyer Richard Cardinal, who seeks to exploit Daniel's death for financial gain.

Judas's Personality

A number of films build upon the Gospels' brief hints about Judas's greed in order to explain Judas's motivation. *Der Galiläer* explicitly describes Judas as someone who loves silver. In Ray's *King of Kings* the camera lingers on Judas as Jesus declares: "No man can serve two masters, either he will hate the one and love the other, or he will cling to the one and despise the other, you cannot serve God and Mammon" (cf. Matthew 6:24; Luke 16:13).

Judas's greed is frequently evident through the camera's eye, which focuses relentlessly on him as he accepts the thirty pieces of silver (e.g., in Heyman's *Jesus*, DeMille's *The King of Kings*, and Gibson's *The Passion of the Christ*). Both DeMille and Gibson emphasize the financial exchange between Caiaphas and Judas. In DeMille, the two are seated across from each other at a small table. Caiaphas talks intently to Judas, asking, "Dost thou swear to betray to us His secret place of prayer, that we may destroy him?" Judas listens, hunched over his knees, hands clasped, the picture of misery. Caiaphas counts out the coins on the table in front of him. The camera slows to focus on this exchange, emphasizing greed as a feature both Caiaphas and Judas share. Gibson, perhaps influenced by the De Mille scene, has Caiaphas slowly toss the bag toward Judas and all the coins fall out slowly and scatter. Judas stares at Caiaphas, stoops, and furtively gathers them up.

In Pasolini's film, Judas counts out coins from his moneybag for food, emphasizing Judas's role as the treasurer for Jesus and the disciples and possibly also foreshadowing the thirty denarii for which he will betray Jesus. Judas later approaches three priests in the Temple square, pulls Caiaphas aside and asks Caiaphas what he will give him for betraying Jesus to them. He smiles when Caiaphas offers him thirty denarii, as the soundtrack plays the melody of *Kol Nidre*, from the liturgy of the Jewish Day of Atonement. Even without specifically describing Judas as greedy, these visual images imply that Judas struggled with greed and lost, even as his conscience plagues him for betraying Jesus for money.

Some films attribute overweening ambition to Judas in addition to his greed. At his first appearance, DeMille introduces him as "Judas Iscariot . . . the Ambitious, who joined the Disciples in the belief that Jesus would be the nation's King, and reward him with honor and high office." Later, when Jesus heals a young blind child, Judas ostentatiously laments: "Would He but shun the Poor and heal the rich we could straightway make Him King—with me on His right hand!" Later in the film, Judas tries to scatter the children who had gathered around, but Jesus stops him: "Suffer little children to come unto Me, and forbid them not for of such is the Kingdom of Heaven."

Divine Plan

In addition to Judas's greed, Gibson's *The Passion of the Christ* suggests that Jesus' suffering and death, and, by implication, Judas's role therein, were part of the divine plan. The scrolling introductory text quotes from the "Suffering Servant song" in Isaiah 53:3–5: "He was wounded for our transgressions, crushed for our iniquities; by His wounds we are healed. Isaiah 53 [dated] 700 BC." In Isaiah, the passage reads as follows:

> He was despised and rejected by men, a man of sorrows, and familiar with suffering. Like one from whom men hide their faces he was despised, and we esteemed him not. Surely he took up our infirmi-ties and carried our sorrows, yet we considered him stricken by God,

smitten by him, and afflicted. But he was pierced for our transgressions, he was crushed for our iniquities; the punishment that brought
us peace was upon him, and by his wounds we are healed.

Although Judas's name or act is not mentioned here, this introduction en-
dorses the view that Jesus' suffering, culminating in death, was part of a
preordained divine plan prophesied many centuries before Jesus came into the
world.

In *Jesus Christ Superstar*, Jesus sees his own death as part of God's plan,
that is, when he is not whining about being forgotten by his followers and
disciples. When Simon urges him to add "a touch of hate at Rome" to mobilize
even more support, Jesus replies:

> Neither you, Simon, nor the fifty thousand
> Nor the Romans, nor the Jews
> Nor Judas, nor the twelve
> Nor the priests, nor the scribes
> Nor doomed Jerusalem itself
> Understand what power is
> Understand what glory is
> Understand at all
> Understand at all
> If you knew all that I knew
> My poor Jerusalem
> You'd see the truth
> But you'd close your eyes
> But you'd close your eyes
> While you live
> Your troubles are many
> Poor Jerusalem
> To conquer death
> You only have to die
> You only have to die

In *Jesus of Montreal*, the notion that Jesus' death is required for salvation is
expressed in the original, tired version of the Passion play that the priest had
asked them to "refresh."

MAN #1 Jesus is sentenced to die.

MAN #2 This just man must die.

WOMAN #1 Why?

MAN #1   Because he is Just and we are not.

WOMAN #1   He will bear our murders.

MAN #1   Our thefts.

WOMAN #1   Our adulteries! He falters under the weight of our sins.

CONSTANCE LAZURE   They chose the heaviest wood!

WOMAN #1   The hardest wood!

MAN #1   Our sins make His cross heavy.

EVERYONE   Our sins! Innocent lamb! See how my pride crushes You!

Yet the fact that Daniel does not appropriate this theme for his own version demonstrates his repudiation of this theology and his disdain for the over-wrought tone and content of the original Passion play as a whole.

In Young's *Jesus* and other films, the inevitability of Jesus' death is evident in Jesus' predictions and his warnings to the disciples. While Judas's role is not specified, the predictions allow viewers to understand Judas's role as despicable yet essential to the working out of God's plan of salvation through the death and resurrection of his son.

In *Godspell* Jesus must encourage, even drive, Judas to betray him; Judas for his part is reluctant but obedient. This dynamic, and the absence of animosity between them, suggests the inevitability and necessity of the story's tragic outcome, but no reason or rationale is presented in the film itself. Similarly, in *Last Temptation*, it is finally Jesus who must persuade Judas to betray him, but this is only one part of a very complex relationship that we will discuss in more detail below.

Satan's Role

The association between Judas and Satan is most prominent in the silent movie *Christus* and in Mel Gibson's *The Passion of the Christ*. In the former, Judas sees Satan lurking in the shadows as he concludes his negotiations with Caiaphas for the thirty pieces of silver. In the latter, Judas is tormented by demons, as two young boys are transformed before his eyes—and ours—into demon children.

Last Temptation makes a more tentative and ambiguous connection between Judas and Satan. This film, like the book upon which it is based, ponders the question of whether Jesus was led by God or Satan. When Jesus is in the wilderness, temptation comes in three forms: the snake, with Mary

Magdalene's voice; the lion, with Judas's voice and red mane; and Satan in a flame, with a voice of his own. The "guardian angel" who removes Jesus from the cross is revealed to be a manifestation of the devil at the end of the dream sequence and disappears in a satanic flame. Judas's red hair maintains the ambiguity regarding the central question of whether the action, and the actors, are playing out Satan's will or God's.[9]

Politics

While personal and divine or satanic motivations are frequent features of Judas's biopic persona, most movies suggest that Judas was motivated by a violent political agenda. While the specific details vary, the biopics portray Judas as a hot-headed young man obsessed with armed revolution against Rome, whether on his own or as part of a revolutionary group under the leadership of Barabbas. Integral to this scenario is the subjugation of first-century Judea, a land occupied and ruled by Rome through a governor, who in Jesus' time was Pontius Pilate.[10] The notion of armed revolution has its basis in Josephus' references to a Fourth Philosophy, the tenets held by the Zealots, a group engaged in guerrilla tactics against Rome.[11]

Establishing a stark opposition between the ordinary people of the land and the oppressive Roman authorities provides an explanation both for Judas's attraction to Jesus and his later disappointment upon learning that Jesus' kingdom is not of this world. Stressing the oppressive burden that Rome laid on ordinary Galilean folk also establishes the longing of the people for freedom. Finally, on a thematic level, the political motif sets up a dichotomy between the sword and love as the means for liberating humanity. Films that present Judas's betrayal as politically motivated contrast political freedom, won through the violence of armed struggle, with spiritual freedom, achieved by faith in Jesus as the son of God who died for the sins of humankind.

The earliest movie that hints at this explanation is *INRI*. In this film, Judas promises Jesus that "the people will minister unto thee, and set thee in power, and hail thee King," a promise that Jesus rejects: "The Son of Man came not to be ministered unto but to minister." This is an allusion to John 6:15 in which the people want to make Jesus king after witnessing the miracle of the loaves and fishes, a move that the Johannine Jesus avoids by withdrawing to the mountain by himself.

The theme is developed in a more detailed way in DeMille's *The King of Kings*. It is epitomized in a scene in which Judas is holding a crown that he had hoped to place on Jesus' head. As music from Handel's *Messiah* plays in the background, an intertitle reads:

> When Jesus perceived that they would take Him by force, to make
> Him king—He withdrew, passing through the midst of them.
>
> —John 6:15

A crowd surrounds Jesus as Judas attempts to crown him king, but Jesus disappears. In the next scene, Satan tempts him with the power of an entire army, but Jesus casts him away. As he walks through the Temple, he picks up a pure white lamb. The lamb symbolizes Jesus' own pure nature and fore-shadows his future sacrificial death.

The camera cuts to Caiaphas, who approaches Judas as he is still holding the crown that he had hoped to place on Jesus' head. Caiaphas threatens Judas: "Hearken thou King Maker! Thou shalt pay with thy life for this—and thy Master, and thy fellow knaves likewise!" Judas trembles with fear. Jesus addresses the crowd: "Do ye not yet understand? My kingdom is not of this world" (cf. John 18:36). The camera cuts back to Judas, who lets the crown drop out of his hands. Judas wipes his hands against his clothes as if to deny that he intended to crown Jesus king.

The epics of the 1960s develop the political theme further. In *King of Kings*, Judas is torn between Barabbas' way of the sword and Jesus' way of peace. Judas attempts to resolve this tension by trying to convince Barabbas to consider Jesus' path seriously. Barabbas protests that their methods are too different: "I am fire, he is water!" Judas persists. Jesus, he tells Barabbas, will come shortly to join his disciples in Jerusalem and to preach in the Temple. Judas urges Barabbas to stand by Jesus: "When his message of peace sweeps the city, let the people proclaim him king of Judea. How can you refuse?" Barabbas finally agrees to Judas's plan: "If he can free the Jews without spilling blood, he deserves the crown. I will shape the crown myself and place it on his brow." Judas is encouraged, even excited, by Barabbas' words. "You will stand beside him in the temple then? You will give him time to speak?" Barabbas gives his assurances. Judas, pleased with what he has accomplished, prepares to depart: "That will be a day to be remembered!" After Judas's exit, Barabbas repeats these words, with an ominous tone: "It will be remembered."

But Barabbas has deceived the gullible Judas. He tells his fellow Zealots: "Judas dreams, and all dreamers are fools. This is the hour that we have waited for. Jesus comes to the temple, let him!" Barabbas plans to wait for Jesus to draw the attention of the Roman soldiers, and then attack. The ominous music heightens the tension and suggests that Barabbas' plan can lead only to death and destruction.

After the intermission and the Sermon on the Mount, the voiceover narrator intones:

> Now the Jewish Passover was near and many went up from the country to Jerusalem to purify themselves and make holiday. Jesus, come from Bethany in the Mount of Olives, did enter Jerusalem on that day to preach in the temple. The Temple was in Judea, his words, spoken here, would echo in Tiberia, Samaria and Caesarea, from here he might speak to the world and the world might listen and the waves be stilled. And as the city prepared for the Passover killing of the lambs, the men of Barabbas planned stranger celebrations, made ready more terrible sacrifices.... And Jesus went into the Temple and the great doors shut out one multitude and within was peace, while outside was the sea that would not be stilled, the tongue which spoke not peace, but the sword.

Barabbas then climbs upon a post and yells, "Long Live Judea! Judea!"

Judas watches in distress as Barabbas and his crew attack the Roman soldiers and kill many of them. The Romans retaliate. Barabbas himself is shot in the leg with a bow and arrow; he surrenders and is led off to jail, from which he will later be rescued by the crowd that chooses him over Jesus. Judas enters the Zealots' hiding place.

> ZEALOTS (*lamenting*) We will never rise again, the glory of Judea is dead, the Romans were waiting for us, we had no chance, so many of us dead for nothing.
>
> ONE ZEALOT, TO JUDAS It was you who told Barabbas that the new rabbi would show us the way.
>
> SECOND ZEALOT He does nothing but pray in the temple.
>
> JUDAS The rabbi will help us.
>
> ZEALOT How will he help us?
>
> JUDAS He has the power of miracles.
>
> ZEALOT He will not use his power except to heal the sick.
>
> JUDAS (*insisting*) And call down hosts to destroy the fortress of Pilate.
>
> ZEALOT He preaches against violence.

> JUDAS   He can with a look, rock the foundations of Herod Antipas'
> palace and brings the walls down on the tyrant's head.
>
> ZEALOT, DISMISSING JUDAS'S PROTESTATIONS   He has never done
> these things before, why will he choose to do them now?
>
> JUDAS (*emphatically*)   I will force his hand...Once he feels the Roman
> sword at his throat, he will strike them down with the wave of one arm.

Judas then runs to Caiaphas as the invisible narrator says: "So Judas Iscariot
went his way to betray Jesus to the chief priests and the captains. To say how
Jesus and Barabbas were the left and the right hands of the same body, thus
Judas thought to test and prove forever the divine power of the Messiah." Judas
betrays Jesus in order to test his messianic identity and to push him into
starting the revolution that will bring political freedom to Judea.

The Judas in Young's *Jesus* betrays his master when he finally realizes that
he has misinterpreted Jesus' message all along. Far from being a revolutionary
leader, Jesus has no intention of leading an armed revolt against Rome. As
Mary and Mary Magdalene sit with Jesus at the table a few days before Passover, Judas urges Jesus to act immediately:

> There will never be a better time to strike against Roman power in
> Jerusalem. There is an army of Zealots waiting. The city is full of
> pilgrims for Passover, they believe in you. Rise up, ask them to at-
> tack the palace, they will. Sheer numbers will overwhelm the Roman
> guard, and once we're in charge, Rome will leave us alone. Now
> is the time. Surely it is your destiny.

But Jesus does not agree. Instead, he announces: "In two days it will be
Passover. In two days, I will be killed." Everyone protests, including Judas, who
repeats that the Zealots are ready and waiting. Jesus explains that his message
is "Freedom not just from the Romans but from all tyranny, the tyranny of sin,
Judas, that is my battle, not the Romans."

> JUDAS   Then you are betraying your people, not saving them. You are
> the one man who has the power and you refuse. That's betrayal.
>
> JESUS   I'm not here to lead a violent revolution, Judas.
>
> JUDAS   You may have no choice.

Young's Judas betrays Jesus: "He's not the man I thought he was." He then
accepts thirty pieces of silver in retribution for an earlier incident in which
Jesus had made him give this sum away to the poor rather than keep it for
himself and his followers.

The above scenarios provide two reasons for Judas's betrayal. One is that he is disappointed in Jesus' refusal or inability to bring about armed revolt against Rome. The other is that Judas acted out of a misguided sense that he was not really betraying Jesus. The betrayal is simply Judas' clumsy attempt to maneuver Jesus into starting a revolution. The films show that the cause is just, given the oppressive measures taken by the imperial power, but the means are wrongheaded. Far from spawning successful revolution, violence results only in tragedy.

The political angle offered the most accessible and plausible explanation for Judas's action, particularly in the postwar period. It is interesting to note the epics' strong emphasis on love as a weapon superior to the sword despite the recent memory of America's military role in liberating Europe from Nazi domination. Perhaps the Johannine account, in which Jesus clearly denies that his kingdom was of this world, acted as a constraint. Perhaps these films are simply expressing the desire for a world—a vaguely Christian one?—in which armed combat was not needed. Or perhaps this approach merely reflects the need for a plausible and acceptable cause-and-effect narrative, while allowing enough on-screen violence to satisfy perceived audience demands.

Jesus and Judas

In the Gospels

The original audience was likely familiar with Judas's role in Jesus' life story. This is apparent from the brevity of the Gospels' references to Judas as one of Jesus' twelve disciples (Matthew 26:14, 47; Mark 14:10, 43; Luke 22:3, 47; John 6:71), and the reminders that appear long before the Passion narrative that it was Judas who betrayed Jesus (Matthew 10:4; Mark 3:19; Luke 6:16; John 6:70–71). If the disciples and other characters in the story are surprised by Judas's betrayal, at least the readers have been forewarned.

Only John refers to Judas's role among the disciples before the betrayal. Coming upon Mary of Bethany anointing Jesus' feet with an expensive oil, Judas gripes: "Why was this perfume not sold for three hundred denarii and the money given to the poor?" The narrator explains that Judas "said this not because he cared about the poor, but because he was a thief; he kept the common purse and used to steal what was put into it" (John 12:4–6). John's reference to Judas as the group's treasurer is not supported by any other texts; the latter claim may have been influenced by the story of his betraying Jesus for thirty pieces of silver.

Not so much the fact of the betrayal but its manner—a kiss, according to the Synoptics—implies a close relationship between Jesus and Judas. The betrayal itself takes place late at night, hours after the meal is over. The accounts of the betrayal are similar, with minor variations. Here is Mark's version:

> Immediately, while he was still speaking, Judas, one of the twelve, arrived; and with him there was a crowd with swords and clubs, from the chief priests, the scribes, and the elders. Now the betrayer had given them a sign, saying, "The one I will kiss is the man; arrest him and lead him away under guard." So when he came, he went up to him at once and said, "Rabbi!" and kissed him. Then they laid hands on him and arrested him. (Mark 14:43–46)

Matthew constructs a brief dialogue between the betrayer and the betrayed: "At once he came up to Jesus and said, 'Greetings, Rabbi!' and kissed him. Jesus said to him, 'Friend, do what you are here to do' " (Matthew 26:49–50). Luke has Jesus reproach Judas at the crucial moment: "While he was still speaking, suddenly a crowd came, and the one called Judas, one of the twelve, was leading them. He approached Jesus to kiss him; but Jesus said to him, 'Judas, is it with a kiss that you are betraying the Son of Man?' (Luke 22:47–48)." In the Synoptics, Judas's role is to identify Jesus to the forces who come to arrest him, suggesting that Jesus was not known to them personally. In John, by contrast, Judas's role is quite different. As is his wont, John amplifies the scene and stresses Jesus' foreknowledge:

> After Jesus had spoken these words, he went out with his disciples across the Kidron valley to a place where there was a garden, which he and his disciples entered. Now Judas, who betrayed him, also knew the place, because Jesus often met there with his disciples. So Judas brought a detachment of soldiers together with police from the chief priests and the Pharisees, and they came there with lanterns and torches and weapons. Then Jesus, knowing all that was to happen to him, came forward and asked them, "Whom are you looking for?" They answered, "Jesus of Nazareth." Jesus replied, "I am he." Judas, who betrayed him, was standing with them. When Jesus said to them, "I am he," they stepped back and fell to the ground. Again he asked them, "Whom are you looking for?" And they said, "Jesus of Nazareth." Jesus answered, "I told you that I am he. So if you are looking for me, let these men go." This was to fulfill the word that he had spoken, "I did not lose a single one of those whom you gave me." (John 18:1–9)

John's Judas does not kiss Jesus, nor does he identify Jesus to the soldiers and police, who must inquire about Jesus not once but twice. His role is to reveal Jesus' location, not his identity.

The betrayal story is the most dramatic portion of the Gospel narrative. One cannot but respond to a tense and emotional scene in which a close associate becomes the instrument of betrayal that leads to death. The use of the kiss—an affectionate greeting if not more than that—is particularly ironic. The kiss opens the door for speculation about the nature and intensity of the relationship between Jesus and Judas, as we shall soon see. The final piece of the Judas subplot is his suicide. According to Matthew:

> When morning came, all the chief priests and the elders of the people conferred together against Jesus in order to bring about his death. They bound him, led him away, and handed him over to Pilate the governor. When Judas, his betrayer, saw that Jesus was condemned, he repented and brought back the thirty pieces of silver to the chief priests and the elders. He said, "I have sinned by betraying innocent blood." But they said, "What is that to us? See to it yourself." Throwing down the pieces of silver in the temple, he departed; and he went and hanged himself. But the chief priests, taking the pieces of silver, said, "It is not lawful to put them into the treasury, since they are blood money." (Matthew 27:1–6)

Acts has a somewhat different story, told by Peter:

> In those days Peter stood up among the believers (together the crowd numbered about one hundred twenty persons) and said, "Friends, the scripture had to be fulfilled, which the Holy Spirit through David foretold concerning Judas, who became a guide for those who arrested Jesus—for he was numbered among us and was allotted his share in this ministry." (Now this man acquired a field with the reward of his wickedness; and falling headlong, he burst open in the middle and all his bowels gushed out. This became known to all the residents of Jerusalem, so that the field was called in their language Hakeldama, that is, Field of Blood.) "For it is written in the book of Psalms, 'Let his homestead become desolate, and let there be no one to live in it'; and 'Let another take his position of overseer.'" (Acts 1:15–20)

From these passages we may surmise the existence of a strong tradition about the fact but not the means of Judas's suicide. The Acts passage is slightly more sympathetic to Judas, as it affirms his place among the disciples and his role in the ministry and views his suicide as the fulfillment of scripture. The notice of

Judas's suicide adds further depth to his characterization; this aspect of the scriptural accounts allows for Judas's portrayal as a man who naively misunderstood the intentions of the Jewish authorities, and whose plan to have Jesus accepted or at least exonerated backfired tragically. This detail thus opens further the possibilities of constructing a detailed picture not only of his (mis)understanding of Jesus but also of his relationship with him.

In the Movies

The biopics almost always draw on all four Gospels as well as Acts in developing their story of Judas. They depict the entry of Judas into the group of disciples, his role as treasurer, and secret meetings with revolutionaries such as Barabbas, followed by his encounters with Caiaphas and/or other Jewish authorities in which he arranges to betray Jesus for the price of thirty pieces of silver. In the biopics, as in the Synoptic Gospels, Judas's act of betrayal is sealed with a kiss. Finally, Judas watches in horror as Jesus is led off for crucifixion, and he commits suicide either by hanging or some other means.

What makes Judas such a dramatic figure, however, is not so much his behavior but what his actions imply about his relationship to Jesus. We turn first to a brief overview of their biopic friendship, and then focus on *The Last Temptation of Christ*, which portrays the relationship between Jesus and Judas with particular intensity.

In *The Greatest Story Ever Told*, Judas is Jesus' first disciple; they meet immediately after Jesus' baptism. This film also inserts Judas into a scene based on Mark 8:27–30:

> Jesus went on with his disciples to the villages of Caesarea Philippi; and on the way he asked his disciples, "Who do people say that I am?" And they answered him, "John the Baptist; and others, Elijah; and still others, one of the prophets." He asked them, "But who do you say that I am?" Peter answered him, "You are the Messiah." And he sternly ordered them not to tell anyone about him.

Whereas Judas is not mentioned in the Markan passage, he becomes a focal point in *The Greatest Story Ever Told*. When Jesus asks his disciples: "But who do you say that I am?" It is Judas who utters the first response: "You are a great leader, the greatest teacher of all." But Jesus bypasses Judas and, as in Matthew 16:18, declares Peter to be the rock upon which he will build his church. Judas is devastated.

In Young's biopic, Jesus persuades Judas to be part of his group, after finding him in the aftermath of a bloody skirmish between Galilean revolutionaries and Roman soldiers. In Zeffirelli's *Jesus of Nazareth*, by contrast, it is Judas who initiates the contact with Jesus, after Jesus has already begun his ministry and gathered his first disciples. Jesus is sitting alone as Judas approaches him eagerly. Jesus is not pleased to see him. Judas struggles to engage him, but Jesus responds only in monotones and avoids eye contact. Judas presents himself as a scholar, a man whose father aimed to give him the best education possible in languages and literature. He is fully literate and numerate, but, alas, has never worked with his hands. Judas believes that this education will be of some use to Jesus. Jesus is neither impressed nor convinced, yet he allows Judas to join his group. By his aloof manner, it is clear that Jesus knows and accepts the role that Judas will play in his life and death but he does not welcome it.

Judas's downfall begins with the betrayal and concludes with his suicide. In DeMille's *The King of Kings*, Judas returns to Caiaphas with the sack of money. "I have sinned, in that I have betrayed innocent blood" (Matthew 27:4). Caiaphas, self-satisfied, dismisses him: "What is that to us? See thou to that!"

Judas's agony is portrayed in excruciating detail. He drops the money, extends his arms in a cruciform position as the camera cuts back and forth between Jesus and Judas. The rope binding Jesus is flung over to Judas. The agonized Judas, clutching the rope, climbs a craggy mountain, in agony. Throughout, the camera continues to cut back and forth between Judas and Jesus, as Jesus carries his cross and is later nailed to it. Judas watches the proceedings from a distance, and, when he sees the three crosses, hangs himself in full view of the crucifixion grounds. The scene is very dramatic; the intercutting between Jesus and Judas contrasts the one who dies in dignity with the one who perishes in shame. This technique also implies the intensity of Judas's feelings for Jesus and of his remorse.

Other films bring the viewer into Judas's consciousness. In *Christus*, Judas' fear-distorted mind envisions the thirty pieces of silver changing into drops of blood that stain his hands forever. In a departure from the usual hanging scene, *The Greatest Story Ever Told* has Judas fling himself into the eternal flame that is burning in the Temple courtyard. Perhaps this modification to Judas's suicide is meant to symbolize that Judas will burn in hellfire eternally.[12]

By far the most interesting aspect of the cinematic treatment of Judas, however, are the homoerotic undertones that occur in a small number of Jesus biopics. These undertones do not rise to the surface, yet in these films the intensity of the relationship between Judas and Jesus positively smolders.

These hints sometimes appear in the kiss scene. In Pasolini's film, the kiss is a moment of strong emotion. Judas approaches Jesus, followed by the chief priests together in a group. Judas then pulls free and runs to Jesus. The two embrace passionately. Judas then watches with concern as Jesus moves toward his death on the cross. Given Pasolini's own homosexuality, his allusion to the homoerotic potential in this intense relationship is not surprising.

In other films, however, the intimacy between Jesus and Judas is not limited to the kiss of betrayal. Nor is such intimacy limited to relatively recent feature films. The early silent film *INRI*, for example, made long before audiences developed a tolerance for viewing homoeroticism in the movies, contains a fleeting but effective sequence in which Jesus approaches Judas, touches his shoulders, looks down slightly, and draws Judas closely to him in passionate embrace.

The suggestion of erotic attraction is exploited by *Monty Python's Life of Brian*. Not being a real messiah, Brian can, and does, have a real lover. Her name is Judith, which is the feminine form of the name "Judas." In a literal sense, Judith betrays Brian to the Romans, but she does so inadvertently. In contrast to Judas, whose act of betrayal is premeditated, Judith simply fails to intervene when Brian is arrested mistakenly, her judgment clouded by her (false) view of him as an ardent revolutionary and now martyr.

Hints of a love triangle among Jesus, Mary Magdalene, and Judas appear in DeMille's *The King of Kings*, in which, as we have seen, Judas abandons his lover Mary in order to follow Jesus. Mary is confident of winning Judas back, and of seducing Jesus at the same time, but fails when she meets him. Judas, in turn, is jealous of Mary's ardent devotion to Jesus after he has exorcised her seven demons.

The relationship between Jesus and Judas come to the fore in two films: *Jesus Christ Superstar*, and *The Last Temptation of Christ*.

JESUS CHRIST SUPERSTAR. In *Superstar*, Judas is a powerfully built, tall, African American with a strong sense of self as well as high expectations of Jesus. While profoundly devoted to Jesus, Judas accuses him of losing track of his own identity and mission.

> At last all too well
> I can see where we all soon will be.
> If you strip away the myth from the man,
> You will see where we all soon will be. Jesus!
> You've started to believe
> The things they say of you.
> You really do believe
> This talk of God is true.

And all the good you've done
Will soon get swept away.
You've begun to matter more
Than the things you say.

Judas objects to Jesus' provocative behavior. In this sequence, Judas evokes the civil rights movement of the 1960s in the United States.

Listen, Jesus, do you care for your race?
Don't you see we must keep in our place?
We are occupied; have you forgotten how put down we are?
I am frightened by the crowd.
For we are getting much too loud.
And they'll crush us if we go too far.
If they go too far....

Judas does not consider Jesus to be the son of God, but he does value Jesus for reasons unspecified in the film. When he sees that Jesus really cannot keep things under control, he becomes so fed up that he calls upon the chief priests. He tells Annas and Caiaphas:

I came because I had to; I'm the one who saw.
Jesus can't control it like he did before.
And furthermore I know that Jesus thinks so too.
Jesus wouldn't mind that I was here with you.
I have no thought at all about my own reward.
I really didn't come here of my own accord.

Of course, we may have our doubts as to whether Judas has no thought at all of his own reward, but it is interesting that, in contrast to the Gospels (e.g., Matthew 27:24), the concern for crowd control is here attributed to Judas and not to Pilate.

Further, in this film it is Judas and not Jesus who experiences resurrection. Soon after his death Judas returns in full regalia, accompanied by an all-female Motown backup group, to deliver a musical reprimand to Jesus for arriving on earth in first-century Judea and not in the twentieth century. "If you'd come today, you could have reached a whole nation. Israel in 4 BC had no mass communication." Of course it is the Jesus movies, including *Jesus Christ Superstar*, that have provided one form of mass communication not accessible to first century Jews like Jesus.

Judas' emotions are also evident in his jealousy of Mary Magdalene. He watches disapprovingly, from slightly above and at a distance from the rest of the group, as Mary fusses over Jesus, and worries over Jesus' obvious enjoyment of her attentions. In one of his songs, Judas confesses that he finds it "mystifying that a man like you can waste his time on women of her kind, but to let her kiss you and stroke your hair, that is hardly in your line." Echoing the story of the adulterous woman, Jesus lashes out at Judas: "Who are you to criticize and despise her?... Leave her alone."

These scenes emphasize the intensity of Judas's feelings for Jesus, his anxieties and his disappointments. It is by no means clear that Jesus reciprocates these emotions, for he is too self-centered to look beyond his own needs.

In *Superstar* the existence of a backstory to the relationship between Judas and Jesus is palpable, but we are not privy to its details. What is clear is that Judas is now disappointed in Jesus for having betrayed his own mission. Jesus, for his part, rejects Judas's concerns, preferring the easy company and unquestioning adulation of Mary and the crowd of followers. In this theme, as in others, *Superstar* is not so much telling a story about Jesus as using the Jesus story to articulate a critique of the cult of celebrity, in which the star begins with some artistic promise then succumbs to the mindless adoration of his fans, losing his soul, and his true friends, in the process.

THE LAST TEMPTATION. Finally, we turn to the most complex and compelling cinematic portrayal of the relationship between Jesus and Judas. Scorsese's *Last Temptation* draws together all of the aspects that we have discussed above, including the political theme and the intense, implicitly homoerotic relationship.

We first meet Judas early on the film. The door to Jesus' carpentry workshop bursts open; a burly, red-haired man barges in, cleans his face and hands, and approaches Jesus, who is sitting down with his back against the wall. The room is thick with tension and fear.

> JUDAS (*shouting*) No, no, no more crosses, we're ready. Jesus, where's your mind, can you hear what I'm saying?
>
> JESUS The Messiah won't come that way.
>
> JUDAS What do you mean by that? Who told you? (*breaks cross*). You're a disgrace! Romans can't find anyone to make crosses except for you. You'll do it! You're worse than them! You're a Jew killing Jews! You're a coward! How will you ever pay for your sins?"
>
> JESUS (*weakly*) With my life, I don't have anything else.

Judas's attitude immediately shifts from contempt to concern. "Look at me, what do you mean?" Then his mood abruptly shifts again; he berates Jesus who has again picked up the cross to continue his work.

JESUS (*begging*)   Don't get in the way. I'm struggling.

JUDAS (*shaking his head*)   I struggle, *you* collaborate!

Judas stalks off.

Like Scorsese's (and Kazantzakis's) Mary Magdalene and Jesus, Judas and Jesus have a prior relationship marked by both tension and love. Judas cares intensely about Jesus, even as he despises his cross-making activities. He himself is committed to a revolutionary cause that he fervently hopes Jesus will join.

Later, after a nocturnal encounter with a dead hermit in the desert, Jesus leaves his hut momentarily and is surprised by Judas, who says, "I've got orders to kill you."

JESUS   Go ahead. Tonight I was purified.... Here's my neck.

JUDAS (*holding his knife to Jesus' neck*)   What kind of a man are you?... These voices... God's voice, only you understand it? You better make me understand it. Power, magic, is there some secret? Tell me your secret.

JESUS   Pity. Pity for men. I feel pity for everything, donkeys, grass, sparrows, ants.... Everything is part of God.

JUDAS   You're not afraid of dying?

JESUS   Why should I be? Death isn't a door that closes, it opens. It opens and you go through it.

Judas returns to the matter at hand: "If I don't kill you, what happens?" Jesus replies, "I'll speak to people.... I'll just open my mouth and God will do the talking. Maybe God didn't send you here to kill me. Maybe he sent you here to follow me."

Judas is torn. On the one hand, he despises Jesus' passivity, so much so that he is ready to kill him for collaborating with the Romans. On the other hand, he is overpowered by love and concern for Jesus. Jesus plays on Judas's ambivalence by inviting him to join with him.

The scene cuts quickly to daylight; Jesus and Judas are walking along at the head of the crowd of followers. Judas has made his decision, for now. He is willing to follow Jesus, but he has not yet completely let go of his hesitations.

"I'll go with you till I understand, but if you stray this much [an iota] from the path, I'll kill you."

The next scene involving Judas takes place as the disciples settle in for a night's sleep under the stars. They bicker quietly; as the cold night settles in, they vie for places close to the fire. Jesus sits alone at some distance from the others. Judas approaches him:

> Rabbi, can I talk to you? I'm not like these other men. They are weak, one is worse than the other. If I love somebody, I die for them, if I hate somebody, I kill them. I could even kill somebody I loved if they did the wrong thing. Do you hear me? Do you understand what I said? The other day you said that if a man hits you, turn the other cheek. I didn't like that. Only an angel could do that, a dog. I'm a free man, I don't turn my cheek to anyone.

Judas is still judging Jesus, trying to decide whether it will be death or life for his friend, even as he acknowledges that his love for Jesus remains unaltered no matter what choice he might make.

Jesus claims that both he and Judas want the same thing, but, as it turns out, he is wrong. Judas wants freedom for Israel, Jesus wants freedom for the soul.

> JUDAS   First you free the body then you free the spirit. The Romans come first. The foundation is the body.
>
> JESUS (*disagreeing*)   The foundation is the soul. You'll only replace the Romans with someone else, nothing ever changes. You have to break the chain of evil. With love.

Their voices rise; Andrew comes over to find out what is going on. Jesus puts him off: "It's alright, Judas and I are talking."

They are quiet for a moment. Then Judas continues: "You know the Zealots ordered me to kill you....I decided to wait...I thought maybe you were the one to unite us and I didn't want to destroy that." Jesus expresses his own doubts: "How could I be the messiah; when those people were torturing Magdalene I wanted to kill them, then I opened my mouth, and all that came out was love. I don't understand." Judas urges Jesus to go to Judea and see John the Baptist. "He'll know..." Then Jesus says to Judas: "I'm afraid. Stay with me." They cuddle up; Jesus shelters in the bulk and strength of his doubting friend. The camera zooms in on their faces, lingering on Jesus. He arises, takes an apple out of his pocket and begins to eat. He opens the apple, removes the seeds and scatters them. An apple tree grows immediately, miraculously, where he has thrown the seeds. Whatever his own doubts might be, Jesus has powers that can only come from the Creator God. The apple also alludes to the forbidden fruit of Genesis, hinting at forbidden sexual desires.

Judas finally comes to believe in Jesus when Jesus turns from the way of love to the way of the axe. Jesus proclaims to his disciples:

> God is inside of us. Devil is outside us in the world all around us.
> We'll pick up an axe and cut the devil's throat, we'll fight him
> wherever he is, in the sick, rich, even in the temple. I'll lead you. If
> you have sheep, give them away, if you have a family, leave them.
> I believed in love, now I believe in the axe. Who's with me?

Judas runs to Jesus, falls to his knees, looks up at Jesus' face, exclaims "Adonai!" (meaning, "my God!"), and kisses his feet. Judas is here uttering a confession of profound faith.

Later, Judas is pulled aside by the Zealot leader Saul (later to become Paul): "Judas, what are you doing with this magician? You had orders to kill him and you haven't done it. Now he acts like a prophet and you follow him." Later, after Saul kills Lazarus, whom Jesus had raised from the dead, Judas tells Jesus, "I'm not surprised. How could they let Lazarus live? He was proof of your greatest miracle. Now there's no more proof. That's what the Zealots want. Their revolution, not yours." Jesus asks: "You want to go back to them?" Judas denies it vehemently: "No. You're the one I follow."

Jesus then tells Judas that of all his disciples, he, Judas, is the strongest. He reveals to him a "terrible secret from God": "Do you know why I came to Jerusalem? ... Last night Isaiah came to me. He had a prophecy. I saw it written. It said: 'He has borne our faults ... he was wounded for our transgressions ... yet he opened not his mouth. Despised and rejected by all ... he went forward without resisting, like a lamb led to the slaughter'" (cf. Isaiah 53:5–7). This is too abstract for Judas, who answers, "I don't understand."

JESUS   Judas, I am the lamb. I'm the one who's going to die.

JUDAS   Die? You mean you're not the Messiah?

JESUS   I am.

JUDAS   That can't be. If you're the Messiah, why do you have to die?

JESUS   Listen. At first, I didn't understand....

JUDAS   No, you, listen! Every day you have a different plan! First it's love, then it's the axe, and now you have to die. What good could that do?

JESUS   I can't help it. God only talks to me a little at a time. He tells me as much as I need to know.... Now I finally understand. All my life I've been followed, by voices, by footsteps, by shadows. And do you know what the shadow is? The cross. I have to die on the cross and I have to die willingly. We have to go back to the Temple.

JUDAS   After you die on the cross, what happens then?

JESUS   I come back to judge the living and the dead.

The final piece is in place when Jesus reveals to Judas his important, and difficult, role in God's plan. They are in the Temple area; Judas urges Jesus to give a sign for the revolution: "They are all waiting for your signal. If you don't give the sign now they'll kill us.... This is the way, do it." Jesus is silent, holds out his hands, showing the blood flowing from the holes that the nails will soon make in them. The silence continues. Jesus looks down, as if he is already dead. He calls Judas to help him. "Stay with me. Don't leave me." They walk away. People start shouting at him, accusing him, he walks as if he is already carrying the cross; Judas supports him. The Romans jump down through the grates. The camera focuses briefly on the eyeless statue of a Roman god, then cuts quickly to Jesus and Judas walking alone through the passageways. They stop and sit down. Judas walks away to center frame and looks around him, then back at Jesus. He walks back to Jesus and sits down beside him. He checks Jesus' forehead, with concern, to see if he has fever.

JESUS   I wish there was another way, I'm sorry, but there isn't. I have to die on the cross.

JUDAS (*vehemently*)   I won't let you die.

JESUS   You have no choice, neither do I. We are bringing God and man together. I'm the sacrifice. Without you there can be no redemption.

JUDAS (*dismissive*)   Get somebody stronger.

Has Judas lost his nerve or been overcome by love?

JESUS   You promised me.... You once told me if I moved one step from revolution you would kill me.... I have strayed, haven't I?

Judas softly, reluctantly, agrees.

JESUS   Then you must keep your promise. You have to kill me.

JUDAS   If that's what God wants, let God do it. I won't.

JESUS   He will do it, through you. The temple guards will be looking for me; go to Gethsemane, make sure they find me there.

Judas is silent, unhappy.

JESUS   I am going to die, after three days I'll come back in victory. You can't leave me, you have to give me strength.

JUDAS   If you were me would you betray your master?

JESUS   No. That's why God gave me the easier job, to be crucified.

In agony, Judas cries into his hands as Jesus sits close by and looks on in sympathy. Judas finally calms down and asks, "What about the others?" Jesus says, "I'll tell them tonight."

The fateful moment arrives during the Last Supper. Jesus distributes the wine, which looks like blood, to each of the disciples. The last one to drink is Judas. He looks carefully into the cup and drinks with great reverence, then takes a blood clot out of his mouth, the blood running down his hand. Judas gets up to leave. A disciple shouts: "We're not finished." Jesus says: "Let him go. I want to tell you something." The camera cuts to Judas walking through the deserted woods.

At the moment of betrayal, Jesus sees Judas at the head of the soldiers. Judas says, "Welcome, Rabbi," and kisses him intensely on the lips. Judas watches as Peter cuts off a man's ear, and Jesus heals it. Jesus turns to look at him. "Take me with you. I'm ready." Judas doesn't respond. The camera moves in to an extreme close-up of Judas as Jesus walks away.

In this film, as in *Godspell*, it is Jesus who demands that Judas betray him.[13] Judas betrays Jesus out of love and devotion not to Jesus' version of the divine plan, but to his master, his rabbi, his God, the one whom he loves. Yet the dream sequence turns this relationship around: in an ironic twist, it is Jesus who betrays Judas.

After a long, satisfying, and entirely ordinary life, Jesus lies weakened, and near death. It is the year 70 CE. The Jews are in the midst of a bloody revolt against Rome that will cost them their Temple, their land, and many lives. Jesus' old friends and disciples come to visit. Among them is Judas, his hands bloody from fighting the Romans. Judas is still furious with Jesus for having stepped off the cross at the behest of his young "guardian angel."

Jesus beckons to Judas: "Judas, come in. I missed you so much." Judas is in no mood to be conciliatory. He shouts:

Traitor! Your place was on the cross. That's where God put you. When death got too close, you got scared and you ran away and you hid yourself in the life of some man.... You're a coward!...You broke my heart. Sometimes I curse the day I ever met you. We held the world in our hands. Remember what you told me? You took me in your arms. Do you remember? And you begged me, "Betray me, betray me. I have to be crucified. I have to be resurrected so I can save the world. I am the lamb," you said. "Death is the door. Judas, my brother, don't be afraid. Help me go through the door." And I loved you so much. I went and betrayed you. And you . . . you . . . What are you doing here? What business do you have here with women, with children? What's good for man isn't good for God. Why weren't you crucified?

Jesus is now lying in near cruciform position; his wounds are bleeding. Judas continues: "He was going to be the new covenant, now there's no more Israel."

JESUS   No, you don't understand. God sent a guardian angel to save me.

JUDAS   What angel? Look at her!

At Judas's words, the girl bursts into flames.

SATAN   I told you we would meet again.

JUDAS   If you die this way you die like a man. You turn against God your father. There's no sacrifice, there's no salvation.

Judas has struck a chord; the dream-spell is broken. Jesus slithers across the floor like the snake of Genesis and returns to the cross.

The story has now come full circle. Judas has been the instrument of Jesus' death, as Jesus, and presumably God, had intended. He becomes the voice of faith, the one through whom God speaks to Jesus and urges him to do what he was supposed to do. He is indeed the strong one; Jesus has been unable to stay focused and carry through on God's plan. In fact, Jesus has succumbed to Satan's Last Temptation: the ordinary life of domesticity and day-to-day pleasures. Judas, in his love for Jesus, has fully comprehended the necessity of Jesus' death, even as he now fights in the armed revolution that he had so long anticipated.

The homoerotic undertones are evident in Jesus' and Judas's body language, their proximity, their tenderness toward one another, the intensity of their relationship, and the fact that they are bound together in the service of God and Israel. Whereas the protests that attended the release of the film focused on the dream sequence in which Jesus is seen making love with Mary Magdalene, the more "scandalous" aspect is in fact this relationship with Judas, which, though it does not come to sexual fruition, remains the driving force behind the plot and the development of Jesus' character.

Conclusion

The Jesus biopics vacillate between seeing Judas as Jesus' friend, his enemy, or his lover. Whereas there are parallels between the movies' treatment of Mary

Magdalene and Judas, these two relationships move in opposite directions. We meet Mary first in her "tainted" state, then witness as Jesus rescues her, whether from stoning, from her demons, or from her unhappy past, and finally as she becomes Jesus' friend, disciple, and apostle. By contrast, we encounter Judas first as Jesus' trusted disciple and we watch in horror as he falls from grace by betraying Jesus and then committing suicide. The intensity of their relationship borders on the erotic, elaborating upon the kiss through which Judas betrays Jesus' whereabouts and/or identity to the soldiers. The biopics do not portray Jesus as a homosexual or as someone with latent homosexual desires, they only allude to the possibility that his relationship with Judas included homoeroticism. They allow us to reflect upon Jesus' humanity by going beyond the pious representation of Jesus in most films. In this regard, the homoerotic potential plays a Christological role similar to that inherent in the erotic undercurrents of Jesus' relationship with Mary Magdalene. If Jesus were truly human, then he would have been capable of sexual desires and needs, and he would have been susceptible to attraction to particular individuals, in addition to his spiritual love for all humankind. In Scorsese's film in particular, Jesus not only loves Judas but needs him profoundly, precisely in his identity as the Son of God, in order to fulfill his human mission in service of the divine. That is what Judas must remind Jesus about when he articulates his own sense of betrayal by Jesus' descent from the cross into the embrace of domestic life.

Judas plays yet another narrative role in the Jesus biopics. Judas is often the onlooker, situated slightly outside the circle formed by Jesus and his associates even before his fateful meeting with the Jewish authorities. As such, he may represent the viewing audience, which also must decide whether to believe Jesus' message or to betray it.

Despite his generally negative portrayal, Judas is a vehicle for overt anti-Semitic stereotypes only in a handful of movies, primarily the silent movies such as *Der Galiläer*, and then only with regard to his greed. In the Jesus biopics, it is Caiaphas far more than Judas who bears the burden of anti-Semitic representation. The reason is likely rooted in their respective narrative roles. Judas's act of betrayal is despicable, to be sure, but it is Caiaphas who is given the main role in the final condemnation of Jesus, leading directly to the deicide charge that was at the foundation of ancient, medieval, and modern Christian anti-Semitism.

PART V

The Story

Jesus' Foes

9
Satan

FIGURE 9.1. *The Greatest Story Ever Told*, 1965

FIGURE 9.2. *The Last Temptation of Christ*, 1988

FIGURE 9.3. *The Passion of the Christ*, 2004

Lurking in the shadows of the Jesus biopics is the figure of Satan. Like God, Satan is a power whose presence can be perceived primarily in his effects upon human beings, their well-being and their behavior. Unlike God, however, Satan is visually present in many of these films.

The most important question about Satan in these films is his relationship to the Son of God. This is a question for which the Gospels have a ready answer: Satan is the cosmic foe whom God vanquishes through Jesus' death. In the movies, however, the answer is not nearly so clearcut.

Filmmakers must decide whether to ignore Satan, on the grounds that many members of their audience do not believe he exists, or whether to treat him realistically, in keeping with the beliefs of the Gospel writers, early Christians, and some contemporary movie viewers as well.[1] Should Satan be treated allegorically, as a stand-in for the evil in the world, or psychologically, as the externalization of anxious, fearful, or evil human thoughts and deeds?

Encounters with Satan

In the Gospels

There is only one Gospel story in which Satan appears as a major character: the temptation in the desert. Mark has only a brief account of this episode, and John none at all, but both Matthew and Luke expand upon the tale of Satan's efforts to lure Jesus away from God by tempting him with worldly goods and desires. Here is Matthew's version (Matthew 4:1–10):

> Then Jesus was led up by the Spirit into the wilderness to be tempted
> by the devil. He fasted forty days and forty nights, and afterwards he
> was famished. The tempter came and said to him, "If you are the Son
> of God, command these stones to become loaves of bread." But he
> answered, "It is written, 'One does not live by bread alone, but by
> every word that comes from the mouth of God.'" Then the devil took
> him to the holy city and placed him on the pinnacle of the temple,
> saying to him, "If you are the Son of God, throw yourself down; for it
> is written, 'He will command his angels concerning you,' and 'On
> their hands they will bear you up, so that you will not dash your
> foot against a stone.'" Jesus said to him, "Again it is written, 'Do not
> put the Lord your God to the test.'" Again, the devil took him to
> a very high mountain and showed him all the kingdoms of the world
> and their splendor; and he said to him, "All these I will give you, if
> you will fall down and worship me." Jesus said to him, "Away with

you, Satan! for it is written, 'Worship the Lord your God, and serve only him.' "

Satan sets up a rivalry between himself and God over Jesus' allegiance, but for God and Jesus neither Satan nor his temptations pose a threat. Yet the Gospels acknowledge that at least some of those who witnessed Jesus' acts believed that his ability to heal the sick and to exorcise demons came from Satan, not from God.

> Then they brought to him a demoniac who was blind and mute; and he cured him, so that the one who had been mute could speak and see. All the crowds were amazed and said, "Can this be the Son of David?" But when the Pharisees heard it, they said, "It is only by Beelzebub, the ruler of the demons, that this fellow casts out the demons." He knew what they were thinking and said to them, "Every kingdom divided against itself is laid waste, and no city or house divided against itself will stand. If Satan casts out Satan, he is divided against himself; how then will his kingdom stand? If I cast out demons by Beelzebub, by whom do your own exorcists cast them out? Therefore they will be your judges. But if it is by the Spirit of God that I cast out demons, then the kingdom of God has come to you." (Matthew 12:22–28)

The demons themselves, who presumably belong to Satan's realm, acknowledge that Jesus is God's son and not Satan's:

> Just then there was in their synagogue a man with an unclean spirit, and he cried out, "What have you to do with us, Jesus of Nazareth? Have you come to destroy us? I know who you are, the Holy One of God." But Jesus rebuked him, saying, "Be silent, and come out of him!" And the unclean spirit, convulsing him and crying with a loud voice, came out of him. (Mark 1:23–26)

Although Satan does not act directly elsewhere in the Gospels, his presence in the world and in people's lives is acknowledged. Satan can work through others to obstruct the divine plan that God is attempting to enact through Jesus. Not only does Satan have a hand in Judas' act of betrayal (Luke 22:3) but he also affects Jesus' other followers. When Peter protests Jesus' prophecy of his own death, Jesus exclaims to Peter: "Get behind me, Satan! You are a stumbling block to me; for you are setting your mind not on divine things but on human things" (Matthew 16:23). He also works against divine purposes by removing belief from fledgling followers. In the Parable of the Sower, Jesus refers to seed that fell on the path "and the birds came and ate it up" (Mark 4:4) and later explains that these are the people who "when they hear, Satan immediately comes and takes away the word that is sown in them" (Mark 4:15). In Luke 13:10-16, Jesus heals a disabled woman "whom Satan bound for eighteen long years" (13:16).

The most problematic passage, however, is found in John 8:44. In this passage, Jesus addresses Jews who do not believe in him: "You are from your father the devil, and you choose to do your father's desires. He was a murderer from the beginning and does not stand in the truth, because there is no truth in him. When he lies, he speaks according to his own nature, for he is a liar and the father of lies." This association of Jews and the devil has persisted in anti-Semitic discourse and art through the ages, including some of the Jesus movies.[2]

In the Movies

Biopic versions of the Temptation narrative range from the literal, in which Satan is a force external to Jesus, to the highly metaphorical, in which Satan is the personification of Jesus' personal "demons." Some movies depict Satan in human form, others afford him only a disembodied voice. The cinematic Satan often expresses the philosophy of the everyday viewer, which contrasts with the asceticism and spirituality attributed to the Son of God.

In Ray's *King of Kings* Satan, like God, does not appear on the screen, but he is heard speaking in voiceover. As the scene begins, Jesus is climbing up a steep rocky incline. The voiceover narrator recounts the baptism and God's declaration that "Thou art my beloved son, in thee I am well pleased" and then recounts Jesus' suffering and deprivation in the desert:

> And Jesus knew the wilderness—its day of heat, its night of cold and solitude—and stayed himself there to commune with God and strengthen himself for the times to come and ate nothing and hungered and brought his soul forth in the light to be seen of himself and know...and was forty days tempted of the devil.

The effect is precisely to contrast the jurisdiction God and Satan have over Jesus. Scenes of grandeur, resembling the grand mosques of Istanbul, illustrate the voice's promises of power. In this version, Jesus enters an altered or heightened state of consciousness, but the film falls short of stating that Satan is a figment of Jesus' imagination.

Ironically, it is Pasolini's allegorical film that provides the most literal account of the Temptation. Here Satan is a simple-looking peasant, dark-haired and bareheaded like the disciples. Jesus is kneeling in the desert sand.

Looking upwards, he sees a huge cloud, then a burning flame, perhaps an allusion to the burning bush that Moses witnesses in Exodus 3. Soon it becomes clear that the flame is an illusion. There is only a man in voluminous black robes walking down the hillside raising up dust behind him that glows in the light. We see his feet as he walks down the hill, and then his back as he approaches Jesus. Jesus stands up and faces him. After the scripted Matthean dialogue with Jesus, Satan walks away as he came.

In other films, however, Satan is an externalization of Jesus' own spiritual torment. In *The Miracle Maker*, this entrance into Jesus' soul is marked by a change in medium. After his baptism, Jesus walks off to the desert and soon begins to suffer from the heat and fatigue. A large bird of prey swoops down behind him and takes on human form. Jesus collapses as claymation turns to animation. The mountains are ominous and tinged with red. Satan's voice rings out: "Command this stone to turn into a loaf of bread to satisfy your hunger." Jesus, famished, visibly struggles with the temptation to eat the bread that Satan has so conveniently placed in his path. He continues climbing, then looks down to see the Roman legions arrayed before him, presided over by Satan, enthroned on the dais before them. Finally, Jesus banishes Satan—"You shall not put your God to the test"—as he stretches out his arms in cruciform position. His posture reminds the viewer that it is the cross that banishes temptation and keeps people focused on the divine will. As throughout this film, the change from claymation to animation signals a shift from external to internal narration; this device indicates clearly that the temptation did not "really" happen but rather reflected a struggle within Jesus' own mind and soul.

THE KING OF KINGS. In DeMille's *The King of Kings* Satan is not so much the force of evil as a metaphor for spiritual distress. The temptation scene takes place within the precincts of the Temple. Jesus, luminous as always in a white robe, is alone, in contemplation as he leans against a column. Up behind him steals a man of similar height and build, dressed in black. He reaches out his hand and points ahead, and recites the temptations according to Matthew: "Behold the kingdoms of the world—and the glory of them" (Matthew 4:8). The music is ominous. Satan points to himself, but Jesus continues to lean against the column, eyes closed, slowly and ceremoniously beating his chest with a closed fist, a gesture used by worshipers in the synagogue during the daily morning prayers and on the Day of Atonement to signify their own repentance.

Jesus is visibly shaken by Satan's presence. The fact that he does not engage Satan directly suggests, however, that Satan is an externalization of Jesus' own inner struggle. After Satan has said his piece, Jesus exclaims in words that the Gospels (Mark 8:33 and parallels) have him address to Peter:

"Get thee behind me, Satan" (though Satan is already behind him!), followed by "It is written: Thou shalt worship the Lord thy God and him only shalt thou serve" (cf. Matthew 4:10). Satan backs off. Suddenly Jesus is alone again. Then he too vanishes from the screen, replaced by a small white lamb that wanders past the column where this encounter took place. At this moment, Jesus reappears from behind the column, bends down to the pet the lamb, picks him up and strokes him. Obviously the lamb is meant to signify Jesus himself, in his role as the pure innocent being that will be sacrificed for the good of humankind in his definitive victory over Satan.

THE LAST TEMPTATION OF CHRIST. For Scorsese's Jesus, Satan is both a metaphor and a real force that threatens Jesus' well-being and sense of identity as the Messiah. Primarily, however, Satan is the externalization of Jesus' ongoing struggle to understand, identify, and come to terms with the forces that are tormenting him from within. Like Honi the Circle-Maker of rabbinic tradition,[3] Jesus draws a circle in the sand and sits down inside it, vowing to stay there until God speaks to him and tells him whether his (Jesus'/God's) weapon is to be love or the axe.

First he is visited by a snake, that has the seductive, liquid voice of Mary Magdalene:

SNAKE   I feel sorry for you. You were lonely, you cried, so I came.

JESUS   I didn't call for you. Who are you?

SNAKE   Your spirit.

JESUS   My spirit?

SNAKE   You're afraid of being alone. You're just like Adam. He called me and I took one of his ribs and made it into a woman.

JESUS   You're here to trick me.

SNAKE   Trick you? To love and care for a woman, to have a family, is this a trick? Why are you trying to save the world? Aren't your own sins enough for you? What arrogance to think you can save the world. The world doesn't have to be saved. Save yourself. Find love.

JESUS   I have love.

SNAKE   Look in my eyes, look at my breasts, do you recognize them? Just nod your head, and we'll be in my bed together (moans) Jesus.

Then she disappears in a burst of thunder. Jesus sobs. Next a lion appears, looking and sounding much like his friend Judas, with similarly broad build, ruddy coloring and earthy language:

LION   Welcome, Jesus. Congratulations. You have passed the small temptations of a woman and family, we're both bigger than that.

JESUS   Who are you?

LION   You don't recognize me? I'm you. I'm your heart. Your heart is so greedy. It pretends to be humble, but it really wants to conquer the world.

JESUS   I never wanted a kingdom on earth, the kingdom of heaven is enough.

LION   You're a liar! When you were making crosses for the Romans in Nazareth, your head was exploding with dreams of power! Power over everyone! You said it was God, but you really wanted power. Now you can have what you want, any country you want. All of them. You could even have Rome.

JESUS   Liar. Step in my circle so I can pull your tongue out.

The lion steps into the circle and disappears. Finally, a fire bursts forth, recalling the burning bush through which God spoke to Moses.

FIRE   Jesus, I'm the one you've been waiting for. Remember? When you were a little boy, you cried "Make me God, God. God, God, make me the god."

JESUS   I was just a child then.

FIRE   You wanted God....You are his son, the only son of God. Join me. Join me. Together we'll rule the living and the dead....Sit in judgment and I'll sit next to you. Imagine how strong we'll be together.

JESUS   Satan?

The bush orders him to take an axe and cut down the apple tree—an allusion to the source of temptation in Genesis 3—that has mysteriously bloomed in the desert.

Scorsese's Jesus faces the temptation of power that the Jesus of the Gospels also had to overcome. In addition, he faces sexual temptation, as symbolized by the snake which, like the apple tree, alludes to the story of Adam and Eve's temptation in Genesis. The third temptation, however, is to see himself as the Son of God. It is impossible to know at this point in the film whether Jesus' intuition that he may indeed be God's son is the truth, given to him by God, or the ultimate sin, inspired by Satan. The parallels between this scene and the Synoptic accounts of the temptation imply the latter, but for the viewer the ambiguity remains.

THE GREATEST STORY EVER TOLD. If Scorsese uses Satan and the temptation narrative as a vehicle for exploring Jesus' psyche, other films employ Jesus' encounter with Satan in order to criticize the materialism and hedonism of western society—hungry for power and for "bread"—to which many of us succumb only too readily.

In *The Greatest Story Ever Told*, Jesus hears a British-sounding voice talking and laughing inside a crevice or a cave. Peering in, Jesus finds a man dressed in dark robes, eating with gusto and chuckling: "A long hard climb, wasn't it?" He motions to Jesus: "Come on in, if you like." As Jesus enters, Satan continues: "Some think the whole of life should be hard like that. An easy life is a sinful life, that's what they think. Not so. Life should be as easy as a man can make it. And it can be easy, friend. If a man knows the way to power and glory in this world." At this, Satan stares intently at the camera, that is, at us the viewers, who may well hold secretly or even overtly to the values that he is articulating here. He chews his food with gusto, his mouth half open.

SATAN   You must be hungry after your long climb. Have some.

JESUS   I'm fasting.

SATAN   A man has to keep his strength up. Are you sure you won't have a little?

The operative word here must be "man" and we viewers are expected to know by now that Jesus is not quite like other men. Satan snorts when Jesus refuses to eat his food, and is even more disdainful when Jesus later refuses the power that Satan offers him. Jesus' spare figure, simple clothing and ascetic behavior contrast with Satan's energetic enjoyment of worldly pleasures. Like the hedonistic life style that he represents, Satan's manner is both seductive and sinister.

JESUS OF MONTREAL. A similarly contemporary message is conveyed by the temptation scene in Arcand's *Jesus of Montreal*. The scene does not appear in the segments from the Passion play that we view in the film, but it is prominent in the frame narrative, in which Satan works through the machinations of an entertainment lawyer named Richard Cardinal, who unsuccessfully tries to tempt Daniel/Jesus to sign on with him.

CARDINAL   Most of my clients, I mean, friends, are in the media: show business, publishing... I look after contracts, tax planning, investments, sometimes even career planning...

DANIEL   What is that?

CARDINAL   If someone's young and not sure how to exploit his talent we sit down and talk about goals. We try to define his dreams and then plan the steps to attain them.

DANIEL   Does it work?

CARDINAL   I know an actress born down in the blue-collar district who now lives in Malibu. There are others from Shawinigan or St. Raymond who own townhouses in Paris or lofts in New York.

DANIEL   What does it take?

CARDINAL   Not much, doing what you like to do.

DANIEL   Even the Passion?

CARDINAL   Jesus is "in" these days, but you'll have to do the weekend talk shows.

DANIEL   I don't believe I was invited.

CARDINAL   I can make a few phone calls. There's always more media space than people with things to say.

DANIEL   I don't have much to say.

CARDINAL   Doesn't matter. You're a good actor.

DANIEL   An actor needs a script.

CARDINAL   We could draft up something. Some ways of saying nothing go over so well. Think of Ronald Reagan. He's not the only one. Actors are everywhere. On TV, radio, in magazines, all you see is actors ... Ever thought of publishing a book?

DANIEL   You mean a novel?

CARDINAL   Yeah. Or your memoirs, travels, your fight against drugs or alcohol—anything.

DANIEL   I'm no writer.

CARDINAL   I said publish, not write. Publishers all have writers with talent and no money.

DANIEL   Of course.

CARDINAL   Do I shock you?

DANIEL   No.

CARDINAL   I'm just trying to show you that with your talent, this city is yours.

With this, both "Jesus" and "Satan" look down upon the bustling city of Montreal. "Satan" tempts "Jesus" with the power, riches, and glory that celebrities crave. At the same time, his very name—Cardinal—ties the corruption that is so evident in his sleazy manner to the more subtle but equally insidious corruption that this film ascribes to the Catholic Church.

After Daniel's death, Richard Cardinal loses no time in contacting his colleagues and offering his services. He suggests that they form a theatre company in Daniel's memory, The Daniel Coulombe Theatre: "It would have to be legally incorporated and all. Martin could be the founding president.... I never said the avant-garde couldn't turn a profit. On the contrary." Three of Daniel's friends nod in agreement; only Mireille realizes that this idea is the very antithesis of everything that Daniel was striving for during his short life. She excuses herself and walks away.

JESUS. In Young's *Jesus*, Satan represents the temptations of modernity and the temptation to judge Christianity by its violent and negative manifestations throughout history. In the temptation scene, Satan appears in modern dress, in the guise of a seductive woman wearing a red dress and flowing red scarf. "The spirit has led you here and allowed you to live ... you must give up everything. Give up your shield." She welcomes him to life, as her scarf blows over her face and then away, resolving itself into Satan, dressed in a black suit. A variation on the Matthean and Lukan dialogue ensues.

SATAN   Command these stones to become bread.

JESUS   You mean call upon my father's power.

SATAN   You have the power to command these stones, don't you?

JESUS   I'm only his son.

SATAN   But you have his power.

JESUS   If I use it in this way I will lose ... he has asked me to use only words.

Suddenly a group of small children appears.

SATAN   Bread could feed these poor children. You have the power to solve mankind's problems. They hunger for bread.

JESUS   They die of hunger because of the hardness of other men.

Satan disappears.

Satan is an anachronistic intrusion from our own era. The scene implies that the temptations that Jesus overcame are no different than those we confront in our own lives. Here too Satan is a product of Jesus' own mind, but Jesus sees far into the future and perceives the various forms that future temptations will take. Moral rectitude, such as the belief in one's ability to solve the problem of world hunger, is seen as moral temptation, as an impulse that must be resisted as Jesus does.

Young's *Jesus* also inserts an encounter between Jesus and Satan in Gethsemane as a way of personalizing or externalizing Jesus' torment as he awaits the inevitable events that will lead to the cross.

SATAN   The final act begins, Jesus. There will be no reprieve handed down from your father. (*Satan walks slowly toward Jesus as he talks. The music is ominous, the lighting cold blue.*) He is willing for you to go through this every painful step of the way. (*Pause*).

JESUS   If it is his will.

SATAN   His will? (*chuckles and kneels down to be face-to-face with Jesus who is sitting on the ground*). His will is for you to be flogged, spit on, humiliated, dragged through the streets, laughed at, tried, convicted, and crucified. You have seen a crucifixion but you have never felt it. You have never felt the pain of nails through your hands, of nails through your feet, it is agony, it's hours in agony, the weight of your own body crushes your lungs, you suffocate slowly, and you will endure this alone. Look at them over there (*tosses his head toward the disciples*), they can't even stay awake! And they will run as soon as Judas shows up, you know I'm right. And (*with emphasis*) it is all in vain, Jesus.

JESUS (*shaking his head vehemently*)   No, no, not in vain. Through me, God will reveal his love for mankind.

SATAN   God? That unseen, heartless, burn-in-hell-watch-your-children-starve God?

JESUS REPEATS   Not in vain.

SATAN   Oh yes, in vain. *Satan stands up, motions behind him.* Let me show you!

Jesus, Satan, and we the viewers watch men on horseback ride toward them.

SATAN   Crusades in your name! "Jesus Christ" they shout when they kill! Killing for Christ will be big business through the centuries, Christ Jesus. This is what you are dying for, this is what your agony will give them. Another reason to kill and torture each other. *Jesus is visibly pained at these words and these scenes from the future.* Don't you think that they have enough reasons already without you going through all this, Jesus? It is so easy, it is so easy, Jesus. Just ask them to come get you.

The scene now switches to modern warfare.

SATAN   The world at war! What a concept!

JESUS   Why?

SATAN   Why? Who knows? That God doesn't like the people of that God. You can stop it.... Come down from that cross they have waiting....You can end poverty and hunger and war. You can do it, it's within your power. Right now!

JESUS   I cannot. It's not God's will.

SATAN   Yes, you can. It is not God's will to end war? What kind of God is that?

JESUS   One who loves mankind so much that he gives them freedom of choice...he gives them the choice of doing good or evil.

SATAN   And this is what they choose! (*he laughs*)

JESUS   Yes.

JESUS, SITTING UP   I forgive you.

SATAN   I don't want your forgiveness. Look, here comes Judas and his mob. (*urgently*) Jesus, you don't even have to bow down to me. I'm not even asking you that. Just call for your father and ask him to deliver you. Tell him you don't want this. He won't make you go through this, you know he won't. Just wave your hand and you'll be home safe. Do it. Now. You know what I showed you is true. You are going to die in vain. You don't know the plan. I do. I've seen it. Nothing changes. They don't have the capacity to love like you want them to, this will never happen. Just lift your hand.... Go home to your father now...don't die in vain, don't die alone.

JESUS (*vehemently*)   No, I am in the hearts of men. I will die for the everlasting kindness of the human heart created by the father. So that man will make his image shine once again and those who will want to will find in me the strength to love until the end.

In this film, Satan, while diabolical, is also perhaps the character whose point of view we movie viewers can most readily comprehend. He articulates the values that our culture holds dear, at least, those to which we pay lip service: stamping out war and poverty. Beside these major projects, Jesus' claim to being in the hearts of men, and making God's image shine sounds vague, and even feeble. While we know that we should distrust Satan and identify with Jesus, the vivid horrors depicted in the film do not make it easy to do so.

THE PASSION OF THE CHRIST. Finally, we turn to a film in which Satan has a starring role: Gibson's *The Passion of the Christ*. Because the movie is not a full biography, it does not contain the temptation scene as such. But the lengthy encounter between Jesus and Satan at Gethsemane, which opens the film, is all about temptation. Jesus prays and expresses his trust in God: "In you I take refuge." He looks up at the full moon.

In the dim light appears Satan, an androgynous figure, with the body, hair, and facial features of a woman, but with shaven eyebrows and a deep masculine voice. She/he says: "No one man can carry this burden, I tell you. It is far too heavy. Saving their souls is too costly. No one ever. No. Never." The camera cuts back and forth between Jesus and Satan. Jesus shields himself against Satan by praying: "Father, you can do all things. If it is possible, let this chalice pass from me." Satan asks the key question: "Who is your father? Jesus kneels in prayer. "Who are you?" he says to him/her. As Jesus continues to pray, a snake slithers out from under her robes, toward Jesus. Satan continues to stare at Jesus as he slays the snake, in effect throwing down the gauntlet in the conflict between God and Satan. Immediately soldiers arrest him. In the absence of Jesus' early temptation, Gethsemane becomes the place in which Jesus and Satan play out the theme of identity and affiliation that will consign them to eternal conflict.

For Gibson, however, this is not the end of Satan's role. Indeed, Satan appears throughout the film, never allowing us to forget that Jesus' story ultimately concerns the struggle between the forces of God/the good and the forces of evil. Satan moves in among the human characters that are her/his instruments of evil: the Roman soldiers and, even more obviously, the Jewish high priests and other Jewish authorities.

Four scenes merit consideration. Two involve Judas, in the aftermath of the betrayal and his realization of the horror that he has unleashed. As he sits, in deep despair, two curious young boys approach.

BOY 1   What's wrong? Are you all right?

BOY 2   Look at his mouth. Hey, can we look at it?

BOY 1   You need help? Can we help?

BOY 2   He's bleeding. Look! Blood!

JUDAS   Leave me alone...you little satans!

BOY 1   Aha! Cursing! Are you cursed?

BOY 2   He's cursed!

Both boys start to taunt him. Yes, a curse! It's inside him!
Look!

BOY 2 *(taking a big juicy bite out of Judas' forearm)*   Watch out! It's like
burning oil from his bones!

JUDAS   Get away from me! Leave me alone! *(He gets up and runs but
cannot escape the boys' jeering voices.)*

Moments later, we see Judas being chased by a group of such children, then
suddenly the children disappear. No doubt these images are meant to be
symbolic; the children are initially sympathetic, and the transformation of
Jewish children into demons is apparently a figment of Judas' guilty and tortured mind. But how chilling that this film, knowingly or not, plays upon the
age-old trope of Jews as the children of the devil, a motif that has its source in
John 8:44, in which Jesus declares that the Jews who do not believe in him
have the devil as their father. The two boys are the only recognizably Jewish
children in the entire film, as evidenced by their skullcaps.

The image of the demon-child returns later on in the film. In a very brief
but highly evocative scene, Satan holds an infant in her arms. The child slowly
turns around to face the camera and smiles wickedly into the camera; we
see that it is a demon child, not a human one. The scene of course both recalls and perverts the traditional Madonna and Child image, and perhaps
also accounts for the physical portrayal of Satan as a woman yet not woman.
(figure 9.4).

Finally, at the moment of Jesus' crucifixion, along with the natural di-
sasters such as earthquakes that everyone experiences, we see the earth split
open, and Satan cast down to her/his hellish abode. The tremendous force
unleashed by the earthquake removes his/her hair from her head. This moment signifies that God's definitive victory over Satan has been achieved by the
death and resurrection of his only son. Gibson here goes far beyond the New
Testament temptation stories and the biopic portrayals of Satan to identify
Satan with the human forces arrayed against Jesus. The close, though not
exclusive, ties between Satan and Caiaphas, are troubling, for it may readily
reinforce the accusation of deicide from which many Christians would now
strongly dissociate themselves.

FIGURE 9.4. "Madonna" and "child" in *The Passion of the Christ*.

Conclusion

Satan provides the Jesus biopic genre with its best opportunity for irony, paradox, and critique. In the Tempation and Gethsemane scenes Satan articulates the enduring questions that people must have raised about Jesus and his claims to divine sonship, and touches on the reasons most people would be unable to emulate Jesus in relinquishing worldly pleasures, aspirations, and even worldly responsibilities such as feeding the poor. It is through Satan that the films articulate their own critique of Jesus as a viable model for behavior for humankind. In doing so, they subtly subvert the Christian evangelical message that at least some of them explicitly set out to deliver.

In this regard, viewers may view Satan either as God's nemesis, the cosmic enemy par excellence, or as humanity's advocate, who is able to articulate the concerns and values of our society over against the nebulous otherworldliness that at least some of our Jesus heroes represent.

IO

The Pharisees

FIGURE 10.1. *Intolerance,* 1916

FIGURE 10.2. *The Gospel According to St. Matthew,* 1964

FIGURE 10.3. *Godspell,* 1973

The conventions of the biopic genre require that our hero confront serious opposition from those who feel threatened by his activities. But how and why did a man who taught peace and love, who healed the sick and raised the dead, arouse hostility so intense that he had to be killed? Although Jesus dies a Roman death—crucifixion being a Roman form of execution—the Gospels insist that he had mortal enemies among the Jewish leaders who resented, feared, and hated him.

Against Jesus are set a bewildering array of Jewish groups: scribes, elders, chief priests, Herodians (Mark 3:6), Pharisees, and Sadducees. During Jesus' ministry, it is the Pharisees who constitute Jesus' most implacable opposition. But Jesus gives as good as he gets. In his long diatribe in Matthew 23, punctuated with the refrain, "Woe to you, scribes, Pharisees, hypocrites," Jesus denounces what he describes as the Pharisees' hypocritical religious behavior and thereby hastens the climax of the plot.

Were the Pharisees merely another long-gone first-century Jewish sect, their portrayal would pose no problem for filmmakers. But, in contrast to the Essenes and the Zealots, the Pharisees, while no longer in existence as such, are considered within the Jewish tradition to be the forerunners of the rabbis who shaped Jewish belief and practice as they are still known today. Specifically, the Pharisees are credited with developing techniques for interpreting the Pentateuch (the Torah or Five Books of Moses) in a way that kept it relevant and provided a focus for Jewish life and worship that would survive the destruction of the Jerusalem Temple in 70 CE.[1]

The filmmaker's dilemma arises from this contradiction between the Pharisees' hateful role as Jesus' enemies within the Christian scriptures and their heroic place in Jewish tradition. The danger is that in portraying the Pharisees as Jesus' harsh enemies, filmmakers become vulnerable to the charge of anti-Semitism.

In the Gospels

In the works of first-century Jewish historian Josephus, the Pharisees appear as highly influential political players from the Hasmonean period in the last two centuries before the common era to the Jewish revolt against Rome in 66–74 CE. Jewish texts spanning the second through the sixth centuries CE regard the Pharisees as meticulous sages who may, or may not, have been proto-rabbis and the progenitors of the rabbinic movement. In our own times, the Pharisees loom large in the scholarly literature. Histories of Second Temple and early rabbinic Judaism, as well as successive quests for the historical Jesus, probe the Pharisees' origins, history, modes of biblical interpretation, and relationships to their contemporaries such as the Dead Sea community, to their successors, and to Jesus of Nazareth.[2]

In the Gospels, however, the Pharisees are simply and primarily Jesus' enemies.The Pharisees as such seem to be of interest only to the Third Evangelist. Luke 16:14 disparages the Pharisees as lovers of money. Acts 23:6–8 briefly refers to their theology:

> When Paul noticed that some were Sadducees and others were Pharisees, he called out in the council, "Brothers, I am a Pharisee, a son of Pharisees. I am on trial concerning the hope of the resurrection of the dead." When he said this, a dissension began between the Pharisees and the Sadducees, and the assembly was divided. (The Sadducees say that there is no resurrection, or angel, or spirit; but the Pharisees acknowledge all three.)[3]

Except for these two passages, the Gospels' only references to the Pharisees recount their conflicts with Jesus. Numerous passages describe the Pharisees' hostility to Jesus. According to Luke 14:1–4, the Pharisees anticipated Jesus' Sabbath healings and hoped to catch him in the act:

> On one occasion when Jesus was going to the house of a leader of the Pharisees to eat a meal on the Sabbath, they were watching him closely. Just then, in front of him, there was a man who had dropsy. And Jesus asked the lawyers and Pharisees, "Is it lawful to cure people on the Sabbath, or not?" But they were silent. So Jesus took him and healed him, and sent him away.

On another occasion, Jesus' followers violated the Sabbath prohibitions against harvesting:

> At that time Jesus went through the grainfields on the Sabbath; his disciples were hungry, and they began to pluck heads of grain and to eat. When the Pharisees saw it, they said to him, "Look, your disciples are doing what is not lawful to do on the sabbath." (Matthew 12:1–2)

Jesus' declaration that "it is not what goes into the mouth that defiles a person, but it is what comes out of the mouth that defiles," also offended them (Matthew 15:11–12).

Yet another problem, according to Luke 7:36–39, was Jesus' willingness to override purity considerations and, with them, social class distinctions. This point is illustrated by the Pharisees' objection to the presence of the anonymous woman who anointed Jesus' feet.[4]

According to John, the Pharisees' hatred of Jesus was rooted in their fear of Roman reprisals, particularly in the wake of Lazarus' resurrection.

> Many of the Jews therefore, who had come with Mary and had seen what Jesus did, believed in him. But some of them went to the Pharisees and told them what he had done. So the chief priests and the Pharisees called a meeting of the council, and said, "What are we to do? This man is performing many signs. If we let him go on like this, everyone will believe in him, and the Romans will come and destroy both our holy place and our nation." (John 11:45–48)

There is, however, at least one Pharisee who is not motivated by hatred for Jesus: "Now there was a Pharisee named Nicodemus, a leader of the Jews. He came to Jesus by night and said to him, 'Rabbi, we know that you are a teacher who has come from God; for no one can do these signs that you do apart from the presence of God'" (John 3:1–2).

In John 7:50–51 Nicodemus defends Jesus to the Pharisees and other Jewish leaders who had planned to have Jesus arrested: "Our law does not judge people without first giving them a hearing to find out what they are doing, does it?" After Jesus' death, Nicodemus, along with Joseph of Arimathea, took Jesus' body and wrapped it with myrrh and aloes in linen cloths, according to the burial custom of the Jews (John 19:38–40).

Jesus, for his part, had some serious differences with the Jewish leaders and what he perceived as their rigid approach to Jewish practice. In Matthew 16:11–12 he warns his listeners to "beware of the yeast of the Pharisees and Sadducees," by which he meant their teachings.[5]

Jesus' sharpest critique occurs in Matthew 23, a lengthy diatribe against hypocrisy. This brief quotation illustrates the flavor of Jesus' invective:

> Then Jesus said to the crowds and to his disciples, "The scribes and the Pharisees sit on Moses' seat; therefore, do whatever they teach you and follow it; but do not do as they do, for they do not practice what they teach.... They love to have the place of honor at banquets and the best seats in the synagogues, and to be greeted with respect in the marketplaces, and to have people call them rabbi. But woe to you, scribes and Pharisees, hypocrites! For you lock people out of the kingdom of heaven. For you do not go in yourselves, and when others are going in, you stop them.... Woe to you, scribes and Pharisees, hypocrites! For you cross sea and land to make a single convert, and you make the new convert twice as much a child of hell as yourselves." (Matthew 23:1–7, 13–15)

According to the Gospels, the Pharisees' hostility toward Jesus was expressed not only verbally but also in action. John states categorically that the Pharisees expelled those who confessed faith in Jesus from the synagogue. "Many, even of the authorities, believed in him. But because of the Pharisees they did not confess it, for fear that they would be put out of the synagogue; for they loved human glory more than the glory that comes from God" (John 12:42–43).

But the Pharisees' primary target was Jesus. In John 7:32 and 7:45, the Pharisees, along with the chief priests, actively sought Jesus' arrest. Matthew 27:62–64 indicates that the Pharisees' concern about Jesus did not abate with his crucifixion and burial.

> The next day, that is, after the day of Preparation, the chief priests and the Pharisees gathered before Pilate and said, "Sir, we remember what that impostor said while he was still alive, 'After three days I will rise again.' Therefore command the tomb to be made secure until the third day; otherwise his disciples may go and steal him away, and tell the people, 'He has been raised from the dead,' and the last deception would be worse than the first."

In contrast to their prominence during Jesus' ministry, the Pharisees are absent from the Passion accounts. Except for John's brief note that "police from the chief priests and the Pharisees" were involved in Jesus' arrest alongside Roman troops (John 18:3), the Pharisees are not mentioned in the final episode of Jesus' life story. From the moment of Jesus' arrest, Caiaphas the High Priest takes over the role of Jesus' chief enemy, and the Pharisees drop out of the picture.

In the Movies

Despite their prominence in the Gospels, the Pharisees do not always appear in the Jesus biopics. In *The Greatest Story Ever Told*, for example, the only reference to the Pharisees occurs sotto voce in the first few words of Matthew 23, which is greatly abbreviated and barely audible. Some films collapse the main Jewish groups into one generic category, in the interests of simplicity. In *Jesus Christ Superstar*, for example, the priests and Pharisees are indistinguishable in appearance; all Jewish leaders are dressed in sinister black outfits.

Godspell takes yet another approach by portraying Jesus' enemies as a huge monster. The monster takes over the lines that the Gospels assign to the Pharisees, and in turn Jesus addresses the diatribe of Matthew 23 against the monster:

> Thou shalt love the lord your God with all your heart and with all your soul. This is the greatest commandment of them all. And the

second is like it. Thou shalt love thy neighbor as thyself. All the rest of the laws and all that the prophets have written is based on these first two. You doctors of the Law and you Pharisees sit in the chair of Moses. But you say one thing and you do another. Everything you do is done for show. Oh you like to have your places of honor at feasts and in the synagogues and to be greeted respectfully and to be called teacher. But you must not be called teacher. For you have one teacher. The messiah. And you must not call any man on earth father. For you have one father. And you are all brothers.

The monster literally blows its stack and finally self-destructs, signifying Jesus' moral victory over his enemies. Portraying the Pharisees as a monster not only circumvents the problem of anti-Judaism but also fits in well with the overall theme of the film, which is at least in part a critique of modern technological civilization and culture.[6]

Neither do the Pharisees figure prominently in Gibson's *The Passion of the Christ*. In a brief conversation, Abenader, Pilate's chief aide, tells Pilate and his wife Claudia that "The Pharisees apparently hate the man [Jesus]," thereby assigning to them at least an implicit role in Jesus' tragic fate. Otherwise, Gibson follows the Gospel accounts in omitting the Pharisees from the Passion account as such.

Films that wish to convey a more nuanced, less monolithic view of the Pharisees often rely upon Nicodemus, whom the Gospel of John presents as sympathetic to Jesus. In Zeffirelli's *Jesus of Nazareth*, for example, Nicodemus seeks Jesus out to warn him of a special meeting of the Sanhedrin and then advocates for him at the meeting as well as at the trial at which Jesus is condemned.

In other films, Nicodemus acts as Jesus' advocate before Caiaphas. Ray's *King of Kings* portrays Caiaphas and Nicodemus in conversation as they walk along the nighttime streets of Jerusalem.

CAIAPHAS   Do you believe in him?

NICODEMUS   I do.

CAIAPHAS   Self-appointed saviors like your Jesus might stir the people up against the Romans.

NICODEMUS   But he is a good man.

CAIAPHAS   You are a fool Nicodemus . . . good or bad he is a threat. If Pilate could use Jesus and his followers as an excuse he would massacre our people. For the present we will bide our time.

In Young's *Jesus*, a more spirited confrontation between the two men takes place against the backdrop of a Roman raid on the Temple courtyard.

NICODEMUS   Rome rules this city and now the temple. They appointed you and now they own you, Caiaphas.

CAIAPHAS   It happened because of Jesus of Nazareth.

NICODEMUS (*contradicting him*)   Because of the Romans.

CAIAPHAS   These men who attacked the priests were from Galilee, Nazareth, they would never have had the strength or the will except for this Jesus. He makes the people think they can overthrow Rome. Have you forgotten what he did at the temple? Kicking over the tables. These Galileans are following his lead. Those speeches inflame the people. He has followers, armed and ready to attack the Romans at any minute. Is that what you want?

NICODEMUS   I want you gone from this council. You blame everyone but yourself. I will not stand by and watch you destroy us. I am withdrawing. Until you come to your senses and resign.

CAIAPHAS TO HIS ADVISOR   As I told you before, if we let this man continue, people will say the messiah is here so they will rise up against Rome again. And the Romans will crush the revolt. It is better for you to have one man die for the good of the people than to have the whole nation destroyed. Jesus of Nazareth must die.

By showing dissension among the Jewish authorities, the film avoids a monolithic portrayal of the Jews and thereby also defuses the anti-Semitic potential inherent in the story's plot. Jesus had his supporters among the Jews as well as his detractors.

When Caiaphas in *The Greatest Story Ever Told* holds a meeting of the Sanhedrin, the Jewish council—to try Jesus without informing Nicodemus, the latter becomes very angry:

NICODEMUS (*entering the proceedings*)   What are you doing?

CAIAPHAS   Lord Nicodemus, my friend, it is good to have you with us.

NICODEMUS   Is that why I and other members of the Sanhedrin have not been informed of the proceedings?

CAIAPHAS   We had to move swiftly, Lord Nicodemus, there was no time to inform everyone.

NICODEMUS   No time? Well, I see Lord Sorak, who lives in Emmaus, I see Lord Hannas who lives a farther distance than I but you say there was no time for your friend Nicodemus who lives right here in Jerusalem, who only lives a shouting distance from this very place. Is my good friend Joseph of Arimathea present? No, I thought not...those who think as I do are absent and those who think as you do are present.

CAIAPHAS   We are trying this man for blasphemy, my Lord Nicodemus. Please be seated.

NICODEMUS   I will not be seated. Are we...are we all Romans now that we disregard decency, justice, hold secret courts, and...and try innocent men in the dead of night?...What you are doing is unlawful, Lord Caiaphas!

The Pharisees come in for more extensive consideration in four films: Griffith's *Intolerance*, Pasolini's *The Gospel According to St. Matthew*, Zeffirelli's *Jesus of Nazareth*, and Arcand's *Jesus of Montreal*.

INTOLERANCE. The Pharisees are central to the theme of this film. There are three aspects to their portrayal: their physical appearance, their role in the plot as Jesus' opponents, and the intertitles that describe them or convey their words. The first appearance of the Pharisees is preceded by an intertitle which describes these men as "Certain hypocrites among the Pharisees" and adds an explanatory footnote: "Pharisees: A Learned Jewish party, the name possibly brought into disrepute later by hypocrites among them." The unstated background here is Matthew 23, the lengthy and powerful discourse punctuated by the refrain, "Woe to you scribes and Pharisees, hypocrites," and the subsequent and pervasive identification of Pharisees as hypocrites that persists to our own day in popular parlance.[7] Nevertheless, the intertitle takes pains to assert that not *all* Pharisees are hypocrites.

This careful distinction disappears under the weight of the subsequent segments of the Judean story. The next appearance of the Pharisees shows two men dressed in traditional fashion, heads covered. One prays publicly and ostentatiously: "O Lord, I thank thee that I am better than other men." Here too the scene is based on a biblical passage that is not acknowledged in the film, in which a Pharisee prays, "God, I thank you that I am not like other people: thieves, rogues, adulterers, or even like this tax collector." This prayer appears in the context of the parable in Luke 18:9–14, which contrasts the self-righteousness of the Pharisee and the humility of the tax collector. In both Luke and *Intolerance*, the line suggests that arrogance is woven into the very fabric of Jewish liturgy.

The negative connotation of this allusion is conveyed by the *tefillin*, or phylacteries, which according to Jewish practice are worn only during the week-day morning prayers. These prayers thank God for a range of things such as opening the eyes of the blind, clothing the naked, and providing for human needs. Included in this long series of blessings are also prayers in which the worshipper thanks God for not making him a Gentile, a slave, or a woman. It is perhaps natural to conclude that a man who utters thanks for being Jewish, freeborn, and male, or, as in Luke, for not being a thief, rogue, adulterer, or tax collector, is in fact thanking God that he is better than other men, though this does not capture the sense and essence of the prayer from a Jewish perspective.[8]

The next cut shows the wedding at Cana. Jesus enters an arched doorway as two Pharisees whisper to one another. The intertitle refers to Jesus as "Scorned and rejected of men." The scene establishes an opposition between Jesus, as the one who is scorned, and the Pharisees, as the instruments of his rejection. At the wedding itself, the two Pharisees comment: "There is too much revelry and pleasure-seeking among the people." That the Pharisees' disdain for revelry did not reflect the common attitude among Jews is indicated by another intertitle that explains, "Wine was deemed a fit offering to God; the drinking of it a part of the Jewish religion." These comments act as a bridge to the film's key tale, "The Modern Story," through which Griffith criticizes the temperance movement as well as what he saw as the rigid and uncompassionate piety of certain groups in American society of the early twentieth century. The drinking of wine should not be forbidden; if it was good enough to be an offering to God, then who are we humans to proscribe it? The Pharisees, however, are the forerunners of the detested "Uplifters" of the temperance movement, who are responsible for the Boy's unjust conviction and death sentence.

The emphasis on wine continues in the third cut to the Judean story, in which a Pharisee complains to his companion: "Behold a man gluttonous, and a winebibber, a friend of publicans and sinners" (Matthew 11:19). The Pharisees do not appear in the remaining cuts to the Judean story, in which Jesus' concern for small children is juxtaposed with the birth of a child to the young couple of The Modern Story, and the sentence of death on Jesus is paralleled to the guilty verdict on the Boy. Shots of the Boy in the Modern Story being led to the gallows are intercut with brief shots of Jesus walking through the streets carrying his cross and of the crucifixion itself. Unlike Jesus, however, the Boy in The Modern Story is saved at the last minute when the real murderer confesses.

The Judean story in Griffith's *Intolerance* narrows Jesus' life story to the conflict between Jesus and the Pharisees, confines that conflict to the issue of pleasure versus temperance, and reduces Jesus to a man devoted to wine and pleasure (though it must be noted that Jesus does not actually imbibe any alcohol on screen). In the process, the Pharisees are portrayed as the hypocritical, supercilious, self-aggrandizing, and powerful Jewish enemies of Jesus.

The hand of Griffith's Jewish advisor, Rabbi Isadore Myers, may be seen in the historical footnotes pointing out that not all Pharisees were hypocrites and that wine was considered a fitting offering to God. No doubt these notes are intended to circumvent potential charges of anti-Semitism that might easily be leveled at a story that focuses so starkly on the Pharisees as Jesus' enemies.

The structure and length of the film were also affected by Griffith's attempt to avoid anti-Semitism, or at least, to respond to Jewish protests. The original film had approximately thirty cuts to the Judean story. After strong protests by the B'nai Brith and other Jewish groups, segments depicting the Jewish leaders persecuting and crucifying Jesus were removed. These changes reduced the Judean story to a mere seven cuts. There are no Jewish authorities, no Caiaphas, no priests, no Judas, and no Pharisees in the final version of the crucifixion sequence.

These efforts, while laudable in the historical context of the film industry in the early years of the last century, do nothing to neutralize the anti-Jewish tone of the film. The note praising Jewish worship for including wine does not convey a sincere appreciation of Judaism but rather promotes Griffith's anti-temperance agenda. The note that not all Pharisees were hypocrites barely conceals Griffith's contempt for this Jewish group. These and other comments strike a pseudoscholarly tone that fails to convince. The omission of Jewish characters from the Passion account, and the inclusion of a number of explanatory points are overshadowed by the overall depiction of Jesus as the victim of the Pharisees, who are consistently portrayed as supercilious and intolerant hypocrites far removed from the common people.

THE GOSPEL ACCORDING TO SAINT MATTHEW. Like *Intolerance*, Pasolini's film distinguishes the Pharisees from other characters by their mode of dress. Pasolini's Pharisees, however, do not wear traditional-looking phylacteries or prayer shawls. Rather, they wear immense hats that look like inverted cones, modeled, somewhat ironically, on the hats worn by Christian figures in Piero della Francesca's painting "The Legend of the True Cross" (1452–66).[9] These hats differentiate them from the priests and Sadducees, who wear large hats that look like giant bishops' mitres. The Romans, in turn, wear helmets, faceguards, and armor.

Not surprisingly, the men who challenge Jesus for breaking the Sabbath by eating wear the headgear of the Pharisees, in keeping with the designation of Jesus' interlocutors in the scriptural passage (Matthew 12:2; 9, 14). Others ask Jesus for a sign to test him (16:1) and are condemned as an evil and adulterous generation (12:38). Matthew's Gospel explicitly associates these episodes with the Pharisees, and, as expected, Pasolini's costuming reflects this association.

But Pasolini is not entirely consistent in his use of headgear; occasionally the distinctive hats of the Pharisees appear on the heads of non-Pharisaic characters. The men who confront Jesus by asking by what authority he does these things (Matthew 21:23) and who plot and then carry out the arrest (26:3, 27:2) are identified as the chief priests and elders in Matthew but they wear the hats of Pasolini's Pharisees. Among these is a man wearing a black version of the outfit. He promises thirty denarii to Judas (26:14) and orders Jesus delivered to Pontius Pilate, which indicates that he is the high priest Caiaphas, though this identification is not made explicit in the film.

The effect of this visual presentation is to blend the Pharisees with the chief priests and elders who are responsible for Jesus' death. In this way, Pasolini can override the text of Matthew's Gospel, in which the Pharisees drop out of the narrative during the Passion account, and he can continue to associate them with the forces that led inexorably to Jesus' crucifixion.

The dialogue too foregrounds the Pharisees. In contrast to other Jesus movies, Pasolini includes the full text of Jesus' diatribe against the scribes and Pharisees in Matthew 23. As in the first Gospel, the key phrase, "Woe to you, scribes and Pharisees, hypocrites" is repeated, passionately and emphatically, seven times. Striking, however, is the absence of the Pharisees or other Jewish figures from the screen during the sermon. Only the Roman soldiers are present on screen, apparently to maintain law and order among the Jewish crowds.

What to make of the Pharisees' visual absence? On the one hand, we might argue that this detail is a sign of Pasolini's intent in the film. For Pasolini, the conflict between Jesus and various groups was not intended as a historical reference, nor did he mean to draw a straight line from first-century Jewish leaders to the Jews of his own day. Rather, Pasolini's stated goal was to draw an analogy between the conflict in first-century Palestine to the conflict between the populace and religious establishment in twentieth century Italy.[10] Filming the movie in southern Italy, explained Pasolini, enabled him to make the transition from the ancient to the modern world without having to reconstruct it either archaeologically or philologically.[11] Hence the visual absence of the Pharisees at this crucial juncture might be intended to draw our attention away from the historical or literary context of Matthew 23 and toward the political and social context of contemporary Italy.[12] As Walsh notes:

> Not surprisingly, the powers-that-be callously do away with this social critic. The leaders' plot, Judas's defection, and the supper follow immediately upon Matthew 23. As a result, Jesus' indictment of the leaders before the crowds, rather than the Temple act or the raising of Lazarus, becomes the reason for Jesus' death.[13]

Doing away with a social revolutionary is far more understandable than dispatching the Son of God, an ethicist, an apocalyptic seer, or a cynic sage.[14]

On the other hand, this point is not apparent to viewers unfamiliar with the Italian context. Whether or not one understands the analogy between ancient Judea and modern Italy, the visual absence of the Pharisees only serves to accentuate their aural presence as the objects of Jesus' diatribe and critique. It is only natural to associate the scribes and Pharisees who are the targets of Matthew 23 with the pompous fellows in elaborate hats who congregate in the area of the Temple and falsely accuse Jesus of various crimes. Completing this picture is the account of the trial before Pontius Pilate, in which Pilate declares himself to be innocent of this man's death, and an unidentified voice in the crowd cries out, "His blood be on our children."

Pasolini's Pharisees stand not only for the forces leading to Jesus' death but also for political leaders who have purposefully distanced themselves from the common people. This estrangement is marked by their exaggerated hats, which contrast with the bare heads and simple dress of Jesus' followers and the crowds. It is also reinforced by the distance that the camerawork often creates between the authorities on the screen and the viewers, including those within the film as well as us at home or in the theater. The Pharisees and other Jewish authority figures watch the proceedings from a window high up in the Temple precincts. This separation between the Jews and the populace is most acute during the trial scene, in which the viewer takes on the perspective of a member of the pro-Jesus crowd, watching the ominous proceedings from a distance. This portrait reflects Matthew's presentation, and particularly, his implicit claim that the Pharisees had a political power base in Jerusalem.

Pasolini himself explicitly disavows any interest in historical accuracy and deliberately did not consult scholars in the process of making the film.[15] He admits to omitting important political and social factors, but justifies this omission by arguing that his purpose was not to reconstruct Jesus as he really was but to "reconsecrate" or "remythicize" him.[16] Nevertheless, the emphasis on the Jewish, and Pharisaic, role in Jesus' death belies Pasolini's adherence to Matthew's text, which gives the Pharisees no role in Jesus' Passion, as well as his own allegorical intention, to which the Pharisees as historical figures are irrelevant.

JESUS OF NAZARETH. In contrast to Pasolini's *Gospel*, Zeffirelli's miniseries goes to great lengths to create a positive representation of the Jews in general and the Pharisees in particular. Where Pasolini's Jesus moves in a black and white, indeterminate landscape, Zeffirelli's Jesus inhabits a richly depicted Jewish Galilee, dominated by the synagogue and the musical strains of Jewish liturgy and ritual. This detailed and positive portrayal of the Jewish landscape of the Gospels, and of Jesus' own identity as a Jew, has an impact on the portrayal of the Pharisees.

First, the film attributes a developed set of beliefs and practices to the Pharisees, some of which are shared by Jesus and some of which are explicitly negated or violated by Jesus' behavior. One central issue is table fellowship. The Pharisees invite Jesus to eat with them but are outraged when Mary Magdalene, the quintessential sinner of this and most other Jesus movies, rushes in uninvited and anoints him. Far from condemning her, as do his Pharisaic hosts, Jesus not only insists on her right to remain but praises her as behaving toward him in a more appropriate and welcoming manner than the Pharisees themselves did.

A second feature that distinguishes Zeffirelli's treatment of the Pharisees from those of both Griffith and Pasolini is the prominent role given to two individual Pharisees—Nicodemus and Joseph of Arimathea—who act as Jesus' advocates.[17] In Zeffirelli's film, Nicodemus warns Jesus of the secret meeting of the Sanhedrin, and, as in Luke 23:51, Joseph of Arimathea is Jesus' staunchest defender at both this pretrial meeting and the trial itself.

Third, the Pharisees are given an active role in the Jewish council, called the Sanhedrin. The film depicts at length the heated but generally respectful debate between Jesus' supporters and detractors on the council. The chief priest Caiaphas presides over the debate on whether to bring charges against Jesus. But Jesus' case is well represented by Joseph of Arimathea and Nicodemus. For example, Nicodemus argues that the Temple saying, interpreted as blasphemy by some, should be understood symbolically rather than literally. Joseph of Arimathea voices the uneasy relationship between the Jewish and Roman authorities and insists that "none of us wants more victims for Pilate." Jesus' fate is sealed by his emphatic response to Caiaphas' direct probing of his messianic identity.

Although the Pharisees are portrayed in a largely favorable manner, they do not entirely escape the charge of hypocrisy. The woes against the scribes and Pharisees are included, albeit in modified form. Even more telling are the criticisms voiced by the Pharisaic representatives themselves. Joseph of Arimathea in the Sanhedrin meeting prior to Jesus' arrest echoes the accusations of hypocrisy and the murder of the prophets (23:30–31) that are voiced in Matthew 23, reminding his colleagues on the council that they are hardly innocent.

Zeffirelli's Pharisees are an elite group concerned with table fellowship, ethics, proper belief, and the delimitation of social boundaries. Although they have membership on the Sanhedrin and participate freely in political debate, they are less powerful, and also more sympathetic to Jesus, than are the priests, whose chief chairs the Sanhedrin and rules on Jesus' culpability. The Sanhedrin has its own political interests, but its power is limited by the oppressive Roman government.

This description of the Pharisees shares some similarities with a number of scholarly reconstructions. Some primary sources attribute to the Pharisees specific views and practices regarding table fellowship. Scholars debate whether all, or maybe only some, Pharisees belonged to a distinct group referred to in some sources as the *havurah*, meaning "fellowship," to which particularly stringent food and table fellowship rules applied, but many ascribe at least some concern for these issues to the Pharisees as a group. Similarly, scholars debate the geographical power base of the Pharisees and its degree of influence in first-century politics. It is plausible that some Pharisees may have been part of a body such as the Sanhedrin, which had some limited decision-making power in the late Second Temple period.[18]

The intersections between Zeffirelli's portrait and the historians' reconstructions of the Pharisees are not coincidental. Unlike Pasolini, who eschewed historical research, Zeffirelli intended his film to be rigorously didactic. To this end he gathered a group of scriptural experts to help him avoid errors and inaccuracies.[19] His research taught him that "Jesus was a Jew, probably a Pharisee (not a Zealot as some have insisted), immersed in the most Jewish practices and customs imaginable. The Christian religion came much later (a schism from Judaism), out of the faith and controversies of his followers."[20]

JESUS OF MONTREAL. The Pharisees as such do not figure as characters in *Jesus of Montreal*, either in the Passion play or the frame narrative. But two references within the Passion play merit our attention. The explicit reference is to the slaughter of eight hundred Pharisees by King Alexander Jannaeus some eighty years before Jesus' time. This reference, which has rabbinic support, is ultimately based on Josephus's *Antiquities of the Jews*. In an effort to quell civil war, Alexander Jannaeus, king of the Hasmonean kingdom of Judea in 103–76 BCE:

shut up and besieged [the most powerful rebels] in the city of Be-
thoma, and after taking the city and getting them into his power, he
brought them back to Jerusalem; and there he did a thing that was as
cruel as could be: while he feasted with his concubines in a conspicuous place, he ordered some eight hundred of the Jews to be
crucified, and slaughtered their children and wives before the eyes of
the still living wretches.[21] (*Antiquities* 13.380)

This text does not specify that the victims were Pharisees. Nevertheless, it is not
an implausible inference, given King Alexander's known hatred of the Pharisees and his deathbed admission to his wife Alexandra that he had treated
them badly (*Antiquities.* 13.402).

The implicit reference to the Pharisees occurs in the Passion play's rein-
terpretation of Matthew 23, which, as we have noted, clearly draws an analogy
between the Pharisees of Matthew's Gospel and the Catholic Church in Quebec.
Unlike Pasolini's film, in which the critique of the contemporary church is not
obvious to most North American viewers, Arcand's point is unmistakable. Just
as the Gospels attribute Jesus' death at least indirectly to the Pharisees' opposition to Jesus, so does Arcand's rendition cast some blame for the death of
Daniel on the church's refusal to allow the play to continue. Arcand's identification of the Pharisees, and the Jewish opposition to Jesus, with the Catholic
Church circumvents the potential anti-Semitism that is problematic in the
Jesus movie genre.

Rather than giving the Pharisees the role of Jesus' opposition, *Jesus of
Montreal* places Father Leclerc and the church he represents in their stead. The
depiction of the Pharisees as victims of persecution aligns them with Jesus
instead of against him.

Conclusion

The Pharisees on film are a rather one-dimensional group, far more powerful
and prominent in first-century Palestine and far more concerned with the
troublesome Jesus than the overall corpus of primary and secondary sources
would suggest. It would seem that the filmmakers themselves are not particularly interested in the historical Pharisees but only in the dramatic purposes
to which they can be put. For Griffith, Pasolini, and Arcand, the Pharisees are
important only insofar as they permit the conflict inherent in the Jesus story to
be translated to the filmmaker's own time and place. For Zeffirelli, the Pharisees count not only as a first-century group that had both affinities and

differences with Jesus, but also as ciphers for modern-day Jews who in Zef-firelli's view should no longer be blamed for the crucifixion. The Pharisees on film simultaneously play themselves, or at least, the filmmakers' version of the Pharisees, and symbolically evoke other groups—the Uplifters, modern Jews, or the Catholic church in Italy or Quebec—in our own era.

Most important, the Pharisees provide a foil for Jesus; they are the background against which he can articulate the values that each film attributes to him, such as the critique of the hypocrisy that adheres to religious and political establishments and the opposition to senseless hatred.

II

Caiaphas

FIGURE 11.1. *Der Galiläer,* 1921

FIGURE 11.2. *The Kings of Kings,* 1927

FIGURE 11.3. *Jesus Christ Superstar,* 1973

With Jesus' arrest, the Pharisees drop out of sight, passing the role of arch-villain on to the high priest Caiaphas. It is Caiaphas who presides over Jesus' trial before the Sanhedrin, pronounces him guilty of blasphemy, and delivers him to Pilate.

Like the Pharisees, Caiaphas challenges filmmakers to maintain the tension and conflict so essential to the biopic genre and yet avoid antagonizing viewers who might be sensitive to the ways in which a Jewish leader, even a long dead one, is brought to life on the silver screen.

During Jesus' Ministry

In the Gospels

In contrast to the Pharisees, who on occasion show Jesus some courtesy, the chief priests are invariably hostile. According to Matthew, "When the chief priests and the scribes saw the amazing things that he did, and heard the children crying out in the Temple, 'Hosanna to the Son of David,' they became angry"(21:15). When Jesus entered the temple "the chief priests and the elders of the people came to him as he was teaching, and said, 'By what authority are you doing these things, and who gave you this authority?' "(21:23).

Under Caiaphas' leadership, the chief priests and elders plot against Jesus (Matthew 26:3; 27:1), and search for false testimony on the basis of which to convict him of a capital crime (Matthew 26:59; Luke 19:4). Mark suggests that they were made extremely uneasy by Jesus' appeal to the masses: "And when the chief priests and the scribes heard it [Jesus' prophetic discourse after the cleansing of the Temple], they kept looking for a way to kill him; for they were afraid of him, because the whole crowd was spellbound by his teaching" (Mark 11:18). When they realized that one of his parables was directed against them, "they wanted to lay hands on him at that very hour, but they feared the people" (Luke 20:19; 22:2).

Opportunity arose when Judas approached them with an offer they could not refuse: to betray Jesus for thirty pieces of silver (Matthew 26:14). Jesus had foreknowledge of this as of all other things, and shared his prophecy with the disciples: "From that time on, Jesus began to show his disciples that he must go to Jerusalem and undergo great suffering at the hands of the elders and chief priests and scribes, and be killed, and on the third day be raised" (Matthew 16:21).

The Gospel trial narratives are carefully crafted to show that Jesus was falsely accused and that events were manipulated to achieve his condemnation and death. Mark begins his version of the story with a summary comment: "It was two days before the Passover and the festival of Unleavened Bread. The chief priests and the scribes were looking for a way to arrest Jesus by stealth and kill him; for they said, 'Not during the festival, or there may be a riot among the people' " (Mark 14:1–2).

Where Mark blames the "chief priests and scribes," Matthew adds the elders, who, according to Matthew 26:3, gathered together with the chief priests in the high priest's palace to confer on the matter. In Luke's version, "the chief priests and the scribes were looking for a way to put Jesus to death, for they were afraid of the people" (Luke 22:1–2).

All three Synoptics thus introduce their accounts of the Passion with a Jewish plot to have Jesus put to death. The Fourth Gospel claims that this plot arose in the aftermath of Jesus' miraculous raising of Lazarus from the dead.

> Many of the Jews therefore, who had come with Mary and had seen what Jesus did, believed in him. But some of them went to the Pharisees and told them what he had done. So the chief priests and the Pharisees called a meeting of the council, and said, "What are we to do? This man is performing many signs. If we let him go on like this, everyone will believe in him, and the Romans will come and destroy both our holy place and our nation." But one of them, Caiaphas, who was high priest that year, said to them, "You know nothing at all! You do not understand that it is better for you to have one man die for the people than to have the whole nation destroyed." He did not say this on his own, but being high priest that year he prophesied that Jesus was about to die for the nation, and not for the nation only, but to gather into one the dispersed children of God. So from that day on they planned to put him to death. (John 11:45–53)

John describes a pre-Passover plot motivated by fear of Roman reprisal should Jesus gather too great a following. Caiaphas' words cast Jesus as the sacrificial lamb who will spare the nation from Roman wrath. For John, Caiaphas is not merely a crafty politician but also an unwitting prophet of Jesus' death and its salvific significance for the end times when all will return to Jerusalem.

In the Movies

In their attempt to create a plausible narrative, the Jesus biopics address the question of what motivated Caiaphas to plot against Jesus. One response that appears in the silent movies is greed. The anti-Semitic cliché that associates Jews and money is abundantly expressed in the German film *Der Galiläer*, in which Caiaphas asks: "Why should we forgo the money that temple commerce brings?" When he turns the thirty pieces of silver over to Judas, Caiaphas says: "Happiness is here, before you, in your hand. You will be rich and a respected man, among the people and before the Sanhedren [sic]." As he hands the money over, the Jews all laugh at Judas.[1]

German silent films are not the only ones that portray Caiaphas as greedy. DeMille too views Caiaphas as the prime example of the money-grubbing Jew for whom the pursuit of profit overrides all other considerations. DeMille introduces the high priest as "The Roman appointee Caiaphas, the High Priest, who cared more for Revenue than for Religion—and saw in Jesus a menace to his rich profits from the Temple." Caiaphas sits in a richly appointed office. The Hebrew script on the walls behind the high priest ensures that we do not mistake him for a Roman. For DeMille, Caiaphas is not only greedy but corrupt; DeMille alleges that the high priest exploited the riches of the Temple for his personal profit: "The Temple ... to the Faithful of Israel, the dwelling place of Jehovah. But to the High Priest, Caiaphas, a corrupt and profitable marketplace." As Stern, Jefford, and DeBona note, DeMille has drawn Caiaphas "with the bold strokes of a medieval and Reformation caricature of the greedy Jews." Caiaphas "represents all things evil about the unwavering hardness of first-century Judaism as it was portrayed by the later church" and "finds an unyielding, corrupt beacon of legalism against which the faithful (and religious pure) Jesus offers the flexible mercy of the loving Father God."[2] Many years later, the theme of Caiaphas's greed is revived in Gibson's *The Passion of the Christ*, in which the camera lingers on the image of Caiaphas handing the blood money over to Judas.

In *Last Temptation*, Caiaphas is not so much greedy as narrowly chauvinistic. Jesus articulates a trenchant critique of the high priest, when he meets up with him in the Temple precincts. "God doesn't need a palace, he doesn't need shekels .... You think God belongs only to you? God's an immortal spirit who belongs to everybody, to the whole world. You think you're special? God is not an Israelite!"

Gibson adds a unique twist by portraying all of Jesus' enemies as instruments of Satan. While the Romans are by no means excused, it is the Jews who are linked most directly to Satan, as they are throughout his main source, *The Dolorous Passion of Our Lord Jesus Christ*, by Anne Catherine of Emmerich. The Jews wear only dark clothing, and move in a red-tinged ambience lit by flaming torches reminiscent of hell-fire. Satan moves smoothly and stealthily among the Jews as they condemn Jesus to death, as they observe the sadistic Roman soldiers scourge and torture Jesus within an inch of his life, and as they watch Jesus carry his cross toward Golgotha. At the moment of Jesus' death,

Caiaphas holds on to his head and screams. Moments later, the camera cuts away to Satan, now banished below the earth, who holds his/her head and screams exactly like Caiaphas does. A fierce wind tears his/her hair off her head and the earth closes over him/her. The synchrony of the priest's and Satan's screams associates them closely and marks the high priest as Jesus' primary human foe.

Caiaphas' determination to bring Jesus down is a staple of the biopics. In *Jesus Christ Superstar*, Caiaphas debates with others the true level of danger Jesus poses. Caiaphas warns: "We've been sitting on the fence for far too long...while he starts a major war we theorize." Others are less concerned: "He's just another scripture-thumping hack from Galilee," but Caiaphas is frightened by the fact that "they call him king." "What about the Romans? When they see King Jesus crowned do you think they will stand around?" Again, someone takes a calmer view: "Why take their toy away? He's a craze." But Caiaphas will not be deterred: "Put yourself in my place. I cannot step aside, let my hands be tied, I am law and order. The priesthood could fall. If we are to last at all, we cannot be divided....Then we are decided?" The others respond: "Then we are decided."

Caiaphas and the Spies

In the Gospels

To effect his plan, Caiaphas required reliable intelligence as to Jesus' activities and whereabouts. The Gospels briefly suggest that Caiaphas had spies to provide him with the necessary information. The role of spies is mentioned briefly in John 11:57: "the chief priests and the Pharisees had given orders that anyone who knew where Jesus was should let them know, so that they might arrest him." Luke 20:19–20 describes the chief priests dispatching spies to trap Jesus:

> When the scribes and chief priests realized that he had told this par-
> able against them, they wanted to lay hands on him at that very hour,
> but they feared the people. So they watched him and sent spies
> who pretended to be honest, in order to trap him by what he said, so
> as to hand him over to the jurisdiction and authority of the governor.

In the Movies

Many biopics exploit these spies for their full dramatic possibilities. In addition to explaining how the authorities knew of Jesus' activities, the spies' reports provide crucial information not only for their masters but for the viewing audience. Films use this device to describe events such as Jesus' miracles that are familiar to readers of the Gospels but that may be too lengthy or too difficult to portray on screen.

The silent movie *INRI* shows Caiaphas giving instructions to the spies. The intertitle states: "The people say the Nazarene shall come unto Jerusalem as king, go ye and spy him out." There follows a lengthy interrogation in which the spies question Jesus about the Temple ("Didst thou say that thou art able to destroy the temple of God and build it again in three days?") and then ask outright: "Art thou the promised messiah?" Jesus holds up his arms and responds, "For God so loved the world . . . " (John 3:16). The camera then cuts to the Temple. In the background there is a large Star of David, in the center of which appears a large ark in the shape of the two tablets of the law, with the Ten Commandments inscribed on them. Other decorations include a stylized menorah. These Jewish symbols leave no doubt as to the priest's jurisdiction over the Temple. Yet Jesus claims that the Temple is his. He strides in and demands, "What have ye made of my father's house?" then upsets the money-changers tables. Caiaphas does not allow the others to seize him just yet. He warns, "Nay, the people yet acclaim him, it would be dangerous," then wonders whether he can find a traitor among the disciples. The spies enter, and speak earnestly with Caiaphas, presumably informing him that Judas is his man.

DeMille's *The King of Kings* asserts that the high priest's spies are "driven by the fury of religious hatred." The spies declare to Caiaphas: "Before our own eyes he broke the Sabbath! And he said, also, that God was His Father—making Himself equal with God! . . . We would have laid hands on Him, but we feared the multitude—because they take Him for a prophet!" Caiaphas castigates them angrily: "Are ye also deceived?" He sends them off and mulls over the problem of how to entrap Jesus. Then he hits upon an idea. He has his soldiers bring in the woman caught in adultery. "This woman hath been convicted of adultery. Wouldst thou that we stone her to death?" Caiaphas looks at her in disgust. "Make him judge her. If he free her, he breaketh the law of Moses and may be stoned in her stead." He sends out his men and rubs his hands in glee.

Later, the spies report to Caiaphas: "He is driving the money-changers from the Temple and those who buy and sell." Caiaphas is alarmed and goes to see for himself. He confronts Jesus: "By what authority doest thou these things?" Jesus answers, "It is written: My house shall be called the house of prayer but ye have made it a den of Thieves." Caiaphas calls out, "Seize him!" He grabs a spear, his eyes burning with rage.

Caiaphas and Pilate

The Gospels do not portray any direct encounters between Caiaphas and Pilate, but many of the Jesus biopics suggest that these two men have a long-standing relationship, sometimes cordial, sometimes hostile, always uneasy. In some moves, Caiaphas is caught up in a vicious power play that required him to act against Jesus against his own will and judgment. This thread is grounded, if insecurely, in historical studies that focus on the role of the high priest as the one who mediated the difficult relationship between Judea and Rome. Caiaphas' tenure as high priest lasted from 18–36 CE, covering Pilate's entire term as governor of Judea and lasting far longer than most other high priests.[3]

This perspective is central to Ray's *King of Kings*, in which Caiaphas is a member of Pilate's "court" and spends much of his time with Pilate, his wife Claudia, Herod, Herodias, and other courtiers. Caiaphas understands well that he has little power, but he does what he can to urge moderation in the Romans' treatment of John the Baptist and other Jewish troublemakers.

HEROD'S WIFE   An agitator!

PILATE (*chuckling*)   Must he agitate me through a palace window? Send him away.

CAIAPHAS   The harangue is directed against you, for mounting graven images on their Temple wall. The incidents in Caesarea were bad.

PILATE   Plaques stay! (*To Herod*) Tell me something about this man.

HEROD   He is harmless. He gives the people the type of entertainment they want. It's not wise to molest him.

PILATE'S WIFE   My husband is afraid of that madman, he thinks he is a holy man. (*Herod gets up.*)

PILATE   A holy man who speaks words of treason. Caiaphas, you are the high priest in that man's house of God. Punish such conduct.

CAIAPHAS   Punishment does not dampen their ardor. Rather it increases their wrath. We have found it better to ignore the ravings of these false prophets than to prosecute them. In my opinion this man seeks martyrdom.

This conversation concerns John the Baptist, but foreshadows the kinds of concerns that Pilate and Caiaphas will soon have about Jesus.

In Young's *Jesus*, Pilate watches Jesus' triumphal entry into Jerusalem with great concern and says, "This man must be arrested." Livio concurs: "He will bring ruin down on his all. He must be stopped; dead. I could kill this messiah tomorrow, there would be another one right behind him. Or, we could see that he becomes a problem for some of his own people. They would solve the problem for us." Here it is Livio, a fictional advisor to Pilate, who plants in Pilate's mind the plot for destroying Jesus.

If in other films Caiaphas persuades Pilate into crucifying Jesus, here it is Pilate who manipulates the high priest into action against Jesus:

PILATE (*as Caiaphas approaches Pilate slowly*)   There are rumors in the streets, priest.

CAIAPHAS   Rumors?

PILATE   Don't be coy with me! This man Jesus rides an ass into town and is welcomed like a king. Herod wants to kill him but does nothing, and you promised me you can keep peace in the temple but I had to use swords! I will not be silent forever! (*Pilate works himself into a highly theatrical temper.*)

CAIAPHAS   These false messiahs....

PILATE (*shouting*)   I don't care about your religion, I care about peace.

CAIAPHAS   Peace, yes, I too care about peace....

PILATE   Well then get control of this man!

CAIAPHAS   I fear my power is...limited.

PILATE   So you want me to do your dirty work for you.

CAIAPHAS   I have no choice. I cannot endanger Israel for one man.

PILATE   Bring him to me. I will eliminate him.

Caiaphas nods in reluctant agreement. As he leaves Pilate's presence, we realize that he is merely an old and worried man. Livio claps bravo to Pilate; his scheme is working marvelously, and they share a good laugh. Through this exchange, Young casts the burden of responsibility upon the Romans, specifically Pilate, and creates sympathy for the Jewish high priest who is caught between Rome and the people.

Many filmmakers have been reluctant to lay the death of Jesus on the Jews as a whole, or even in many cases on particular groups among the Jewish authorities, and focus instead on the Romans' role in Jesus' death. The expansion of the Romans' role is an effort to present the Jesus story in such a way as to avoid vilifying Jews and Judaism. As film historian Gerald Eugene Forshey puts it, "To choose any interpretation other than one that mitigated the scriptural contention of Jewish culpability was to risk being a bigot."[4]

Jesus' Trial before Caiaphas

In the Gospels

The Passion narrative recounts the working out of the plot against Jesus. The four versions vary to some extent but have the same overall shape: Judas betrays Jesus; Jewish and Roman troops arrest him; Jewish authorities and then Pilate either interrogate him or formally try him;[5] Pilate sentences him to crucifixion after the Jews refuse Pilate's offer to release him. Jesus then undergoes mocking and torture, proceeds to Golgotha bearing his cross, suffers crucifixion and death, then disappears from the tomb on the third day.

Matthew, Mark, and Luke tell similar versions of the Jewish interrogation. Mark describes an assembly of the high priest, chief priests, elders, and scribes (14:53) at which "the chief priests and the whole council were looking for testimony against Jesus to put him to death; but they found none" (14:55). Witnesses gave false and contradictory testimony. Whereas some testified that he declared, "I will destroy this temple that is made with hands, and in three days I will build another, not made with hands," others gave contradictory testimony (14:58–59).

The high priest then stood up and demanded that Jesus respond to this testimony, but Jesus remained silent. Finally the high priest asked him directly: "Are you the Messiah, the Son of the Blessed One?" To this direct question Jesus responded: "I am; and you will see the Son of Man seated at the right hand of the Power and coming with the clouds of heaven." Now, finally, the high priest had his evidence, straight from Jesus' own mouth.

> The high priest tore his clothes and said, "Why do we still need witnesses? You have heard his blasphemy! What is your decision?"
> All of them condemned him as deserving death. Some began to spit on him, to blindfold him, and to strike him, saying to him, 'Prophesy!'
> The guards also took him over and beat him." (Mark 14:55–63)

Matthew's account adds two details that make the situation even more explicit. First, he specifies that two witnesses came forward to testify to Jesus' statement that he would rebuild the Temple, presumably because two witnesses are required for a capital case according to Jewish law (Matthew 26:59–60).[6] Second, he has the high priest put Jesus under oath to respond to the question of whether he is the Messiah: "I put you under oath before the living God, tell us if you are the Messiah, the Son of God" (26:63). In this way, Matthew explains why Jesus finally speaks up after remaining silent throughout the interrogation.

Luke omits the first section in which the Jewish authorities seek testimony and presents a different version of the exchange with Jesus about his messianic identity:

> They said, "If you are the Messiah, tell us." He replied, "If I tell you, you will not believe; and if I question you, you will not answer. But from now on the Son of Man will be seated at the right hand of the power of God." All of them asked, "Are you, then, the Son of God?" He said to them, "You say that I am." Then they said, "What further testimony do we need? We have heard it ourselves from his own lips!" (Luke 23:67–71)

John recounts an interrogation before Annas, the father-in-law of Caiaphas, who, according to John, was the high priest that year (John 18:18).[7] The line of questioning differs from that in the Synoptics:

> Then the high priest questioned Jesus about his disciples and about his teaching. Jesus answered, "I have spoken openly to the world; I have always taught in synagogues and in the temple, where all the Jews come together. I have said nothing in secret. Why do you ask me? Ask those who heard what I said to them; they know what I said." When he had said this, one of the police standing nearby struck Jesus on the face, saying, "Is that how you answer the high priest?" Jesus answered, "If I have spoken wrongly, testify to the wrong. But if I have spoken rightly, why do you strike me?" Then Annas sent him bound to Caiaphas the high priest. (John 18:19–24)

In contrast to the Synoptics, John's Jesus is his usual loquacious self even under interrogation. The Gospel narrative itself illustrates the accuracy of Jesus' statement that he has always spoken openly, for until the Farewell Discourses, Jesus' discourses take place out in the open air (e.g., John 12:17–36), in the Temple (7:14, 10:23), or in the synagogue at Capernaum (6:59). In John's version, there is no formal condemnation at this stage, nor is there a record of what occurred during his interview with Caiaphas. Most important, the questioning by Annas does not address the issue of blasphemy, though this issue does appear elsewhere in the Gospel (10:33, 36).

When these accounts are harmonized, this stage of the narrative conveys two main points: Caiaphas and his minions falsely accuse Jesus of blasphemy and teaching secretively; and it is their plotting that finally leads to Jesus' death.

In the Movies

Like the Gospel of John, DeMille's *The King of Kings* does not depict a trial before Caiaphas. After a title stating "And they led him away to Caiaphas, the High Priest," the curtains open and behind them, in the distance, the council sits in a semicircle with Caiaphas at the midpoint. Jesus enters in the foreground and faces the court, his back to the viewer. His large figure in the foreground of the shot overshadows the council as he walks toward Caiaphas. Then the screen goes black, and the next intertitle appears: "In the morning they brought Jesus before Pontius Pilate, the Roman Governor of Judea, who alone had authority to pass sentence of death" (Mark 15:1).

By contrast, and in keeping with its overall tenor, *Der Galiläer* overplays the trial before Caiaphas. Far from being an objective, dignified process, the trial is nothing less than a political rally in which Caiaphas vigorously incites his council to condemn Jesus to death. The high priest is enthroned in his chambers, laughing and carrying on with his associates, as a bound Jesus stands there in front of them. The contrast in the appearance and behavior between the judge and the accused could not be greater. Whereas the former and his supporters are vocal, Jesus says not a word.

> CAIAPHAS   What does he deserve, then, the one who scorns God's priests? (*Was trifft den, der verachtet Gottes Priester?*)
>
> THE COUNCIL   Death! (*Der Tod!*)
>
> CAIAPHAS   What does he deserve, the one who desecrates the Sabbath? The one who defends sinners! (*Was trifft den Sabbathschänder?! Den, der Sünder schützt!*)
>
> THE COUNCIL   Death! (*Der Tod!*)
>
> CAIAPHAS   And the one who has slandered God himself? (*Und den, der Gott selbst frech gelästert?*)
>
> THE COUNCIL   Death and Death again! (*Der Tod und abermals der Tod!*)
>
> CAIAPHAS TO JESUS   So hear your fate, you heretic and blasphemer— death! (*So hör'dein Urtail, Ketzer, Lästerer! Und sei des Todes.*)

Zeffirelli, by contrast, deflects blame from Caiaphas onto the fictional scribe Zerah. It is Zerah who orchestrates a "meeting" between Jesus and the high priest that in fact is his trial before the Sanhedrin on charges of blasphemy. The Council hears testimony both for and against Jesus, and Caiaphas, far from being a greedy schemer, is portrayed as a wise leader seeking to do what is right in God's eyes. Then Caiaphas asks Jesus formally: "I ask you now, in the name of the Eternal: Are you the Messiah, the Son of God?" Jesus pauses at length, as the camera focuses on his face in extreme close-up: "I am . . . and you shall see the Son of Man sitting at the right hand of the power of God." Caiaphas closes his eyes and the camera scans the room to show the stunned reaction of the Sanhedrin. The high priest then recites, slowly and solemnly, yet with great emotion, "Hear O Israel the Lord our God the Lord is One" (Deuteronomy 6:4). He rips his garment, in the ritual sign of mourning. Zerah steps in: "We have heard enough. Let him be taken before the Procurator Pontius Pilate in whose hands lies the final authority for trial and judgment."

In the movies, in contrast to the Gospels, Caiaphas appears yet again, this time in the trial before Pilate. But we save this discussion for the next chapter.

Conclusion

The Gospel accounts of Jesus' enemies leave many gaps. They do not distinguish clearly or consistently among the various Jewish groups that were arrayed against Jesus, nor do they provide many details about the Jews' role in Jesus' suffering and death, their relationship to each other, or their stance toward the Roman authorities. It would not be realistic to expect feature films to be more precise than the Gospels themselves in these matters, for films tend to simplify rather than complicate the story lines of their textual sources. It suits the movie medium to have the conflict as simple and as stark as possible, so that viewers are clear on the identities of the adversaries. In the case of the Jesus biopic, it is obvious that the "good guy" is Jesus. For most films, the role of the "bad guy" is shared by the Romans and the Jews.

The portioning out of relative blame varied over time. Most films made prior to World War II readily viewed Jewish individuals or groups as Jesus' main opponents, even if they tried to avoid blaming the Jews as a whole (Griffith, DeMille) for Jesus' death. In addition to cohering well with the Gospel accounts, this approach made for a better story, as it is more dramatic to have Jesus' own people turn against him than to have him face off directly with the large and anonymous Roman imperial machinery. Films made after the Holocaust present a more nuanced scenario, no doubt influenced at least in part by a marked decrease in the acceptability of public anti-Semitism and also by new studies of the historical Jesus that reassess the question of Jewish responsibility.[8] These films tend to portray the Jewish authorities as being caught between their people and the Romans, and as motivated in the case of Jesus not by animosity but by the strong and not unreasonable fear that disorder or disobedience will lead to a more terrible punishment from the Romans. This representation is reminiscent of the moral dilemma faced by the Judenrat, or Jewish council, in the ghettoes of the Nazi period, though there is no direct evidence that filmmakers had such detailed knowledge about the Nazi regime.[9]

12

Pilate

FIGURE 12.1. *The King of Kings*, 1927

FIGURE 12.2. *Jesus of Montreal*, 1989

FIGURE 12.3. *The Passion of the Christ*, 2004

The Roman governor Pilate has gone down in history as the man who condemned Jesus to death on the cross. The Gospels portray him as a fair-minded and weak-willed leader who was easily manipulated by Caiaphas and the Jewish crowds into executing Jesus despite his own belief in Jesus' innocence. This image contrasts rather starkly with the portrait of a ruthless, even vicious man that is to be found in noncanonical sources. In crafting a coherent and dramatic depiction of the events that lead inexorably to Jesus' crucifixion, filmmakers must address this discrepancy and, more specifically, assign responsibility for Jesus' death, either to Pilate, who formally pronounces the death sentence, or to one or more Jewish participants in this tragic affair. In doing so, they must also decide whether to introduce Pilate only in the trial scene, as the Gospels uniformly do, or to bring him into the story at an early point, in order to build a context and create momentum for his role in the trial story.

Before Jesus' Trial

In the Gospels

The only Gospel references to Pilate prior to the trial narrative are two brief notes in Luke. Luke 3:1 dates John the Baptist's activities to "the fifteenth year of the reign of Emperor Tiberius, when Pontius Pilate was governor of Judea, and Herod was ruler of Galilee, and his brother Philip ruler of the region of Ituraea and Trachonitis, and Lysanias ruler of Abilene." Luke 13:1–5 refers to Pilate's actions against a group of Galileans:

> At that very time there were some present who told him [Jesus] about the Galileans whose blood Pilate had mingled with their sacrifices. He asked them, "Do you think that because these Galileans suffered in this way they were worse sinners than all other Galileans? No, I tell you; but unless you repent, you will all perish as they did. Or those eighteen who were killed when the tower of Siloam fell on them—do you think that they were worse offenders than all the others living in Jerusalem? No, I tell you; but unless you repent, you will all perish just as they did."

While we know nothing about this event apart from this passage, it is not inconsistent with what Josephus tells us about Pilate's character. According to Josephus, Pilate slaughtered a group of Samaritans during a religious gathering on Mt. Gerizim (*Antiquities* 18.86–87) and, on another occasion, killed the Jews who opposed his efforts to appropriate money from the Temple treasury to build an aqueduct in Jerusalem (*Jewish War* 2.175–77; *Antiquities* 18.60–62).

In the Movies

While some films take their lead from the Gospels and turn to Pilate only in the Passion sequence, most introduce him in the course of developing the political theme which presents Jesus as the answer to Jewish suffering under Roman domination. In doing so, these films also prepare the way for Pilate's condemnation of Jesus.

In *The Greatest Story Ever Told*, the Romans report to the incoming governor that the eagle of Rome has been torn down and desecrated by a Jerusalem mob. The scene is filled with Roman soldiers; Jerusalem is overcome with smoke and fire and rows of crosses can be seen in the background as the Roman legions march along. The scene visually expresses the oppressiveness of the Roman regime and the suffering of the Judeans at the hands of Rome. The failure of the younger Herod to keep order has forced Rome to send a governor, Pilate, to accomplish this task. Upon his arrival, Pilate meets with Herod Antipas as follows:

HEROD   Greetings in the name of Augustus Caesar.... You may be sure that Caesar will not regret what he has done for the son of his old friend, King Herod.

PILATE   Your father kept the people in order. In this you have failed. I must inform you that we will take over.

HEROD   My father's kingdom was guaranteed by Caesar.

PILATE   From now on a Roman legion directed by a Roman governor will govern Judea.

Herod is extremely displeased at this announcement. To add insult to injury, the Romans take the vestments of the high priest. "From now on those vestments will stay in my headquarters... And those who defy us will not be allowed to wear them."

This last incident is not present in the Gospels but has its source in the writings of Josephus. In *Jewish Antiquities* 15.405, Josephus describes how the kings and high priests of the Hasmonean family deposited the priestly robe, which the high priest donned only when he had to offer sacrifice, in Herod's citadel. After Herod's death, the robe was in the custody of the Romans until the time of Tiberius Caesar. Later the governor of Syria, Vitellius, at the request of the populace of Jerusalem, interceded with Tiberius Caesar. Tiberius Caesar returned to them authority over the robe, which remained with them until the death of King Agrippa (45–50 CE), at which time it was again the subject of much dispute (Josephus, *Antiquities* 15.401–405).

In Young's *Jesus,* Herod Antipas welcomes Pilate to Jerusalem. Their encounter commences cordially enough. Pilate accepts Herod's welcome, and conveys Caesar's blessings on the land; he praises the architecture of Jerusalem, for which Herod Antipas proudly takes the credit on behalf of his father, "Herod the Great, Beloved of his people."

LIVIO (*whispering to Pilate*)   They hated him.

PILATE   A vicious man, I'm told.

HEROD ANTIPAS   How distasteful to speak of my father this way. As his son I am a hero to the people.

LIVIO (*whispering to Pilate again*)   Butt of all their jokes.

PILATE   You must understand. In Rome we call your father's way of ruling statesmanship.

HEROD ANTIPAS   Perhaps Pontius Pilate would like to see the grandest of all structures in Israel, the Temple. Built by my father, a personal friend of Augustus. As I am a personal friend of Tiberius.

PILATE   Strange. I never heard him mention you. I thank you for your welcome. I will take your suggestion and visit the Temple.

HEROD ANTIPAS (*shouting after him*)   Make sure you take your troops and show their insignia proudly.

PILATE   Livio, what does he mean, show their insignia?

LIVIO   I could tell you but it would spoil all the fun.

Young's *Jesus* is sympathetic to the difficult situation in which Caiaphas and the other Jewish leaders found themselves. As Pilate and his troops enter Jerusalem for the first time, the Jews watch the Romans stream in. The camera shows a panoramic shot from above, then returns to street level. Pilate enters the scene and surveys his surroundings with curiosity. Livio, his aide and self-proclaimed historian to Caesar, is by his side and draws Pilate's attention to Caiaphas. He identifies him to Pilate as the high priest appointed by Rome and observes, "On the one hand he has to appear to be a presider of his own people, on the other hand he owes his position to Rome. Narrow path to tread."

CAIAPHAS   Welcome, Pontius Pilate. I am Caiaphas the high priest of this temple. We come to wish you well, as you undertake the post of governor of Judea.

PILATE   I thank you, priest. Allow me to get right to the point. Rome is displeased with the number of legions it has to keep in this barren land in order to maintain peace. Your taxes don't begin to pay back the cost.

CAIAPHAS   You speak of the past.

PILATE   This disorder derives directly from your current religion that derives directly from this temple. This ends today. My soldiers will be posted here every minute of every day from now on.

CAIAPHAS   This order defiles the Temple.

ANOTHER JEW   Our religion forbids graven images in the Temple. Your soldiers are an abomination to the Temple. Even their flags break our laws. We allow no graven images and your images carry...

PILATE   These shields are symbols of Roman dominion. No building in Judea, not even the Temple, is exempt from the display of these symbols. What your religion forbids, Rome demands.

(*Caiaphas looks on grimly, hanging on to his staff as a potent symbol. They are all quiet. The music is ominous.*)

CAIAPHAS   We submit...to your swords.

CAIAPHAS (*kneeling down*)   Here is my bare neck. Let Rome cut it. We will die before we allow the temple to be defiled.

Pilate, flabbergasted, is unsure of what to do. Livio approaches him and says, "Governor, an awful lot of blood for your first day. I am not sure Rome would be happy if you were to murder every priest in the temple." Pilate stands down—this time.

This scene portrays Caiaphas in a highly favorable light, as a leader of integrity, who is willing to die for the principle of religious freedom, and who has the confidence and trust of his own community. This episode is based on an anecdote told by Josephus:

Now Pilate, the procurator of Judea, when he brought his army from Caesarea and removed it to winter quarters in Jerusalem, took a bold step in subversion of the Jewish practices, by introducing into the city the busts of the emperor that were attached to the military standards, for our law forbids the making of images.... Pilate was the first to bring the images into Jerusalem and set them up, doing it without the knowledge of the people, for he entered at night. But when the people discovered it, they went in a throng to Caesarea and for many days entreated him to take away the images. He refused to yield, since to do so would be an outrage to the emperor; however, since they did not cease entreating him, on the sixth day he secretly armed and placed his troops in position, while he himself came to the speaker's stand ... surrounded them with his soldiers and threatened to punish them at once with death if they did not put an end to their tumult and return to their own places. But they, casting themselves prostrate and baring their throats, declared that they had gladly welcomed death rather than make bold to transgress the wise provisions of the laws. Pilate, astonished at the strength of their devotion to the laws, straightway removed the images from Jerusalem and brought them back to Caesarea. (*Antiquities* 18: 55–62; cf. *Jewish War* 2.169–74)

Note, however, that Caiaphas is not mentioned explicitly in Josephus's account, though this does not mean that he was not present, assuming that these events are historical.

In Ray's *King of Kings*, Pilate places the responsibility for handling John the Baptist and his disciples on Caiaphas. "You must punish them," he orders. Caiaphas is more cautious: "Punishment does not dampen their ardor. Better to ignore the ravings of these people rather than to prosecute. In my opinion this man seeks martyrdom." Caiaphas, though clearly an underling, also has enough power and status to object, perhaps as a guise for his own distaste for taking the life of a fellow Jew.

In *The Miracle Maker*, Pilate explains the festival of Passover to the new chief centurion of the twelfth legion in a manner that conveys Rome's disdain.

PILATE   Did the garrison commander brief you on the curious customs of the Jews?

CENTURION   Sir?

PILATE   Passover, for example.

CENTURION   Passover? No.

PILATE   (*sniff*) I'm surprised. Well, the Jewish Passover is their festival of freedom. They celebrate their day of freedom. Oh, and they say some—something about the Egyptians, some old story.

CENTURION   Sir? (*Soldiers rush up the stairs.*)

PILATE   There are Jews from all over the empire gathering here along with the whole of Judea and the disgusting pilgrims from the North, they're the worst. The Galileans. Oh, but I hear you've already put down the little revolt up there.

CENTURION   117 crucified, sir.

PILATE   Mmhmm. Mmhmm. And the ringleader?

CENTURION   Barabbas and the others? We've—(*Pilate cuts him off.*)

PILATE   Ah. We will have a public execution of rebels on the day of freedom. You may go, Tribune.

CENTURION   Hail Caesar, son of the Gods.

PILATE   Hail Caesar but don't let them hear you talk of "the Gods" (*chuckles*).

Judging by the Jesus biopics, the Romans saw keeping order as the main task of Caiaphas and the other Jewish leaders. The leaders themselves were highly conscious of this responsibility and expectation. At the triumphal entry, they are very concerned about the huge crowds that have gathered to welcome Jesus. They give orders to assemble as many guards as needed to prevent an uproar.

The dialogue, visuals, voiceovers, and scrolled texts all help to depict the political context, the tension between Romans and Jews, and the difficult position of the Jewish leadership caught between the ordinary Judeans and the Roman empire.

The Trial before Pilate

We know how the story ends: Jesus is condemned and crucified. There are numerous gaps in the Gospel accounts of this last trial. The most important one, from the point of view of both Gospel and film, is the question of moral responsibility. From the perspective of the evangelists and Christian tradition, Jesus is innocent of all charges against him, from blasphemy to sedition. His condemnation is a serious violation of human law, a grotesque perversion of justice, even if his death is required by God's plan of salvation.

The question of who bears the blame is a crucial and highly freighted question with repercussions both in the temporal world and in the divine realm. Crucifixion is the end-point of a Roman legal process for those accused of violating the Roman laws against treason.[1] The Gospels unanimously portray Pilate as judge and jury. But the Gospels also insist that Jesus' trial was by no means impartial; rather, there were individuals or groups that had powerful political and security interests in Jesus' removal and who exerted their own power to move events in that direction.[2] The real culprits are the "chief priests" and the Jewish crowds. Significantly, Caiaphas himself is not mentioned, though he may be included implicitly in the group identified as the "chief priests."

In the Gospels

The trial before Pilate, the Roman governor, is described in all four Gospels.[3] Here is Mark's account:

> As soon as it was morning, the chief priests held a consultation with the elders and scribes and the whole council. They bound Jesus, led him away, and handed him over to Pilate. Pilate asked him, "Are you the King of the Jews?" He answered him, "You say so." Then the chief priests accused him of many things. Pilate asked him again, "Have you no answer? See how many charges they bring against you." (Mark 15:1–4)

Although we are not privy to the exchange between the chief priests and Pilate, Pilate's question implies that the charge against Jesus is treason. But Pilate is not terribly concerned about Jesus' putative claim to kingship.

Matthew's account places greater emphasis on the role of the Jewish leaders in this Roman proceeding. Their goal is to manipulate Pilate into carrying out the death sentence: "When morning came, all the chief priests and the elders of the people conferred together against Jesus in order to bring about his death. They bound him, led him away, and handed him over to Pilate the governor" (Matthew 27:1–3). Luke adds details about the Jews' testimony before Pilate:

> Then the assembly rose as a body and brought Jesus before Pilate. They began to accuse him, saying, "We found this man perverting our nation, forbidding us to pay taxes to the emperor, and saying that he himself is the Messiah, a king." Then Pilate asked him, "Are you the king of the Jews?" He answered, "You say so." Then Pilate said to the chief priests and the crowds, "I find no basis for an accusation against this man." But they were insistent and said, "He stirs up the people by teaching throughout all Judea, from Galilee where he began even to this place." (23:1–5)

The assembly impresses upon Pilate the gravity of the charges in both political and economic terms. But Pilate is not interested; according to Mark and Matthew, "he realized that it was out of jealousy that the chief priests had handed him over" (Mark 15:10; Matthew 27:18).

In Matthew, Pilate's reluctance is reinforced by his wife: "While he was sitting on the judgment seat, his wife sent word to him, 'Have nothing to do with that innocent man, for today I have suffered a great deal because of a dream about him'" (Matthew 27:19).

Luke's Pilate is so anxious to stay out of this messy situation that he sends Jesus off to Herod Antipas of Galilee, who happened to be in Jerusalem, on the grounds that as a Galilean, Jesus should be tried by the Galilean ruler instead of himself. Herod does not play along, however, and sends Jesus back to Pilate (Luke 23:6–11).

At this point Pilate "called together the chief priests, the leaders, and the people" and said to them:

> You brought me this man as one who was perverting the people; and
> here I have examined him in your presence and have not found this
> man guilty of any of your charges against him. Neither has Herod, for
> he sent him back to us. Indeed, he has done nothing to deserve death.
> I will therefore have him flogged and release him. (Luke 23:13–16)

But the people are not satisfied. In a last-ditch effort to salvage the situation, Pilate offers to release someone at the Passover: either Barabbas or Jesus. To his dismay, the Jewish crowds call for Barabbas' release and, repeatedly, insistently, cry out for Jesus' crucifixion (Mark 15:13, 14; Matthew 27:22, 23; Luke 23:21; John 19:6, 15). Mark's account is typical:

> But the chief priests stirred up the crowd to have him release
> Barabbas for them instead. Pilate spoke to them again, "Then what
> do you wish me to do with the man you call the King of the Jews?"
> They shouted back, "Crucify him!" Pilate asked them, "Why, what
> evil has he done?" But they shouted all the more, "Crucify him!" So
> Pilate, wishing to satisfy the crowd, released Barabbas for them;
> and after flogging Jesus, he handed him over to be crucified. (Mark
> 15:11–15)

John describes a tug of war between Pilate and the Jewish crowds. The Jews try to convince Pilate that Jesus is a political threat; Pilate tries to have him released, to no avail. The Jews insist: "If you release this man, you are no friend of the emperor. Everyone who claims to be a king sets himself against the emperor" (John 18:12).

Matthew is even more explicit about Jewish responsibility and Pilate's lack of culpability:[4]

> Now the chief priests and the elders persuaded the crowds to ask for
> Barabbas and to have Jesus killed. The governor again said to them,
> "Which of the two do you want me to release for you?" And they said,
> "Barabbas." Pilate said to them, "Then what should I do with Jesus who
> is called the Messiah?" All of them said, "Let him be crucified!" Then

he asked, "Why, what evil has he done?" But they shouted all the more, "Let him be crucified!" So when Pilate saw that he could do nothing, but rather that a riot was beginning, he took some water and washed his hands before the crowd, saying, "I am innocent of this man's blood; see to it yourselves." Then the people as a whole answered, "His blood be on us and on our children!" (Matthew 27:20–25)

In crying out "His blood be on us and on our children," the Jewish crowd takes the responsibility for Jesus' death not only upon themselves but also upon subsequent generations. This passage is the source for the notion that the Jews, for all time, are guilty of deicide, a perennial cornerstone of anti-Semitism.[5] The taunt of "Christ-killer" is one to which Jews have been subjected for centuries, down to this very day.[6]

Crossan puts the Gospel trial accounts into historical perspective:

Those first Christians were relatively powerless Jews, and compared to them the Jewish authorities represented serious and threatening power. As long as Christians were the marginalized and disenfranchised ones, such passion fiction about Jewish responsibility and Roman innocence did nobody much harm. But, once the Roman Empire became Christian, that fiction turned lethal.... However explicable its origins, defensible its invectives, and understandable its motives among Christians fighting for survival, its repetition has now become the longest lie, and for our own integrity, we Christians must at last name it as such.[7]

While differing in detail, the Gospels present the same overall narrative: the Jewish authorities plan to have Jesus killed, whether for religious reasons (blasphemy) or political reasons (fear of Roman reprisal for the unrest that Jesus and his followers are causing). They are unable to execute Jesus themselves, perhaps because Roman law does not permit them to try capital cases (John 18:31). They therefore devise a scheme to compel Pilate to act as their executioner. They inform Pilate that Jesus has claimed kingship for himself. When this accusation fails to impress Pilate, they simply call repeatedly for Jesus' crucifixion. In each case, the narrative emphasizes Jesus' innocence, Pilate's reluctance, and the Jews' guilt.

The Gospel accounts are susceptible to different interpretations. According to Sanders, for example, Pilate ordered Jesus' execution on the high priest's recommendation. In doing so, Pilate accepted Caiaphas' charge that Jesus claimed to be King of the Jews:

He [Caiaphas] probably regarded him as a religious fanatic whose
fanaticism had become so extreme that it posed a threat to law and
order.... Pilate was eventually dismissed from office because of large-
scale and ill-judged executions (*Antiquities* 18.88ff.).... The stories of
Pilate's reluctance and weakness of will are best explained as Christian propaganda; they are a kind of excuse for Pilate's action which
reduces the conflict between the Christian movement and Roman
authority. [8]

Crossan, on the other hand, blames both parties; in his view, Jesus was executed by a conjunction of Jewish and Roman authority: "Caiaphas and Pilate
were dismissed around the same time in late 36 and early 37. It is not unfairly
cynical to presume that there was close cooperation between Caiaphas and
Pilate, that it often offended Jewish sensibilities and that eventually it became
necessary to break up that cooperation in Rome's best interests."[9]

Read together, as filmmakers are wont to do, the Gospels present a consistent account. They do not deny that it was Pilate who pronounced the death
sentence, but they claim that his pronouncement was instigated by the Jewish
leaders, who had a plan intended to lead to precisely this outcome. Matthew is
the most telling. He has Pilate absolve himself of moral responsibility by
washing his hands of the affair, declaring Jesus innocent even as he sentences
him to death, and the Jewish crowd assuming culpability for themselves and
subsequent generations.

In the Movies

The Gospel versions of the Passion narrative contain fewer narrative gaps than
do most other episodes. Nevertheless, they pose a serious challenge to filmmakers. Here the problem lies not so much within the story, as in the disso-
nance between the attitudes reflected in the Gospel accounts, in which the Jews
are assigned moral responsibility for Jesus' death, and our contemporary sensibilities, in which overt anti-Semitism—and especially the deicide charge—
are unacceptable.

Jesus filmmakers are in a difficult position. To remain true to their source
texts requires them to portray the event in a manner that many would construe
as anti-Semitic; to refrain from casting blame on the Jews or their leaders
requires them to depart significantly from the texts upon which their films are
based. Several important decisions must be made: To differentiate Caiaphas or
other individual Jewish leaders from the crowd and, if so, how? To have Pilate
wash his hands of the whole affair or not? And most important, to include or

omit the Jewish crowds' outcry in Matthew 27:25: "Let his blood be on us and on our children"?

Movies of the Silent Era

The trial scene in *From the Manger to the Cross* harmonizes the accounts in Matthew and John. Through the trial, Pilate is greatly distressed and unsure of himself; Jesus is silent. The crowds call for crucifixion; Pilate attempts to evade the situation by demanding of the Jews: "Take ye him and crucify him for I find no fault in him" (John 19:6). In the end, the Romans do take Jesus, and Pilate adopts an angry posture toward the crowd. An aide brings him water in a pitcher and a towel but there is no intertitle or scriptural reference at this point; the visual cue is enough as the audience is expected to know the reference. The scene ends as soldiers take Jesus away and Pilate looks contemptuously at the crowd. This film softens the Gospel accounts subtly by avoiding the words of Matthew 27:24–25, including the "blood" pronouncement.

INRI, by contrast, amplifies Pilate's self-proclaimed innocence in a lengthy scenario that humanizes Pilate and demonstrates his compassion for Jesus in contrast to the bloodthirstiness of the clamoring crowds. As soon as the Jewish council pronounces Jesus guilty of blasphemy, the camera cuts abruptly to the Roman court. Pilate is napping peacefully in his private quarters when he is interrupted by a centurion who announces: "Caiaphas and the High Council demand the sentence of death on a prisoner." Pilate waves him off, and drifts off again, but the centurion persists: "They say he hath conspired against the Emperor." Alarmed, Pilate springs out of bed, and hastens to interview Jesus: "Where is thy kingdom, O Nazarene? Where are thy armies? Knowest thou not that I have power to crucify thee?"

The camera then cuts to Pilate's wife as she reaches out to embrace her husband. She tells him that she has had a frightening dream and begs him: "Have thou nothing to do with that just man." Pilate looks up to heaven, clasps her hand, and then rises. She beseeches him as he leaves her side and returns to Jesus (Matthew 27:19).

Pilate then declares: "I find no fault in this man" (Luke 23:4), and the camera cuts to a huge crowd clamoring for Jesus' death. Pilate offers to release either Barabbas or Jesus. Barabbas is dirty and swarthy, in contrast to Jesus who is slim and refined. Pilate is dismayed when the crowd chooses Barabbas. His servants bring him a bowl of water; he washes his hands and declares himself "innocent of the blood of this just person; see ye to it." Jesus is immediately seized by Roman soldiers and hauled away.

This version enacts the handwashing and includes Pilate's declaration of innocence, but omits the blood curse. Yet the overall image of the Jewish crowds is highly negative as they clamor loudly for Jesus' crucifixion despite the sensitive Pilate's best efforts.

Der Galiläer provides the most anti-Jewish depiction of the trial before Pilate. Outside the Temple, Caiaphas whips a huge Jewish crowd into a blood-thirsty frenzy. The crowd rushes to Pilate's palace screaming for Jesus' death. Pilate, filled with compassion, offers to release him, but the crowd demands Barabbas alive and Jesus dead. Pilate does not wash his hands but puts the blood curse on the Jews: "On you comes his blood" [auf euch komme sein blut].[10] The huge crowd takes Jesus' blood upon themselves and their children, not once, as in Matthew, but twice: "On us and on our children comes his blood. We take it upon ourselves" (auf uns und unsere Kinder komm' sein Blut. Wir nehmen es auf uns).

In this film, the blood curse is repeated three times. The film is not merely faithful to the words of scripture; it magnifies the elements upon which the deicide charge is based. Also noteworthy is the visual appearance of Caiaphas and the other Jewish leaders, who wear headgear that looks suspiciously like horns, another prevalent anti-Semitic image.[11]

Cecil B. DeMille's The King of Kings presents the most complex and no doubt the most influential silent version of the trial. This film consistently portrays Caiaphas as a money-hungry power monger, but it clears the Jewish crowds of major moral responsibility. When Pilate asks: "Shall I crucify your king?" it is Caiaphas, not the crowd (as it is in John 19:15) who declares, "We have no king but Caesar." After Pilate washes his hands of the affair, it is the high priest and not the crowd who proclaims a version of Matthew 27:25: "If thou, imperial Pilate, wouldst wash thy hands of this Man's death, let it be upon me and me alone!"

The contrast between Pilate and Caiaphas is nowhere more apparent than in their behavior in the final frames of the scene. Pilate pronounces himself "innocent of the blood of this just Man" and then stalks off to sob alone in his throne room. Caiaphas, self-satisfied, legs astride, arms folded, smirks, savoring his victory. By reassigning to Caiaphas the lines that Matthew's Gospel attributes to the Jewish crowd as a whole, DeMille reconfigures the trial scene to place blame squarely—and solely—upon the high priest.

Babington and Evans describe DeMille's Caiaphas as "the Romans' Jew," an "anti-Semite's dream caricature of wickedness: obese, cynical, rubbing his plump fingers together in gleeful anticipation of his plots, appearing like a well-fed devil at Pilate's side to whisper 'Crucify him!' The scapegoat...is the living epitome of ethnic guilt." DeMille's portrait is at home in 1920s America, in which anti-Semitism was an almost respectable response to waves of Eastern European immigration and to labor unrest in which many Jewish workers were involved, a response fed by well-established anti-Semitic caricature.[12]

The treatment of the trial narrative in the silent Jesus biopics shows that long before the Holocaust, filmmakers were conscious of the anti-Semitic potential of this scene. All of these films employ some anti-Semitic stereotypes in their representation of Caiaphas, from his grotesque physical appearance to his imputed greed. And all take Pilate's declaration of innocence at face value; contrary to the historical record, the silent Pilate is a deeply emotional and compassionate person, susceptible to his wife's influence. He ordered Jesus' crucifixion under extreme duress, bowing to the shrill demands of the Jewish leadership. But at the same time, all the silents except *Der Galiläer* make some attempt to soften the anti-Semitic potential of the scriptural scenes. No doubt at least some were motivated by a desire to avoid or deflect charges of anti-Semitism, as DeMille's autobiography indicates.[13] But they do not fundamentally offer an alternate interpretation of Jesus' death. In the final analysis they leave intact the Gospels' own assignment of guilt to the Jewish authorities and, by extension, the Jewish people as a whole.

Epics

The post-Holocaust epics of the 1960s demonstrate more determination in deflecting blame for Jesus' death from the Jews. Their usual strategy was to assign greater blame to Caiaphas than the Gospels would suggest.[14] This approach is obvious in Ray's *King of Kings*, which departs from the image of the reluctant Pilate. Ray's Pilate conducts a legal proceeding that owes more to other films and television shows from the 1960s than to what we know about Roman legal processes.[15] Pilate explains to Jesus (and the movie audience):

> You have just been interrogated by Caiaphas. They have judged you
> guilty on two counts: blasphemy and sedition. This court takes no
> cognizance of your blasphemy, but the charge of sedition is a major
> offense. The rules of Roman law will prevail. I, Pontius Pilate, Governor of Judea, by grace of the Emperor the divine Tiberius of
> Rome will judge your case. No matter what you've done up to this
> moment, no matter what others have accused you of doing, I and
> I alone have authority to sentence you to be crucified or flogged
> or to set you free. How you conduct yourself here and now will
> determine your fate. Do you understand?

He gives Jesus two opportunities to state his defense but, as in the Synoptics, Jesus remains silent.

Pilate then calls on his aide, the fictitious Lucius, to advocate for Jesus, rather like the public defender in an American legal television series. Lucius begins: "For the benefit of the accused, so that he comprehends the gravity of his case, I request that the charge against him be repeated." Lucius does a convincing job of defending Jesus. He argues that Jesus was not guilty of sedition but rather spoke only of a kingdom of God that poses no challenge to Rome's authority.

When Pilate proposes to send Jesus to Herod Antipas, Lucius counters that Herod Antipas is prejudiced against him. Pilate's will prevails. As in Luke, Herod quickly tires of Jesus and sends him back to Pilate. Pilate orders Lucius to force a confession from Jesus. Here, as in Matthew, Pilate's wife is favorably disposed toward Jesus, a development that backfires, as Pilate concludes that Jesus must truly be dangerous if he can influence even the daughter of Caesar. Pilate takes responsibility. He neither washes his hands of the affair, nor proclaims his innocence.

Stevens's *The Greatest Story Ever Told* copes with the problem by simply omitting Caiaphas from the trial scene. Pilate washes his hands but does not declare himself "innocent of this man's blood." Nor does the crowd declare its responsibility. Instead the film offers a voiceover that recites from the Apostles' Creed: "He suffered under Pontius Pilate, was crucified, dead and buried...." The omissions and the voiceover point to Pilate as the major culprit in Jesus' suffering and death.

Musicals

Of the musicals, *Godspell* has no trial before Pilate; though New York may stand in for the Roman Empire, there is no governor and also no Jewish high priest to wrangle over Jesus' fate. In *Jesus Christ Superstar*, all the *dramatis personae* of the trial scenes are equally despicable. Caiaphas, the other priests, and the Pharisees are indistinguishable; they all resemble large dark birds of prey ready to swoop down on Jesus at any moment. Herod is a foppish fool, and Pilate has no patience for Jesus whatsoever. The crowd urges Pilate to pronounce the death sentence, and Pilate shows no reluctance to do so. When Jesus refuses to speak, Pilate dismisses him: "Die, if you want to, you misguided martyr." He washes his hands in red water and continues, "I wash my hands of your demolition, you innocent puppet." Even as he declares Jesus' innocence, Pilate displays his contempt for this Superstar. Yet despite the negative depiction of all those involved, the portrayal of the Pharisees, Caiaphas, and others is disturbing.

As Baugh notes:

> If *Jesus Christ Superstar* can be defended against the charges of racism [a reference to the controversy created by having a black actor play Judas], it is much more difficult to dismiss the repeated charges of anti-Semitism leveled at the film. Clearly, the film places the blame for the death of Jesus on the Jews. Shifting the account of the Gospel, neither Webber and Rice nor Jewison attempt to attenuate the responsibility of the Sanhedrin for the death of Jesus. They make Pilate a weak and fearful man and Herod a spoiled child and a comic figure. Their responsibility for Jesus' death is diminished by these characterizations. On the other hand, the Sanhedrin, first appearing in black cloaks on the scaffolding above the ruin, "like giant vultures roosting on the branches of a tree," are portrayed as strong, determined, politically astute and sadistically evil.[16]

Nevertheless, we must remember that Jewison's Jesus is also not a particularly appealing figure. The overall unrealistic nature of this film—its studied absence of authenticity despite its setting in Israel's Negev desert—does attenuate its anti-Semitic potential.

Dramas

John Heyman's *Jesus* (1979), a film created and used primarily for evangelical purposes, sends a self-contradictory message. *Jesus* claims to be based entirely on the Gospel of Luke. Although the film strays from the Third Gospel upon occasion, its rendition of the trial before Pilate follows Luke very closely, including Pilate's attempt to have Herod take care of the matter. A voiceover introduction to this segment declares solemnly: "And they took him before Pontius Pilate, the most vicious of all Roman procurators, alone responsible for the crucifixion of thousands."

While this comment would seem to hold Pilate morally culpable, other details of the scene work against this verdict. Indeed, the reluctance that Pilate expresses in Luke is accentuated by the final detail of the scene, in which Pilate grudgingly tosses the crucifixion order down from his balcony to the pavement below.

In keeping with his positive portrayal of Judaism, Zeffirelli's *Jesus of Nazareth* goes to great lengths to avoid blaming Caiaphas or the Jews. His principal strategy is to create an entirely fictional character, the scribe Zerah, and to hold him responsible for the plot against Jesus and ultimately his death. When Pilate moves to acquit Jesus, Zerah intervenes:

ZERAH   Procurator, we, the leaders of the Sanhedrin, have always had the same aim as you, peaceful administration of our country for the good of our people.

PILATE   Please, please, please, please, don't talk to me about the people. As long as they obey, we care as much about your children of Israel as we do the mob in Rome. Let us speak directly. Why does the Sanhedrin consider this man so dangerous that they send you yourself here to make sure that he is condemned?

ZERAH   ... If you knew him as well as we do, you would also find him dangerous.

After the crowd chooses Barabbas over Jesus, Pilate pronounces the death sentence. The camera zooms in on Jesus, cuts to Pilate as he walks away, then turns slightly to watch Jesus being taken away for crucifixion. Zeffirelli reproduces the stereotypical portrait of Pilate as mildly sympathetic and the Jewish authorities as hostile. But the role normally played by Caiaphas is here assumed by the fictional Zerah. Zeffirelli's Pilate does not wash his hands nor do his Jews take collective responsibility. By these means, Zeffirelli aims not only to portray a Jewish Jesus but to evoke the tragedy of blaming the Jews for Jesus' death.[17]

Like the silents and epics of the 1960s, later dramas such as *Jesus of Nazareth* employ a limited number of strategies for addressing the deicide charge. Most often, they omit the blood curse and soften the notion of collective responsibility. The films portray the Jews somewhat sympathetically and attempt to provide some insight into why Jesus was so irritating to the Jewish leaders. In this context, Zeffirelli's invention of Zerah is a unique and equivocal strategy. Though Zerah takes some of the pressure off Caiaphas and the other leaders who are implicated in the Gospel accounts, it is not at all clear that inventing a nefarious Jew mitigates the anti-Semitic potential of the trial account.

The skillful camera work in Pier Paolo Pasolini's *The Gospel According to Saint Matthew* offers a more subtle approach than do most other Jesus biopics. In the trial scene, the camera places the viewer among the crowd that has gathered at the Temple compound to witness the trials before the high priest and Pilate. We crane our necks to see above the heads of the bystanders; we can distinguish the main players but we are too far away to see them clearly.

The effect of the camera work is to erase any differentiation between the Jewish and Roman authorities and simultaneously to emphasize the gap between the governing elites and the crowd of commoners. This visual gap symbolizes the social, political, economic, and ideological chasm between these two groups.

By situating his viewers among the crowd on the screen, Pasolini engages their support in opposition to social hierarchy and political authority. We watch helplessly as a gross injustice is committed. We hear Pilate declare himself innocent of Jesus' blood, and we hear a lone and disembodied voice cry out: "His blood be on us and on our children!" The speaker, whom we can neither locate nor identify, does not represent either the watching crowd as a whole or any faction among them. Pasolini would have us view this scene not as a faithful rendition of history or scripture, but as an allegory of contemporary Italian society. The opposition between political and religious authorities on the one hand, and the people on the other, reflects Pasolini's own Marxist worldview and his critique of the social and political institutions in Italy at this time.[18]

In contrast to Pasolini's *Gospel According to Saint Matthew*, Rossellini's *The Messiah* takes the conventional route well trod by the silents and epics. Pilate is sympathetic to Jesus; Caiaphas is accusatory and manipulative. When Caiaphas brings Jesus to him, Pilate is highly annoyed.

> PILATE   I want a concrete accusation against this man.... Don't think it is enough for me that he has insulted your religion... Rome is not interested if someone breaks the laws of your fathers!
>
> CAIAPHAS (*anxious not to make Pilate too angry*)   It is not only this that makes him guilty. We brought him here as token of our friendship. We found him inciting our people to revolt against your government.... He was telling people not to pay the tribute to Caesar and proclaiming himself king and messiah.

Pilate finds no case against him and informs the Jewish authorities that if they bring this man for judgment, they must provide proof and motives. He concludes:

> As far as I am concerned, as far as my authority and legal power are concerned, you have brought this man before me under the accusation of subverting the people. As you saw, I have interrogated him in your presence and could not find him guilty of any of the charges you have brought against him. Therefore according to the law of Rome, he has done nothing to merit being put to death.

Yet the priests persist, and Pilate gives in; he washes his hands and dries them with a white towel.

The films made since the 1970s vary considerably, both in their treatment of this issue and in their explicit claims to historicity and fidelity to scripture. Martin Scorsese's *The Last Temptation of Christ* (1988) omits Caiaphas and any Jewish participants completely. There is no trial before the Sanhedrin, only a private conversation between Pilate and Jesus. Scorsese's radical departure from the Gospel accounts is anticipated by his initial claim that his movie is an adaptation of a work of fiction, not of a scriptural canon.

The trial scene takes place where Pilate is having his horse groomed. Pilate sends his groom away before speaking with Jesus, so there are no witnesses to the scene. Scorsese's Roman governor is momentarily amused by the opportunity for conversation with this "king of the Jews." When Jesus refuses to perform tricks on Pilate's demand—a demand that Luke associates with Herod (Luke 22:8)—Pilate dismisses Jesus as "just another Jewish politician." He admonishes Jesus:

> You know, it's one thing to want to change the way the people live. But you want to change how they think and how they feel.... Killing or loving, it's all the same. It simply doesn't matter how you want to change things, we don't want them changed. You do understand what has to happen. We have a space for you up on Golgotha. Three thousand skulls there by now, probably more.

As Pilate walks away, he tells Jesus, "I do wish you people would go out and count them some time. Maybe you'd learn a lesson. No, probably not."

Caiaphas is nowhere in sight; Pilate is calm, polite, aloof, and alone. The Roman governor neither knows nor cares if Jesus is a thorn in the side of the Jewish authorities. For him, Jesus is just another Jewish troublemaker, and he applies the usual remedy: crucifixion. In this film, then, no Jews are involved in Jesus' condemnation, and there is no hint of any Jewish responsibility.

Denys Arcand's *Jesus of Montreal* also has a complex view of the trial scene. In Daniel's Passion play, Caiaphas and Pilate are both present at Jesus' trial. Pilate is clearly the key player; Caiaphas hovers at his side, prayer shawl draped over his head. Pilate interviews Jesus—is he a member of a sect, or perhaps a prophet?—and mocks Jesus' emphasis on love: "Isn't that a bit optimistic? You wouldn't last a week in Rome."

Pilate declares Jesus harmless and hands the file back to Caiaphas. Pilate expresses his disdain for priests, who, he says, are either idiots or profiteers.

CAIAPHAS   The priests support Rome. You wouldn't want rumors to spread. Tiberius is a suspicious ruler. We want to help you govern, but one must set an example. He attracts crowds. He has disciples.

PILATE   Who are unarmed.

CAIAPHAS   He performs miracles. He's caused riots in the temple. Crucify him.

CAIAPHAS (*smiling superciliously as he walks away*)   It's better to sacrifice one man... [cf. John 11:50].

Pilate returns to Jesus and informs him calmly of what will now transpire:

My soldiers will take you. They're brutes, of course. We don't get the elite. You'll be whipped, then crucified. It won't be pleasant. You're not Roman, but try to be brave. Who knows, I may be doing you a favor. A philosopher said the freedom to kill oneself during hardship is the greatest gift man has. In a few hours you'll cross the Styx, the River of Death, whence no one has returned, except Orpheus, it is said. Perhaps your kingdom lies on the far shore. Or maybe Jupiter Capitolinus awaits you, or Athena, or the god of the Germans or the Franks. There are so many gods. Perhaps the river has no other shore and vanishes into darkness. You at least will know. Courage.

He then orders the soldiers to take Jesus away.

Arcand's Pilate is indifferent to Jesus. He does not particularly desire Jesus' death, but neither does he lament it. Certainly he finds it simpler to give in to Caiaphas than to resist him. Physically, the Caiaphas of the Passion play resembles DeMille's high priest; he has a similarly stocky build, carries the same arrogant expression on his smiling face, and oozes the same ostentatious piety. But if we view this scene in the context of the film as a whole, a different interpretation emerges. Like all other aspects of Daniel's Passion play, the trial is allegorical, pointing beyond the details of the Passion narratives to a devastating critique of contemporary Quebecois society. Pilate's invective against the priests is not directed at the high priesthood in first-century Judea, but at what the movie consistently portrays as the corrupt and hypocritical Catholic priesthood in late twentieth-century Quebec.

Also relevant is one of the final scenes of the frame narrative. During the final performance of the Passion play, Daniel sustains a terrible injury when the cross on which he is suspended falls and crushes his head. He is first taken to St. Mark's Hospital, where he is made to wait in a crowded hallway with dozens of other patients. He is later taken to the Montreal Jewish General, where he is immediately taken into the operating room. His companions, Constance and Mireille, are treated with utmost compassion and genuine concern. Once it is clear that Daniel is going to die, the Jewish doctor gently suggests to the women that some good might come from transplanting his corneas and heart. It is not the Jews who killed this Jesus but the callous Roman Catholic establishment, through the hypocrisy of the church and the indifference of its hospital. The Jewish doctors and nurses, on the other hand, allow him to die with dignity and, more than this, resurrect him, or at least, offer his body parts, so that others might live a better life. Conspicuous through-out this lengthy scene is the Star of David on the uniforms of the doctors and nurses. This detail evokes the Jewish badge worn by Jewish residents of the ghettos and concentration camps of the Nazi regime. This scene powerfully asserts that the Christians—St. Mark's—have rejected the dying Jesus, whereas the Jews, who have suffered so much, have taken him in.

The 2003 film *The Gospel of John* demonstrates a sincere attempt to di-minish the Jews' role in the trial, a difficult task given its commitment to reproducing every word of the Johannine text. Any modification to the por-trayal of the Jews in the trial scene must therefore come, as in the Pasolini film, from elements other than the dialogue. In this regard, the film makes some attempts to deflect attention from the Jews.

Caiaphas is present, but he is not singled out as the sole or principal culprit, nor does he confer directly with Pilate as do his counterparts in the films of DeMille and Arcand. Still, there is palpable antagonism between the two leaders, and the crowd is unmistakably Jewish, as the men's fringed gar-ments make obvious. The dark garments worn by some members of the Jewish crowd convey a rather sinister impression, as does the zeal with which some clamor for Jesus' death. At least the crowd is relatively small in size, suggesting that it was not all or even the majority of Jews in Jerusalem who pressed for Jesus' death.

The film's production team and the academic advisory committee recog-nized that using the entire Gospel of John as the script for the movie created serious problems, particularly in the Passion scenes. Because this film un-dertook to reproduce faithfully virtually every word in the Good News Bible translation of the Gospel of John, it was not possible to omit dialogue or to reassign it to other characters, as other filmmakers have done. Under this constraint, the academic advisory committee composed a brief text that would scroll at the very beginning of the film. This text emphasized that Jesus was tried and executed under Roman auspices, and that the way in which the Fourth Gospel tells its story reflects Jewish/proto-Christian hostility at the time it was written, not necessarily the realities of Jesus' own lifetime.[19]

By contrast, not only does Gibson's *The Passion of the Christ* include all of the problematic elements of the Gospel sources, but it also inserts extraneous elements that exacerbate the anti-Jewish potential of the Gospels' accounts. In Gibson's version of the trial before Pilate, the Roman governor attempts to please the crowd, as in Mark. He washes his hands of Jesus' blood, as in Matthew. He sends Jesus off to Herod Agrippa, as in Luke. And he dithers at length before finally ordering Jesus' execution, as in John.

Like his counterparts in DeMille's *The King of Kings* and *The Greatest Story Ever Told*, Gibson's Pilate is a compassionate man who does his utmost to exonerate Jesus. It is the Jewish crowds and, above all, Caiaphas and his fellow priests who orchestrate Jesus' extreme suffering and his death, even if it is the Romans who inflict the most savage blows, extract the most blood, and nail him to the cross.

Gibson defended himself against the charge of anti-Semitism numerous times in the media. Here is how he explained himself to Diane Sawyer (ABC, February 18, 2004):

> He [Jesus] was born into Judea, into the House of David. He was a child of Israel among other children of Israel. The Jewish Sanhedrin and those who they held sway over and the Romans were the material agents of his demise. Critics who have a problem with me don't really have a problem with *me*, they have a problem with the four Gospels.

Granted that the Gospels are hardly reticent in blaming the Jewish authorities and the frenzied crowds for Jesus' death. Nevertheless, what is troubling about Gibson's film are the ways in which it, much like *Der Galiläer*, exaggerates the Jews' role, going far beyond the Gospel accounts. *The Passion*, like this early silent film, accentuates the role of Caiaphas and his fellow Jewish leaders. Caiaphas is a bloodthirsty, scheming, vicious villain who will do everything in his power to persuade the suave, compassionate Pilate to order Jesus' crucifixion. Richly clothed, Caiaphas is not only physically ugly, but morally repugnant as well in his hatred for Jesus, and in his disdain for truth, justice, or God. The Jewish crowds are huge, as in almost all of the Jesus movies. The occasional voices that speak in Jesus' favor all belong to his disciples; the crowd easily overwhelms them.

In his defense against charges of anti-Semitism, Gibson points to his removal of the English subtitle for Matthew 27:25 ("Let his blood be on us and on our children").[20] With or without this line, however, the villainy of the Jews is made abundantly clear. And the line is still present in Aramaic on the soundtrack, hence comprehensible to any viewer who knows this Semitic language. Given the worldwide distribution of the film and diversity of its global audience, the absence of this line from the subtitles may or may not have the desired effect.

Does Gibson's film, do any of these films, foment anti-Semitism? If this question means: do Jesus movies intend to stir up hostile feelings toward Jews that under certain conditions might lead to physical violence? then the answer is probably not, with the possible exception of *Der Galiläer*. Each film has its own theme and emphasis, but it is doubtful that the Jesus biopics set out to provoke anti-Semitism. But if the real question is, can these films help to perpetuate certain beliefs, images, and stereotypes that have been implicated in anti-Semitism? then the answer must be yes. This is particularly true in the case of films such as Gibson's that explicitly claim to be telling a story that is faithful both to scripture and to history. According to Reinhold Zwick, in the more than century-long history of cinema, Jesus movies have been a major vehicle for anti-Semitism.[21] This trend can only increase with the ready availability of most of these films on television, on VHS and DVD, and, in the near future, on demand through the Internet.

Whatever filmmakers' intentions might be, they cannot exert complete control over the message that people will take away from their films. Viewers who enter the theater without prejudice toward Jews will not exit two hours later as anti-Semites. But those who enter with blatant or latent anti-Semitic feelings or opinions will find plenty of reinforcement in Gibson's movie and in at least a few others of its genre.

Conclusion

The trial of Jesus before Pilate is the pivotal moment in the Passion narrative. After Pilate pronounces the death sentence, there is no turning back on the path to Golgotha. The story is so familiar in our culture that we may overlook an astonishing paradox: Pilate sentences Jesus to execution upon the cross but is not held morally responsible for his death. It is always possible, of course, that the events occurred more or less as recorded in the Gospels. Yet the blaming of the Jews, including subsequent generations, according to Matthew 27:25, may be the result of other factors than the historical events, whether it be the strained relationship between those who believed Jesus to be the Messiah and those who did not, the need for fledgling communities of believers to differentiate themselves from other groups within the overall Jewish community, or other factors as yet unknown.

Filmmakers must resolve the tension between their adherence to scripture and the norms of the social context in which they are working. Films that do not claim to be true to scripture—*Godspell, Last Temptation, Jesus of Montreal*—can pick and choose from the Gospel accounts. Other films face a trickier situation. Some simply do not attempt to avoid anti-Semitic intimations; *Der Galiläer* and *The Passion of the Christ*, separated by nine decades or more, fall into this category, Gibson's disclaimers notwithstanding. Other films attempt various strategies to mitigate the harshness of the Gospel accounts, such as omitting one verse or another, creating a fictional character, or laying the blame on one individual rather than the Jewish people as a whole.

These strategies do not alter the overall impression that it is ultimately the Jewish leaders, and perhaps even the Jewish people as a whole, who bear primary responsibility for Jesus' death. While Pilate acts as Jesus' judge and jury, he rarely acts alone. In most biopics, he is joined in an unholy, and uneasy, alliance with Caiaphas, without whom there would have been no trial, and, tentatively, fleetingly, with Jesus, foreshadowing the eventual conversion of the Gentiles and the Roman Empire as a whole. Unlike biopics in which a climactic trial provides the opportunity for the hero to speak, Jesus' trial is the point at which the story apportions guilt and responsibility among those implicated in his death. Yet at the same time as Pilate judges Jesus, the Jesus biopics, and their viewers, judge the authorities, Jewish and Roman alike.

13

Afterword: Jesus of Hollywood

FIGURE 13.1. *Godspell, 1973*

FIGURE 13.2. *The Last Tempta-tion of Christ, 1988*

FIGURE 13.3. *Jesus of Montreal, 1989*

If the historical Jesus of Nazareth was the unique and only Son of God, as the Gospels proclaim, then Jesus of Hollywood is his opposite—multiple, diverse, and born of many parents. These include not only the directors of the Jesus biopics over the course of a century, but the numerous other professionals, including screenwriters, producers, camera operators, costume and set designers, whose creative and technical work is essential for the production of any film.

As the products of multiple authors, the biopic Jesuses have more in common with the main character of the Gospel narratives, who varies somewhat from text to text. Yet while some of the movie Saviors' actions and words resemble those attributed to Jesus in the Gospels, it is unlikely that the Evangelists would recognize their own particular Jesus in any of the films we have discussed.

Nevertheless, in his multiple and diverse forms, Jesus of Hollywood has much in common with the Jesus of history and the Jesus(es) of scripture. In the first place, they are all shaped by the history, society, religion and culture of their own time and place, whether this be early first-century Palestine (Jesus of Nazareth), late first-century Asia Minor (Jesus of Scripture) or twenty- and twenty-first-century North America and Europe (Jesus of Hollywood).

Second, scripture and cinema alike aim to make Jesus known to those who could not witness him in person. Nevertheless, the Jesus figures of scripture and silver screen are constructs, created by and ultimately encased within a medium that tries but cannot fully manage to reproduce the Jesus of history. Just as the evangelists used the cultural norms and icons of their own time to tell their stories of Jesus, so do the creators of the biopic Jesuses draw not only upon the Gospels but also upon the vast store of other texts, works of art, practices, and beliefs about Jesus that have accumulated throughout two millennia.

Third, the historical Jesus, the canonical Jesus and the biopic Jesus are equally preoccupied with the interests, concerns, and anxieties of their own time and place. Jesus of Nazareth, as far as we may reconstruct him from the Gospel accounts, addressed the concerns of the people of his own time and place: how to balance their obligations to God, to Rome and to one another, and how to get along economically, spiritually, socially and emotionally. So also the Jesus of the Gospels, but he added concerns that were specific to a post–70 situation, including the question of how to worship God after the destruction of the Jerusalem Temple, and how to construct an identity for those who engaged in a Christ-focused piety. For his part, Jesus of Hollywood speaks to his twentieth and twenty-first century viewers, who have witnessed and continue to be part of tremendous social change in family structures, in technology, in the physical, social and political environment, and in numerous other facets of life.

Finally, whether in the Gospels or on the silver screen, Jesus is an admirable, if distant, individual. If his fundamental message is love, it is a generalized, even universalized love of humanity. This love undergirds his commitment to justice for all human beings. But for the most part, he has few intimates. The Gospels are silent on his emotional ties, even with his mother or closest followers; the movies almost always portray Jesus as celibate and either uninterested in romance or completely convinced that romance is incompatible with his divine mission. Though surrounded by disciples and followers, Jesus of Hollywood is essentially a loner whom others try but fail to understand.

While Jesus does not perpetrate violence—except upon the money-changers who have defiled his Father's house (John 2:16) —he is a victim of Roman violence. From the point of view of those who believe him to be the Messiah, this violence, however graphically displayed, is not gratuitous or meaningless. Rather, it is a consequence of his self-offering as a divinely sanctioned sacrifice on behalf of humankind.

Finally, and paradoxically, the Jesus of scripture and of screen has an ambivalent, sometimes antagonist attitude to those of his own ethnic group. He criticized Jewish institutions, or, more to the point, the ways these have been interpreted and practiced, but he observed them, as Jesus of Nazareth surely did, in a manner that does not differ appreciably from the Jews around him.

Despite these similarities, the biopic Jesus is fundamentally different from his historical and scriptural counterparts. For one thing, cinematic Saviors are assigned one task that Jesus of the Gospels and, I believe, Jesus of Nazareth, did not have to undertake: the liberation of his people from the shackles of Roman oppression. This task is required not by the primary sources or by Christian theology or the history of interpretation but by the narrative template of the biopic genre as such. Alas, Jesus of Hollywood, in any of his guises, is simply not up to the task. His failure is not due to any inherent weakness on his part, but, ironically, to the constraints of history. Even if Jesus of Hollywood is ultimately a fictional character, neither he nor his creators can override the fact that Roman rule over Judea and Galilee continued for centuries after his death, and affected Jews and Gentiles, believers in Christ as well as those whose faith took other forms, until the situation changed radically in the fourth century with the conversion of the Roman Empire to Christianity. While almost all biopics present Jesus as God's response to the Jews' suffering under Rome, none address his failure to deliver.

It is the film medium itself that transforms Jesus of Nazareth, via the Gospels and two thousand years of art, theology and interpretation, into Jesus of Hollywood. Its visual, aural and narrative elements require an imaginative exercise that goes well beyond the data available to us from the Gospels or any other ancient sources. In addition, filmmaking involves financial, technical, societal and other considerations that affect the final product, even for those who attempt to depart from the path well-trodden by DeMille and the epics.

Yet the very label "Jesus of Hollywood" is a misnomer. Just as the Gospels present four different portraits of Jesus, so does each of the films discussed in this book present its own unique Jesus. Though these Jesuses by and large share the features we have just described, they differ in appearance, in voice, in message, and in their impact upon us as viewers. Their behavior varies also. While they all talk at length and do wonderful things for those around them, they project different modes and engage in a variety of activities. One or two of them sing and dance, some of them play, some long for the normal pleasures of human existence, and others look only to their heavenly father for companionship.

And while we have grouped all of these films within the biopic genre and referred to their heroes collectively as "Jesus of Hollywood," these elements properly describe only some of the films, namely, such as DeMille's *The King of Kings*, the epics of the 1960s, and several of the major dramas and television series since then. Many of the most thought-provoking films, such as Pasolini's *The Gospel According to Saint Matthew*, Scorsese's *The Last Temptation of Christ* and Arcand's *Jesus of Montreal*, to say nothing of the entertaining spoofs by Monty Python and Luis Buñuel, are strictly speaking not biopics nor were they made in Hollywood. But, I would argue, these films all take the biopic genre, and the conventions of the epic form both as a starting point and as a foil for their own creative, allegorical and ironic presentations. Without Jesus of Hollywood, there could be no Brian or Daniel Coulombe, nor would we have Pasolini's angry young prophet or Scorsese's tormented crossmaker to contend with.

For this reason, the Jesus biopic category must be wide and complex enough to include the entire range of feature films that seek to retell all or part of the biography of Jesus of Nazareth. If so, we can identify three principal features of the genre. First and foremost, of course, is the claim to historicity.

Second, at the same time as these films proclaim their historicity, they undermine that very claim in every frame and scene. Even as these movies introduce themselves as Gospel truth, even if they take their footage in Jerusalem and Bethlehem, and dress their characters in flowing robes and sandals, they inevitably undo their self-proclaimed historical goals by casting a particular actor as Jesus, having him speak in English, anglicized Aramaic or Latin, and provide a rationale for his behavior and the actions of those around him. It is precisely because the undermining of historicity is inseparable from the claim to historicity that the Jesus biopics should not be judged on the basis of historical accuracy at all. We must not forget that these movies reflect the dependence of Jesus of Hollywood upon the entertainment industry.[1]

The third, and perhaps most interesting aspect of the Jesus biopic genre is the use of history to reflect, and reflect upon, contemporary concerns. In these films, we can recognize a number of themes that have preoccupied us over the century-long history of the genre. One major area concerns the nature of the family and the role of sexuality, specifically an acknowledgement of the diversity in family structures and flexibility in gender roles, at the same time as the nuclear family continues to be seen by many as the formative influence on our well-being and success as adults. Also reflected in these films, if less directly, are changing attitudes toward sexuality, monogamy, and homosexuality. A second area is theological. These films testify to an entire range of theological tensions. Are there forces for both good and evil at work in the world beyond what we can see and touch? Does science explain all phenomena or should we accept the possibility of miracles that transcend scientific explanation? A third area concerns racism, specifically, anti-Semitism. Because the Gospels implicate the Jewish authorities and Jewish crowds in Jesus' condemnation and death, any attempt to tell Jesus' story must also make some difficult decisions. In most cases, the Jesus biopics assign a major role to all or some Jews, even where responsibility is shared by Pilate and the Romans. This is due at least in part to the desire on the part of most filmmakers to remain close to the Gospels as their source texts. Yet this feature of the genre remains disturbing. It may be too harsh to say that Jesus of Hollywood is an anti-Semite, or, more accurately, a self-hating Jew. But one may safely conclude that the Jesus biopics exhibit a discomfort with Jews and Judaism whether they portray Jewish characters in negative, positive, or mixed ways. What remains unresolved is not only the question of the role of Jews or the Jewish leaders in Jesus' death, but what the answer to that question should mean for Christians and Jews today.[2]

For the most part, the heroes of these biopics reinforce the dominant values of their era. In this regard, Jesus is no different from any other biopic subject. Hollywood, says Custen, sustains the status quo, by portraying life as it should be and eliminating realities that create discomfort or uneasiness.[3]

Some may long for a truly accurate historical drama about Jesus; others may hope that there may in the future be a Jesus biopic that offers a more nuanced theology. For my part, I would be happy for another Jesus like

Arcand's or Scorsese's, who will bring a third dimension to the usual cardboard Jesus figures that Hollywood likes to offer. But whatever our wishes in this regard, we can be certain that new offerings will appear sooner or later, and they will join the other films in this genre to offer us yet another view on who we are and what we care about.

Notes

CHAPTER I

1. See William R. Telford, "Jesus Christ Movie Star: The Depiction of Jesus in the Cinema," in *Explorations in Theology and Film: Movies and Meaning*, ed. Clive Marsh and Gaye Ortiz (Malden, Mass.: Blackwell, 1998), 122.

2. Lloyd Baugh comments extensively on the historical distortions of the films as part of his critique of their lack of historicity. Cf. Lloyd Baugh, *Imaging the Divine: Jesus and Christ-Figures in Film, Communication, Culture and Theology* (Kansas City, Mo.: Sheed & Ward, 1997), 18–19.

3. For an account of this controversy, see Cindy Wooden, "Pope Never Commented on Gibson's 'Passion' Film, Says Papal Secretary," *Catholic News Service*, January 19, 2004.

4. Note that often our conception, or our judgment, of authenticity is not based on firsthand knowledge but on other images we have seen, such as famous photographs of the Middle East, newsreels and documentaries.

5. George F. Custen, *Bio/Pics: How Hollywood Constructed Public History* (New Brunswick, N.J.: Rutgers University Press, 1992), 144.

6. Ibid., 7.

7. Solomon refers to "cinematic boredom," along with cheap piety, causing audiences to ridicule at least some Jesus films, including Zeffirelli's *Jesus of Nazareth*. Jon Solomon, *The Ancient World in the Cinema*, rev. and expanded ed. (New Haven: Yale University Press, 2001), 25.

8. John Ivan Simon, "Christ in Concrete," in *Private Screenings* (New York: Macmillan, 1967), 150.

9. Leger Grindon, *Shadows on the Past: Studies in the Historical Fiction Film, Culture and the Moving Image* (Philadelphia: Temple University Press, 1994), 1.

10. Cf. Lloyd Baugh, *Imaging the Divine*, 27.

11. See, for example, the relevant scenes in *The Greatest Story Ever Told.*

12. That the Jesus movies reflect contemporary concerns is evident to most commentators. Margaret Miles describes her approach as "cultural studies," in that her interest is not so much in the films as such as in the "social, political, and cultural matrix in which the film was produced and distributed." Margaret Ruth Miles, *Seeing and Believing: Religion and Values in the Movies* (Boston: Beacon Press, 1996), xii. My approach differs from that of Miles in that it does not bracket out the films as such but also looks closely at the relationship between the film and the Gospels, characterization, and other features of the film as a text.

13. On the Gospel genre, see, for example, Philip L. Shuler, *A Genre for the Gospels: The Biographical Character of Matthew* (Philadelphia: Fortress, 1982).

14. Richard Walsh adopts this approach, as he compares each film with one of the Gospels rather than all four. See Richard Walsh, *Reading the Gospels in the Dark: Portrayals of Jesus in Film* (Harrisburg, PA: Trinity Press International, 2003).

15. For thought-provoking reflections on the differences between American and European film, see the December 2001 edition of p.o.v., an on-line film journal (http://pov.imv.au.dk/Issue_12/POV_12cnt.html).

16. Roy Kinnard and Tim Davis, *Divine Images: A History of Jesus on the Screen* (New York: Carol Pub. Group, 1992); Baugh, *Imaging the Divine*; W. Barnes Tatum, *Jesus at the Movies: A Guide to the First Hundred Years*, rev. and expanded ed. (Santa Rosa, Calif.: Polebridge Press, 2004); Reinhold Zwick, *Evangelienrezeption im Jesusfilm: Ein Beitrag Zur Intermedialen Wirkungsgeschichte Des Neuen Testaments*, Studien Zur Theologie Und Praxis Der Seelsorge, 25 (Würzburg: Seelsorge/Echter, 1997); Richard C. Stern, Clayton N. Jefford, and Guerric DeBona, *Savior on the Silver Screen* (New York: Paulist Press, 1999).

17. Bruce Babington and Peter William Evans. *Biblical Epics: Sacred Narrative in the Hollywood Cinema* (Manchester: Manchester University Press, 1993). Eric S. Christianson, Peter Francis, and William R. Telford, *Cinéma Divinité: Religion, Theology and the Bible in Film* (London: SCM Press, 2005); Walsh, *Reading the Gospels in the Dark.*

18. As this book goes to press, a new film, entitled *The Nativity Story*, directed by Catherine Hardwicke, has been announced. The projected release date is December 1, 2006. For details, see www.thenativitystory.com.

19. According to Baugh, the term "peplum" refers to the loose-fitting clothing worn by the women in these films. Cf. Baugh, *Imaging the Divine*, 241. For detailed studies of this genre, see Gerald Forshey, *American Religious and Biblical Spectaculars* (Westport, Conn.: Praeger, 1992), Solomon, *The Ancient World in Cinema*, and Maria Wyke, *Projecting the Past: Ancient Rome, Cinema, and History* (New York: Routledge, 1997).

20. For an excellent discussion of the Passion play at Oberammergau, see James S. Shapiro, *Oberammergau: The Troubling Story of the World's Most Famous Passion Play*, 1st ed. (New York: Pantheon, 2000).

21. Kinnard and Davis, *Divine Images*, 20.

22. Ibid., 32.

23. Everett Carter, "Cultural History Written with Lightning: The Significance of *The Birth of a Nation*," in *Hollywood as Historian: American Film in a Cultural Context*, ed. Peter C. Rollins (Lexington: University of Kentucky Press, 1983), 9–19; Len F. Litwack, "*The Birth of a Nation*," in *Past Imperfect: History According to the Movies*, ed. Mark C. Carnes (New York: Henry Holt, 1996), 136–141.

24. Tatum, *Jesus at the Movies*, 58–59.

25. The most detailed study of the biographical film genre is Custen, *Bio/Pics*. Custen's book examines all biographical movies made in the studio era of Hollywood. Yet one searches in vain for a single reference to a Jesus movie. In fact, the only "Bible" movie in Custen's index is DeMille's *The Ten Commandments* (1956). This omission is explained by the fact that no Jesus biopics appeared within the time frame of Custen's study.

26. As Tatum notes, Ray's film is not a remake of the 1927 film. While it borrows its title from DeMille's opus, and in some scenes "quotes" or pays tribute to the earlier film, it is a completely different film. Originally Ray had planned to call his film *The King of Kings*, as DeMille had done, but revised it slightly in the aftermath of legal problems with the corporation that controlled DeMille's movie. See Tatum, *Jesus at the Movies*, 77.

27. Solomon, *The Ancient World in the Cinema*, 3; Stern, Jefford, and DeBona, *Savior on the Silver Screen*, 62.

28. In addition to the exigencies of the Production Code and the popularity of DeMille's film, Tatum suggests that the development of the peplum film, in which Jesus' story is a subplot of a fictional story, may have been a factor. See Tatum, *Jesus at the Movies*, 61–62.

29. This period in American cinematic history is alluded to in Martin Scorsese's 2004 film *The Aviator*, in which director Howard Hughes must defend the size of Jane Russell's "mammaries" (only her cleavage, in fact) in his film *The Outlaw*.

30. The full text of the Code is available in the appendix to Leonard J. Leff and Jerold L. Simmons, *The Dame in the Kimono: Hollywood, Censorship, and the Production Code from the 1920s to the 1960s* (New York: Doubleday, 1990), 283–292.

31. James M. Skinner, *The Cross and the Cinema: The Legion of Decency and the National Catholic Office for Motion Pictures, 1933–1970* (Westport, Conn.: Praeger, 1993), 1–2.

32. Telford, "Jesus Christ Movie Star," 130.

33. Tatum, *Jesus at the Movies*, 86, citing the unattributed film review in *Time*, October 1961, 27.

34. Telford, "Jesus Christ Movie Star," 121.

35. Cf. Babington and Evans, *Biblical Epics*, 5, 9–10.

36. In 2000 another filmed version of *Jesus Christ Superstar*, made for television, appeared, directed by Gale Edwards and Nick Morris. Discussion of this musical in the present study is based on the 1973 Norman Jewison version.

37. In 2004, full-stage productions of *Jesus Christ Superstar* took place in Los Angeles, Houston, and Toronto, among other North American and European venues.

Other musicals exist but have not been commercially released. See, for example, http://www.jesus-musical.de/ for information about a German musical production.

38. Tag Gallagher, *The Adventures of Roberto Rossellini: His Life and Films* (New York: Da Capo Press, 1998), 669.

39. Some nineteenth- and twentieth-century critics saw Jesus' comment in 5:39 that Jairus' daughter is not dead but sleeping as a sign that she was in a coma. As Joel Marcus points out, however, Jesus is using a common biblical and Jewish metaphor here. A reference to death as a form of sleep also appears in the story of Lazarus, for example, in John 11:5–16. Joel Marcus, *Mark 1–8: A New Translation with Introduction and Commentary*, ed. William Foxwell Albright and David Noel Freedman, vol. 27, *The Anchor Bible* (New York: Doubleday, 2000), 362.

40. See Tatum's acknowledgments in the second edition of his book, in which he explains how he changed his mind and therefore added a chapter on this film in the second edition of his book. Tatum, *Jesus at the Movies*, x.

41. The term "Palestine" is currently associated with the anticipated homeland of the Palestinians. For scholars of first-century Judaism and Christianity, however, the term denotes the Roman province including Judea. From the conquest of Pompeii until Herod the Great, Palestine was a client kingdom under a local monarch; after Herod's death, it became a Roman province under the authority of a governor.

42. Cf. Michael Medved, *Hollywood vs. America: Popular Culture and the War on Traditional Values*, 1st ed. (New York: HarperCollins, 1992), 37–49; Tatum, *Jesus at the Movies*, 188–92; Babington and Evans, *Biblical Epics*, 106.

43. Shapiro, *Oberammergau*, 4–5.

44. Not all viewers, however, remain engaged throughout Jesus' long discourses. As the "special advisor" to the academic advisory committee for this film, I received a ticket to its premiere at the Toronto International Film Festival on September 11, 2003, and brought my mother along as my guest. About halfway through Jesus' farewell discourse, my mother turned to me and asked, "Why does he have to talk so much?" Good question!

45. Richard Wightman Fox, *Jesus in America: Personal Savior, Cultural Hero, National Obsession*, 1st ed. (San Francisco: HarperSanFrancisco, 2004), 11.

CHAPTER 2

1. Sarah Kozloff, *Invisible Story-Tellers: Voice-Over Narration in American Fiction Film* (Berkeley: University of California Press, 1988), 76–79.

2. Rossellini's words are quoted on the box of the VHS version.

3. Mark Goodacre, "The Power of the Passion: Reacting and Over-Reacting to Gibson's Artistic Vision," in *Jesus and Mel Gibson's "The Passion of the Christ": The Film, the Gospels and the Claims of History*, ed. Kathleen E. Corley and Robert L. Webb (London: Continuum, 2004), 33.

4. Theophilus was a common proper name for both Jews and Gentiles from the third century BCE onward. The reference is unlikely to be symbolic rather than historical. It is possible that Theophilus was Luke's patron. Joseph A. Fitzmyer, *The*

Gospel According to Luke: Introduction, Translation, and Notes, 2d ed., 2 vols. (Garden City, N.Y.: Doubleday, 1983), 299–300.

5. Unless otherwise indicated, all English translations of biblical passages are from the New Revised Standard Version.

6. New Testament scholars generally view the Gospels as anonymous writings that have been ascribed to particular individuals in the course of canonization, reflecting traditions that had arisen in the interim, as well as the need to establish the authoritative nature of these different versions of Jesus' life story. I will refer to them throughout as Matthew, Mark, Luke, and John, as shorthand for "the Gospel of...." Because the authors are anonymous, it is not possible to know whether they are male or female. I have used the masculine pronoun, as in my view it is more likely that they were male, but certainty in this regard is not possible.

7. Not to be confused with the computer game of the same name (cf. http://www .templetantrum.com). To my knowledge, this apt description of the "cleansing of the Temple" episode originates with Paula Fredriksen, personal communication.

8. Indeed, there are scholars who argue that John does not refer to the institution of the Eucharist at all. See Rudolf Schnackenburg, *The Gospel According to St. John* (New York: Seabury Press, 1980), 2: 65–69.

9. For discussion of the discrepancy between Johannine and Synoptic chronologies, see D. Moody Smith, *John among the Gospels*, 2d ed. (Columbia: University of South Carolina Press, 2001).

10. Most historical Jesus scholars rely more on the Synoptics than on John. See, for example, Gerd Theissen and Annette Merz, *The Historical Jesus: A Comprehensive Guide* (Minneapolis: Fortress, 1998), 36. An exception is Paula Fredriksen, *Jesus of Nazareth, King of the Jews: A Jewish Life and the Emergence of Christianity*, 1st ed. (New York: Knopf, 1999).

11. There are numerous books and articles on the Synoptic problem. A good starting point can be found on the Web: http://www.ntgateway.com/synoptic/. This site has links to many other good sites that contain bibliographies, synopses of the Gospels (that is, passage-by-passage comparisons among the three Synoptic Gospels), and other resources.

12. For a critique of the two-source hypothesis and a plausible alternative, see Mark Goodacre, *The Case against Q: Studies in Markan Priority and the Synoptic Problem* (Harrisburg, Pa.: Trinity Press International, 2002).

13. In the absence of a straightforward, reliable historical source, historical Jesus scholars have developed a variety of criteria for evaluating the Gospel materials with respect to their historicity. These criteria include multiple attestation and dissimilarity. The criterion of multiple attestation assumes that if an event appears in more than one source it is more likely to be historical. The criterion of dissimilarity assumes that Jesus was unique and his teachings entirely original, so that the sayings that are *least* similar to those attributed to other sages in ancient texts are the ones that are *most* likely to be authentically his. Both of these criteria are vulnerable to criticism. For example, the presence of the same event or saying in two sources may reflect authenticity or it may reflect a widespread oral tradition. The criterion of dissimilarity

fails to take into account the likelihood that Jesus would have spoken in the idiom of his day and that there may well have been overlap between his stories, sayings, and teachings, and those attributed to other Jewish leaders. To give but one example, the fact that the prohibition of divorce on any grounds but adultery is associated in ancient literature with a Pharisee named Shammai does not either support or rule out the possibility that Jesus also may have held this view (cf. Matthew 5:32). For detailed discussion and evaluation of the criteria for determining authenticity, see E. P. Sanders and Margaret Davies, *Studying the Synoptic Gospels* (London: SCM Press, 1989).

14. See William Wrede, *The Messianic Secret*, Library of Theological Translations (Greenwood, S.C.: Attic Press, 1971).

15. An exhaustive list of the Matthean passages used and reordered by Pasolini was compiled by Jeffrey L. Staley in 1997 for the Society of Biblical Literature, "Literary Aspects of the Gospels and Acts: Panel on Pasolini's Matthew." To my knowledge this list has not been published.

16. According to the information on http://www.jesusfilm.org/faqs/, 54.5% of the film is taken verbatim from Luke, and 2.7% verbatim from other scriptures (John 3:16; Revelation 3:20; Matthew 28:19). An additional 23.8% is paraphrased or summarized from Luke and 1.8% from other scriptures, leaving 17.6% not taken from scripture at all.

17. Underlying the harmonizing approach is the assumption that biopics can present only one version of the Jesus story; to date no Jesus movie has appeared that adopts the Rashomon-like approach of presenting several versions of the same sequence of events, each from the perspective of a different character in the drama. It would be an interesting exercise for some enterprising filmmaker.

18. Lew Wallace, *Ben-Hur: A Tale of the Christ* (New York: Harper and Brothers, 1901); Edward Bulwer Lytton, *Last Days of Pompeii* (London: R. Bentley, 1834); Lloyd C. Douglas, *The Robe* (Toronto: Thomas Allen, 1942).

19. Luke Timothy Johnson, *The Real Jesus: The Misguided Quest for the Historical Jesus and the Truth of the Traditional Gospels* (San Francisco: HarperSanFrancisco, 1996), 1.

20. As in all film adaptations, Scorsese has shaped his source text, Kazantzakis's novel, and in doing so has adopted and also responded to the conventions of the Jesus biopic genre.

21. While the other transcriptions from *Jesus of Montreal* are taken from the subtitles, I have modified this one as the subtitles did not reflect the French original, which, incorrectly, translated "territories" as "the Left Bank," creating an inadvertent conflation of the West Bank of the Jordan with the Left Bank of the Seine River in Paris.

22. Daniel appears to be consulting a color version of plate 24, bound between pages 128 and 129, pertaining to N. Haas, "Anthropological Observations on the Skeletal Remains from Giv'at Hamivtar," *Israel Exploration Journal* 20 (1970), 38–59.

23. For sources and discussion, see R. Travers Herford, *Christianity in Talmud and Midrash* (London: Williams, 1903; reprint. New York: Ktav Publishing House, 1975), 35–48.

24. For Judas of Galilee, see Acts 5:37 and Josephus, Jewish *War*, 2.118. For Simon the Magician, see Justin, *First Apology*, xxvi, and Pseudo-Clementine, *Homilies*, II, xxii. The standard work on Jesus as magician is Morton Smith, *Jesus the Magician*, 1st ed. (New York: Harper and Row, 1978).

25. See Josephus, *Antiquities*, 13. 3–83, *Jewish War*, 1.97–98.

26. Among Arcand's documentaries are *On est au coton* (1976), *Quebec: Duplessis et après . . .* (1972) and *Le confort et l'indifférence* (1981).

27. The Stations are as follows: 1. Jesus is condemned to death; 2. the cross is laid upon him; 3. His first fall; 4. He meets his mother; 5. Simon of Cyrene is made to bear the cross; 6. Jesus' face is wiped by Veronica; 7. His second fall; 8. He meets the women of Jerusalem; 9. His third fall; 10. He is stripped of His garments; 11. His crucifixion; 12. His death on the cross; 13. His body is taken down from the cross; and 14. He is laid in the tomb.

28. Stern, Jefford, and DeBona conclude that *Jesus of Montreal* brings us to the end of the "possibility of the Christian metanarrative." "The world that constructed the Jesus film is at an end because, in a certain sense, the humanist culture that assembled an image called 'Jesus Christ' has disappeared." Stern, Jefford, and DeBona, *Savior on the Silver Screen*, 333. Little did they know that within a few years, *The Gospel of John* and *The Passion of the Christ* would require a revision to this pre-diction. Tatum concludes the second edition of his book with the following proph-ecy: "Based on past experience, the viewers of this film and the readers of this book are left with a certainty: the cinematic Jesus will come again." Tatum, *Jesus at the Movies*, 225.

CHAPTER 3

1. On the "parting of the ways," see Adam H. Becker and Annette Y. Reed, eds., *The Ways that Never Parted: Jews and Christians in Late Antiquity and the Early Middle Ages* (Tübingen: Mohr-Siebeck, 2003); Adele Reinhartz, "A Fork in the Road or a Multi-Lane Highway?: New Perspectives on 'The Parting of the Ways' Between Ju-daism and Christianity." *The Changing Face of Judaism, Christianity and Other Greco-Roman Religions in Antiquity*, Studien zu den Jüdischen Schriften aus hellenistisch-römischer Zeit, Bd 2. (Gütersloh: Gütersloher Verlagshaus GmbH, 2005), 278–293, and bibliography.

2. Geza Vermes, *Jesus and the World of Judaism* (London: SCM Press, 1983), 1. While it is true that "Christianity," and therefore "Christians" as such did not yet exist in the time of Jesus, I have often noticed that Christians and non-Christians alike assume that Jesus was a "Christian."

3. One of the most pervasive ways of describing, referring to, or calling upon God employs the formula "God of Abraham, Isaac, and Jacob." See, for example, The Eighteen Benedictions, recited three times daily, which begin: "Blessed art thou, Lord our God and god of our fathers, God of Abraham, God of Isaac, and God of Jacob." Philip Birnbaum, *Ha-Sidur Ha-Shalem* (New York: Hebrew Publishing Co., 1949), 88. This translation is from an orthodox prayer book; the prayer books

of other denominations include this formula as well, sometimes with the addition of the matriarchs. See, for example, a prayer book of the Reconstructionist movement, Federation of Reconstructionist Congregations and Havurot., *Kol Haneshamah: Shabbat Ve-hagim*, 3d ed. (Wyncote, Pa.: Reconstructionist Press, 1994), 98.

4. Cf. E. P. Sanders, *Jewish Law from Jesus to the Mishnah: Five Studies* (Philadelphia: Trinity Press International, 1990), 23. Mary C. Boys, *Has God Only One Blessing? Judaism as a Source of Christian Self-Understanding* (Mahwah, N.J.: Paulist Press, 2000), 126.

5. Vermes, *Jesus and the World of Judaism*, 54, sees these passages as an example of overt, even extreme chauvinism. This chauvinism sits uncomfortably with the overall Christian construction of Jesus as sinless, universal, and perfect.

6. E. P. Sanders, *The Historical Figure of Jesus* (London: Penguin, 1993), and idem *Jesus and Judaism* (Philadelphia: Fortress, 1985); Vermes, *Jesus and the World of Judaism*; Sean Freyne, *Galilee, Jesus, and the Gospels: Literary Approaches and Historical Investigations* (Dublin: Gill and MacMillan, 1988); Paula Fredriksen, "What You See Is What You Get: Context and Content in Current Research on the Historical Jesus," *Theology Today* 52 (1995): 75–95.

7. E. P. Sanders, "Jesus and the First Table of the Jewish Law," in *Jews and Christians Speak of Jesus*, ed. Arthur E. Zannoni (Minneapolis: Fortress, 1994), 71.

8. William E. Arnal, "Making and Re-Making the Jesus-Sign: Contemporary Markings on the Body of Christ," in *Whose Historical Jesus?* ed. William E. Arnal and Michel R. Desjardins, Studies in Christianity and Judaism, 7, (Waterloo, Ont.: Wilfrid Laurier University Press, 1997), 310.

9. Lawrence Schiffman, "The Jewishness of Jesus: Commandments Concerning Interpersonal Relations," in *Jews & Christians Speak of Jesus*, ed. Arthur E. Zannoni (Minneapolis: Fortress, 1994), 39.

10. Sanders, *The Historical Figure of Jesus*, 254–64.

11. Fredriksen, "What You See Is What You Get," 80.

12. John Dominic Crossan, *The Historical Jesus: The Life of a Mediterranean Jewish Peasant*, 1st ed. (San Francisco: HarperSanFrancisco, 1991), 263.

13. Fredriksen, "What You See Is What You Get," 81–82.

14. Marcus J. Borg, *Jesus in Contemporary Scholarship* (Valley Forge, Pa.: Trinity Press International, 1994); N. T. Wright, *Christian Origins and the Question of God*, 2 vols., 2d impression with corrections (London: SPCK, 1993).

15. Fredriksen, "What You See Is What You Get," 86.

16. Wright, *Christian Origins and the Question of God*, 2: 228.

17. Borg, *Jesus in Contemporary Scholarship*, 26.

18. Fredriksen, "What You See Is What You Get," 88.

19. Custen, *Bio/Pics*, 78.

20. Transcriptions from Arcand's *Jesus of Montreal* are taken from the subtitles on the video version of the film.

21. The image appears at http://www.lightplanet.com/mormons/basic/christ/physical_appearance.htm.

22. See, for example, the Baptism of Jesus, Gustave Doré, *The Doré Bible Illustrations* (New York: Dover Publications, 1974), 168. James Jacques Joseph Tissot, *The Life of Our Saviour Jesus Christ: Three Hundred and Sixty-Five Compositions from the Four Gospels, with Notes and Explanatory Drawings* (London: Sampson Low, Marston & Co., 1899), plate in volume 1, between 62–63.

23. Stephen R. Prothero, *American Jesus: How the Son of God Became a National Icon*, 1st American ed. (New York: Farrar, Straus and Giroux, 2003), 118.

24. http://www.godweb.org/sallman.htm. For more detailed discussion of the Sallmann image, see Prothero, *American Jesus*, 116–123.

25. Franco Zeffirelli, *Franco Zeffirelli's Jesus: A Spiritual Diary*, trans. Willis J. Egan (San Francisco: Harper and Row, 1984), 101.

26. The destruction of the Temple looms large within traditional Jewish historiography, as the major turning point from the sacrificial system to prayer-based worship, and for a radical transformation of the social and political order. The Pharisees are seen as the ones who enabled Jewish continuity, in that their exegetical activities allowed Judaism to survive this catastrophe. For a presentation of this view, see Lawrence H. Schiffman, *From Text to Tradition: A History of Second Temple and Rabbinic Judaism* (Hoboken, N.J.: Ktav Publishing House, 1991), 158–171.

27. Sanders, *The Historical Figure of Jesus*, 272–73.

28. Cf. Josephus, *Antiquities*, books 17–18, and *Jewish War*, book 2.

29. For essays on Jesus' attitude to Rome, see Ernst Bammel and C. F. D. Moule, eds., *Jesus and the Politics of His Day* (Cambridge: Cambridge University Press, 1985).

30. George F. Custen, "The Mechanical Life in the Age of Human Reproduction: American Biopics, 1961–1980," *Biography* 23 (2000): 132.

31. For a discussion of Jesus in the Galilean context, see Sean Freyne, *Galilee and Gospel: Collected Essays* (Tubingen: Mohr Siebeck, 2000), and *Galilee, Jesus, and the Gospels: Literary Approaches and Historical Investigations* (Dublin: Gill and MacMillan, 1988).

32. On the international scene, Ray's introduction is rivaled only by the detailed overview of all of biblical history up to the time of Jesus given by the anonymous narrator in Rossellini's *The Messiah*.

33. Jewish books were burned in Nazi Germany on May 10, 1933. See Edward Alexander, *The Holocaust and the War of Ideas* (New Brunswick, N.J.: Transaction Publishers, 1994), 221.

34. On the echoes of the Holocaust and the Nazi regime in the introduction to *King of Kings*, see Stern, Jefford, and DeBona, *Savior on the Silver Screen*, 85.

35. For more detailed discussion, see Emil Schürer, Geza Vermes, and Fergus Millar, *The History of the Jewish People in the Age of Jesus Christ (175 B.C.–A.D. 135)*, rev. ed., vol. 1 (Edinburgh: T.&T. Clark, 1973), 1: 236–242.

36. For an excellent summary of Herod's biography, see Lee Israel Levine, "Herod the Great," in *The Anchor Bible Dictionary*, ed. David Noel Freedman (New York: Doubleday, 1992), 161–169. For a more detailed study, see Peter Richardson, *Herod: King of the Jews and Friend of the Romans*, Studies on Personalities of the New Testament (Columbia: University of South Carolina Press, 1996).

37. It may be that the film's identification of Herod as a Bedouin Arab is intended primarily to simplify matters so that they will be less obscure to the audience, but in light of Herod's sinister appearance and his despotic behavior it may also reflect an anti-Arab, pro-Israel stance at the time that the film was made. Bruce Babington and Peter William Evans, *Biblical Epics: Sacred Narrative in the Hollywood Cinema* (Manchester: Manchester University Press, 1993), 130.

38. This transcription is taken from http://www.mwscomp.com/movies/brian/brian.htm#script, which justifiably claims to be the most complete and accurate transcription of this film available.

39. Isidore Epstein, ed. *The Babylonian Talmud., Seder Mo'ed* 1 (London: Soncino Press, 1938), 156.

40. On the archaeological evidence for the Roman occupation of Palestine, see the articles in Louis Finkelstein, ed., *The Cambridge History of Judaism, Volume 3: The Early Roman Period* (Cambridge: Cambridge University Press, 1999).

CHAPTER 4

1. George F. Custen, *Bio/Pics: How Hollywood Constructed Public History* (New Brunswick, N.J.: Rutgers University Press, 1992), 149.

2. For discussion of the influence of the Christian apocrypha on the history of Christian art, see David R. Cartlidge and J. K. Elliott, *Art and the Christian Apocrypha* (London: Routledge, 2001), 21–46.

3. Many interpreters attempt to read John 2:4 in a way that minimizes or explains away what to our ears may sound rude. For an example, see Raymond E. Brown, *The Gospel According to John*, 1st ed., 2 vols. (Garden City, N.Y.: Doubleday, 1966), 2: 99–100.

4. E. Elizabeth Johnson, "Who Is My Mother?: Family Values in the Gospel of Mark," in *Blessed One: Protestant Perspectives on Mary*, ed. Beverly Roberts Gaventa and Cynthia L. Rigby Gaventa (Louisville, Ky.: Westminster John Knox, 2002), 32–46.

5. Peter Brunette, *Roberto Rossellini* (Berkeley: University of California Press, 1996), 346–347.

6. Bertrand Buby, *Mary of Galilee: A Trilogy of Marian Studies*, 3 vols. (New York: Alba House, 1994), 170.

7. There is no explicit indication, however, that this woman was identified as Mary in Revelation. See Pheme Perkins, "Mary in Johannine Traditions," in *Mary, Woman of Nazareth: Biblical and Theological Perspectives*, ed. Doris Donnelly (New York: Paulist Press, 1989), 109–122.

8. Buby, *Mary of Galilee*, 168.

9. Rosemary Radford Ruether, *Mary, the Feminine Face of the Church* (London: SCM Press, 1977), 53.

10. Leo Steinberg has argued that the sexuality of Jesus and the erotic dimensions of his relationship with his mother as depicted in western art tend to be ignored in the scholarly literature. In his book on the sexuality of Christ, Steinberg demonstrates the broad range of devotional imagery that emphasizes Jesus' genitalia. The most

frequent themes are the Madonna and Child, in which Mary's hand is often touching or covering her son's genitals, and the Pietà. The intention, in Steinberg's view, is the "humanation" of God. Leo Steinberg, *The Sexuality of Christ in Renaissance Art and in Modern Oblivion*, 2d ed. (Chicago: University of Chicago Press, 1996).

11. Buby, *Mary of Galilee*, 169.

CHAPTER 5

1. *The Protoevangelium of James* is dated approximately 140–170. The material is quoted from http://www.newadvent.org/fathers/0847.htm. This site, and several others, provide full texts of standard translation of the New Testament Apocrypha and Patrisitc literautre and are cited in these notes for the convenience of the reader.

2. See http://gnosis.org/library/psudomat.htm.

3. For a summary of apocryphal texts and traditions about Joseph, see Jane Schaberg, *The Illegitimacy of Jesus: A Feminist Theological Interpretation of the Infancy Narratives*, Biblical Seminar, 28 (Sheffield: Sheffield Academic Press, 1995).

4. They also reflect specific interests of the filmmakers. The screenwriter of *From the Manger to the Cross*, for example, was Gene Gauntier, who also played the role of Mary and may have had an ideological and professional interest in augmenting her role. Tatum, *Jesus at the Movies*, 26. Rossellini often had very positive female characters in his films. Peter Brunette, *Roberto Rossellini* (Berkeley: University of California Press, 1996), 346.

5. The actor who plays Joseph in Young's *Jesus* is Armin Mueller-Stahl, who was born in Tilsit, East Prussia, now Sovetsk, Russia. It is his Eastern European accent that evokes twentieth-century Eastern European immigrants to the United States. Cf. Jonathan D. Sarna, *American Judaism: A History* (New Haven: Yale University Press, 2004).

6. See Ronald P. Rohner and Robert A. Veneziano, "The Importance of Father Love: History and Contemporary Evidence," *Review of General Psychology* 5 (2001): 382–405. Cf. also John W. Miller, *Jesus at Thirty: A Psychological and Historical Portrait* (Minneapolis: Fortress, 1997).

7. In maintaining conservative family values, the Jesus movie genre conforms to the conventions of the biopic genre as a whole, which combines "homage" to traditional family and religious values with the "safely prurient." George F. Custen, "The Mechanical Life in the Age of Human Reproduction: American Biopics, 1961–1980," *Biography* 23 (2000): 138.

CHAPTER 6

1. On ancient notions of reproduction and their impact on the New Testament conception of Jesus as God's son, see Adele Reinhartz, "And the Word Was Begotten": Divine Epigenesis in the Gospel of John," *Semeia* 85: *God the Father in the Gospel of John*, ed. Adele Reinhartz (Atlanta: Society of Biblical Literature, 1999), 83–103.

2. In most of these paintings, the angel, a large-winged, but otherwise human male figure, is to Mary's left. For detailed analysis of this positioning (to the right or to

the left), see Don Denny, *The Annunciation from the Right: From Early Christian Times to the Sixteenth Century*, Outstanding Dissertations in the Fine Arts (New York: Garland, 1977). Mary is often reading a book, probably the Gospels, or spinning, as she is described in the *Protoevangelium of James* and as depicted in DeMille's *The King of Kings*. Sometimes the spirit is represented by a dove, perhaps because of the baptism scene, in which John the Baptist declares that he saw the spirit descend upon Jesus as a dove; some of the movie versions show a dove or other birds in the scene as well.

3. Herford, *Christianity in Talmud and Midrash*, 35. Rabbinic sources for this claim are found in segments censored from the printed versions of Babylonian Talmud, Tractate Shabbat 104b, and Tractate Sanhedrin 67a.

4. *The Acts of Pilate* is dated between the middle of the second to the middle of the third century CE. http://www.ccel.org/fathers2/ANF-08/anfo8-77.htm#p6602 _1993239.

5. Origin lived from 185–254 CE in Alexandria, Egypt. http://www.newadvent.org/fathers/04161.htm.

6. The image is also an allusion to the story of the Holy Grail, which features a glowing chalice. Cynthia Read, personal communication.

7. Cf. Aaron Kirschenbaum, *Self-Incrimination in Jewish Law* (New York: Burning Bush Press, 1970).

8. The Fourth Gospel uses the term "sign" (*semeion*; see, e.g., John 2:11, 2:18, 4:54, 6:2) to refer to Jesus' miracles, but it exhibits a certain amount of ambivalence not so much about Jesus' ability to perform the signs but about their efficacy in bringing people to faith based on a true understanding of who Jesus is. While the signs reveal Jesus' glory (2:11), they may also be grossly misinterpreted (cf. 2:23). In 4:48, Jesus gently chides the nobleman who has sought help for his sick son: "Then Jesus said to him, 'Unless you see signs and wonders you will not believe'."

9. Cf. *The Infancy Story of Thomas* 2:1–5, in which Jesus shapes twelve birds out of clay and brings them to life Wilhelm Schneemelcher and R. McL Wilson, eds. *New Testament Apocrypha*. Rev. ed. Vol. 1 (Louisville, Ky.: Westminster John Knox Press, 1991), 444.

10. Lloyd Baugh, *Imaging the Divine: Jesus and Christ Figures in Film, Communication, Culture and Theology* (Kansas City, Mo.: Sheed & Ward, 1997), 53.

11. John Dominic Crossan, personal communication. See also David Denby, who refers to the film as a "sickening death trap." David Denby, "Nailed: Mel Gibson's 'The Passion of the Christ'," *New Yorker*, March 1, 2004. http://www.newyorker.com/critics/cinema/?040301crci_cinema.

CHAPTER 7

1. On the representation of women in the Jesus movies, see William R. Telford, "Jesus and Women in Fiction and Film," in *Transformative Encounters: Jesus and Women Re-Viewed*, ed. Ingrid Rosa Kitzberger (Leiden: Brill, 2000), 353–81.

2. The latter passage is part of the so-called "longer ending" of Mark, which scholars generally view as a later addition. Discussion of the various endings of Mark can be found in all the major commentaries on Mark, such as John R. Donahue and Daniel J. Harrington, *The Gospel of Mark* (Collegeville, Minn.: Liturgical Press, 2002), 462.

3. Marianne Sawicki, "Magdalenes and Tiberiennes: City Women in the Entourage of Jesus," in *Transformative Encounters: Jesus and Women Re-Viewed*, ed. Ingrid Rosa Kitzberger (Leiden: Brill, 2000), 193, 196.

4. Luise Schottroff, "Women as Followers of Jesus in New Testament Times," in *The Bible and Liberation: Political and Social Hermeneutics*, ed. Norman K. Gottwald and Richard A. Horsley (Maryknoll, N.Y.: Orbis Books, 1993), 455.

5. Sawicki, "Magdalenes and Tiberiennes," 219–221.

6. Carla Ricci, *Mary Magdalene and Many Others: Women Who Followed Jesus* (Minneapolis: Fortress, 1994), 135. These comments lead into a lengthy discussion of the downtrodden role of women in Judaism, which is apparently Mary's true affliction, and one that only Jesus could cure. On anti-Judaism in Christian feminist analyses such as Ricci's, see Judith Plaskow, "Anti-Judaism in Feminist Christian Interpretation," in *Searching the Scriptures*, ed. Elisabeth Schüssler Fiorenza (New York: Crossroad, 1993), 117–129.

7. John 7:53–8:11 was not originally part of the Gospel of John. For discussion, see Brown, *The Gospel According to John*, 1.335–36.

8. Marjorie M. Malvern, *Venus in Sackcloth: The Magdalen's Origins and Metamorphoses* (Carbondale: Southern Illinois University Press, 1975), 39.

9. Malvern, *Venus in Sackcloth*, 39.

10. Ibid.

11. Ibid., 55.

12. In these films, Mary evokes the prostitute or vamp as the image appears in other silent movies. See Sumiko Higashi, *Virgins, Vamps and Flappers: The American Silent Movie Heroine*, Monographs in Women's Studies (St. Albans, Vt.: Eden Press Women's Publications, 1978).

13. Michael W. Cuneo, *American Exorcism: Expelling Demons in the Land of Plenty*, 1st ed. (New York: Doubleday, 2001).

14. The abundance of sex, sexuality, and nudity in the silent era was an impetus for the institution of a production code. See Leff and Simmons, *The Dame in the Kimono*, 6; Robert Sklar, *Movie-Made America: A Cultural History of American Movies*, rev. and updated. ed. (New York: Vintage, 1994), 90–103.

15. Here, however, Mary Magdalene is not dressed entirely in red, as she is in many films, but rather wears a dress that is blue except for its red sleeves and bodice. This outfit implies that her promiscuity, symbolized by the red outfit, is not all there is to her character.

16. James Robert Parish, *Prostitution in Hollywood Films: Plots, Critiques, Casts, and Credits for 389 Theatrical and Made-for-Television Releases* (Jefferson, N.C.: McFarland, 1992). This book is primarily a summary of plots of films that feature

prostitutes, but there are some useful introductory comments that place the portrayal of prostitutes in film in the context of the censorship codes.

17. Richard Burridge, personal communication. Burridge was an advisor to the filmmakers.

18. See Adele Reinhartz, "From Narrative to History: The Resurrection of Mary and Martha," in *"Women Like This": New Perspectives on Jewish Women in the Greco-Roman World*, ed. Amy-Jill Levine, Early Judaism and Its Literature (Atlanta: Society of Biblical Literature, 1991), 161–184.

19. See Mary Rose D'Angelo, "Reconstructing 'Real' Women in Gospel Literature," in *Women and Christian Origins*, ed. Ross Shepard Kraemer and Mary Rose D'Angelo (New York: Oxford University Press, 1999), 105–128.

20. Katherine Ludwig Jansen, "Maria Magdalena: *Apostolorum Apostola*," in *Women Preachers and Prophets through Two Millennia of Christianity*, ed. Beverly Mayne Kienzle and Pamela J. Walker (Berkeley and Los Angeles: University of California Press, 1998), 57–75.

21. Da Vinci's painting does not include her, despite assertions to the contrary in Dan Brown's work of fiction, *The Da Vinci Code* (New York: Doubleday, 2003).

22. This man is likely meant to be the Beloved Disciple whom John places at the foot of the cross and whom tradition identifies as John son of Zebedee.

23. Cf, for example, Heidi Bright Parales, *Hidden Voices: Biblical Women and Our Christian Heritage* (Macon, Ga.: Smyth and Helwys, 1998), 45.

24. Jane Schaberg, "Fast Forwarding to the Magdalene," in *Semeia 74: Biblical Glamour and Hollywood Glitz*, ed. Alice Bach (Atlanta: Society of Biblical Literature, 1996), 42.

25. With this speech, Daniel fulfills his commitment to the actor, who agreed to join the troupe on condition that he be given the opportunity to recite Hamlet's famous soliloquy (*Hamlet*, Act III, Scene I, Lines 64ff).

26. See Mary Rose D'Angelo, "A Critical Note: John 20:17 and Apocalypse of Moses 31," *Journal of Theological Studies* 4 (1990): 529–36; Michael McGehee, "A Less Theological Reading of John 20:17," *Journal of Biblical Literature* 105 (1986): 299–302.

27. Sandra Schneiders argues that the encounter between Jesus and Mary Magdalene is intended to evoke both the garden of Genesis 2:15–17 and 3:8 and the garden of Canticles, which has been traditionally as portraying the covenant between Israel and Yahweh. Sandra M. Schneiders, "John 20:11–18: The Encounter of the Easter Jesus with Mary Magdalene—A Transformative Feminist Reading," in *What Is John? Readers and Readings of the Fourth Gospel*, ed. Fernando F. Segovia (Atlanta: Scholars Press, 1996), 161. For detailed discussion of John 20's allusions to Song of Songs, see Adele Reinhartz, "To Love the Lord: An Intertextual Reading of John 20," in *The Labour of Reading: Desire, Alienation, and Biblical Interpretation*, ed. Fiona C. Black, Erin Runions, and Roland Boer (Atlanta: Society of Biblical Literature, 1999), 53–69.Cf. also Ann Robert Winsor in *A King is Bound in the Tresses: Allusions to the Song of Songs in the Fourth Gospel*, Studies in Biblical Literature (New York: Peter Lang, 1999).

28. When I taught this film in class, I asked my students to vote on whether they read the relationship between Daniel and Mireille as sexual or not. The group was

split, half voting yes, and the other half voting no. This result may well be typical, and testifies to the successful ambiguity of Arcand's presentation.

29. As part of the academic advisory team for Saville's *The Gospel of John*, I can report that the question of Mary Magdalene's inclusion or exclusion was discussed and the decision made that given the Gospels' silence it would not violate the integrity of the film project to include Mary as much as possible among the group of disciples and followers of Jesus. Thus she is present in many of the group scenes, including the Last Supper.

30. The theme of unrequited love, that is, the unrequited love that Mary Magdalene has for Jesus, is developed in most detail by *The Book of Life* (dir. Hal Hartley, 1998) in which Jesus and Mary Magdalene return to earth in order to open the seven seals to the Book of Life. By contrast, José Saramago's fascinating novel, *The Gospel According to Jesus Christ*, trans. Giovanni Pontiero, 1st Harvest ed (San Diego: Harcourt, 1991) portrays Jesus and Mary Magdalene in a long-term intimate relationship, from the time Jesus is eighteen years old until his death at thirty.

31. For a comprehensive study of the history of interpretation of Mary Magdalene, see Jane Schaberg, *The Resurrection of Mary Magdalene: Legends, Apocrypha, and the Christian Testament* (New York: Continuum, 2002).

CHAPTER 8

1. Cf. Hyam Maccoby, *Judas Iscariot and the Myth of Jewish Evil* (London: Peter Halban, 1992).

2. The most detailed historical study of Judas is William Klassen, *Judas: Betrayer or Friend of Jesus?* (Minneapolis: Fortress, 1996).

3. Klassen, *Judas*, 73.

4. On the demonization of Judas, see Klassen, *Judas*, 15, 203, and Maccoby, *Judas Iscariot*.

5. Maccoby, *Judas Iscariot*, 3; Klassen, *Judas*, 74. Sanders, *Jesus and Judaism*, 230.

6. Kim Paffenroth, "Film Depictions of Judas," *Journal of Religion and Film* 5 (2001): 1–11.

7. R. E. Brown, *The Death of the Messiah: From Gethsemane to the Grave; A Commentary on the Passion Narratives in the Four Gospels*; 2 vols., Anchor Bible Reference Library (New York: Doubleday, 1994), 1399–1401.

8. Kim Paffenroth, *Judas: Images of the Lost Disciple* (Louisville, Ky.: Westminster John Knox Press, 2001).

9. It is not clear whether Judas's ruddiness is meant to connect him to the Jewish people as such, as this is not a major theme in the film. On the use of red hair as a marker for Judas, Jews, and Satan, see Ruth Mellinkoff, "Judas's Red Hair and the Jews," *Journal of Jewish Art* 9 (1982): 31–46. See also her excellent study on the representation of the other in western art. Ruth Mellinkoff, *Outcasts: Signs of Otherness in Northern European Art of the Late Middle Ages*, 2 vols., California Studies in the History of Art (Berkeley: University of California Press, 1993), and Ruth Mellinkoff,

Antisemitic Hate Signs in Hebrew Illuminated Manuscripts from Medieval Germany (Jerusalem: Center for Jewish Art, Hebrew University of Jerusalem, 1999). See also W. R. Telford, "The Two Faces of Betrayal: The Characterization of Peter and Judas in the Biblical Epic or Christ Film," in E. Christianson, P. Francis, and W. R. Telford, eds., *Cinéma Divinité: Religion, Theology and the Bible in Film* (London: SCM-Canterbury, 2005), 219, 220, 232 and notes.

10. Pilate is often referred to as a procurator but he was in fact a governor, as Judea did not have a procurator until 44 CE.

11. Josephus, *Antiquities*, 18. 225.

12. Tatum, in *Jesus at the Movies*, 94, refers to Judas' incineration as a "holocaust," referring to the Israelite sacrifice by that name and perhaps also suggesting that Judas' form of suicide in this film is an allusion to the Nazi Holocaust.

13. The idea that Judas's betrayal was in fulfillment of Jesus' own wishes is not unique to modern works of fiction and film, but is apparent also in the recently discovered *Gospel of Judas*, a Coptic manuscript dating from the third or fourth century. For an introduction, see http://www.nationalgeographic.com/lostgospel/?fs=www9. nationalgeographic.com. For analysis, see Bart D. Ehrman, *The Lost Gospel of Judas Iscariot: A New Look at Betrayer and Betrayed* (New York: Oxford University Press, 2006).

CHAPTER 9

1. On the image of the devil throughout antiquity, see Jeffrey Burton Russell, *The Devil: Perceptions of Evil from Antiquity to Primitive Christianity* (Ithaca, N.Y.: Cornell University Press, 1977), and *Satan: The Early Christian Tradition* (Ithaca: Cornell University Press, 1981).

2. For further discussion, see Adele Reinhartz, "A Nice Jewish Girl Reads the Gospel of John," *Semeia 77: Ethics and Reading the Bible*, ed. Gary Phillips and Danna Nolan Fewell (Atlanta: Scholars Press, 1998), 177–193; idem, "'Jews' and Jews in the Fourth Gospel," in *Anti-Judaism and the Fourth Gospel: Papers of the Leuven Colloquium, 2000*, ed. R. Bieringer et al. (Assen: Van Gorcum, 2001), 341–356; and idem, "John 8:31–59 from a Jewish Perspective," in *Remembering for the Future 2000: The Holocaust in an Age of Genocides*, vol. 2, ed. John K. Roth and Elisabeth Maxwell-Meynard (London: Palgrave, 2001), 787–797.

3. On Honi the Circle-Maker, see Babylonian Talmud, Tractate Ta'anit 23a. For an English translation, see Isidore Epstein, *The Babylonian Talmud. Translated into English with Notes, Glossary and Indices, under the Editorship of I. Epstein* (London: Soncino Press, 1961). Seder Mo'ed vol. 4, 115–120.

CHAPTER 10

1. For a comprehensive examination of the Pharisees and their portrayals in ancient Jewish and Christian sources, see Jacob Neusner and Bruce D. Chilton, eds., *In Quest of the Historical Pharisees* (Waco, Texas: Baylor University Press, 2006).

2. One example of many is Günter Stemberger, *Jewish Contemporaries of Jesus: Pharisees, Sadducees, Essenes* (Minneapolis: Fortress, 1995).

3. Acts is the "second volume" of the Gospel of Luke and was written by the same author.

4. See Judith K. Applegate, "'And She Wet His Feet with Her Tears': A Feminist Interpretation of Luke 7.36–50," and Teresa J. Hornsby, "Why Is She Crying? A Feminist Interpretation of Luke 7.36–50,"in *Escaping Eden: New Feminist Perspectives on the Bible*, ed. Harold C. Washington, Susan Lochrie Graham, and Pamela Lee Thimmes, Biblical Seminar 65 (Sheffield, England: Sheffield Academic Press, 1998), 69–90; 91–103.

5. In the Markan parallel, Mark 8:15, the Pharisees are paired with the little-known Herodians: "And he cautioned them, saying, 'Watch out—beware of the yeast of the Pharisees and the yeast of Herod,'" suggesting that even the early Christian traditions did not distinguish definitively among these various groups (cf. also Mark 3:6).

6. Richard Walsh comments that the monster, or robot as he calls it, "suggests romantic fears about industrial and bureaucratic society. The institution that troubles *Godspell* is modern civilization. Once again, we have arrived at the American Romantic aversion to the city and a desire to escape the city for a peaceable garden. The robot is the revenge of industrial society." Walsh, *Reading the Gospels in the Dark*, 87.

7. Even in modern dictionaries, such as the Oxford English Dictionary, "hypocrite" is still given as one of the definitions of "Pharisee."

8. In this prayer, Jews are acknowledging their covenantal relationship with God, which is expressed through the effort to live their lives according to Jewish law. See Hayim Donin, *To Pray as a Jew: A Guide to the Prayer Book and the Synagogue Service.* (New York: Basic Books, 1980), 195.

9. Heinz Schreckenberg notes that the medieval Jewish hat, as well as the Jewish ring, "became defamatory marks of identification." Heinz Schreckenberg, *The Jews in Christian Art: An Illustrated History* (New York: Continuum, 1996), 15.

10. Tatum, *Jesus at the Movies*, 113–114.

11. Oswald Stack and Pier Paolo Pasolini, *Pasolini on Pasolini: Interviews with Oswald Stack* (London: Thames and Hudson, 1969), 82.

12. Walsh, *Reading the Gospels in the Dark*, 104.

13. Ibid., 111.

14. Ibid.

15. Stack and Pasolini, *Pasolini on Pasolini*, 82.

16. Ibid., 83.

17. Nicodemus is identified as a Pharisee in John 3:1. Joseph of Arimathea is nowhere explicitly called a Pharisee but may have received such status by his association with Nicodemus in John 19:38. In Matthew 27:57 Joseph of Arimathea is Jesus' disciple; in Mark 15:43 he is described as a member of council and in Luke 23:51 as a member of council who did not agree with the plot against Jesus.

18. For a detailed historical study of the Pharisees, see Albert I. Baumgarten, *The Flourishing of Jewish Sects in the Maccabean Era: An Interpretation*, Supplements to the Journal for the Study of Judaism, 55 (New York: Brill, 1997). On the question of Pharisaic observance of Jewish law, see Sanders, *Jewish Law from Jesus to the Mishnah*, 131–254.

19. Zeffirelli, *Franco Zeffirelli's Jesus*, 39.

20. Ibid., 45.

CHAPTER 11

1. For a detailed analysis of this film, particularly with regard to its anti-Semitism, see Reinhold Zwick, "Antijüdische Tendenzen im Jesusfilm," *Communicatio Socialis* 30 (1997), 227–246.

2. Richard C. Stern, Clayton N. Jefford, and Guerric De Bona, *Savior on the Silver Screen*, (New York: Paulist Press, 1999).

3. For historical studies of Caiaphas, see Helen K. Bond, *Caiaphas: Friend of Rome and Judge of Jesus?* (Louisville, Ky.: Westminster John Knox Press, 2004); James VanderKam, *From Joshua to Caiaphas: High Priests after the Exile* (Assen: Van Gorcum, 2004).

4. Gerald Eugene Forshey, *American Religious and Biblical Spectaculars*, Media and Society Series (Westport, Conn.: Praeger, 1992), 93.

5. Luke adds an extra interrogation, before Herod Antipas, the tetrarch of Galilee, who was visiting Jerusalem at the time (Luke 23:6–11).

6. The bringing of multiple witnesses is based on the biblical law requiring more than a single witness to a capital crime (Numbers 35:30).

7. R. E. Brown comments that some scholars suggest that the Gospel writer did not know Palestinian customs, given that Jewish high priests generally held office for life while pagan ones were chosen every year. In Brown's view, the reference to Caiaphas as high priest "that year" is intended to emphasize that he was the high priest during the fateful year of Jesus' crucifixion. Brown, *The Gospel According to John*, 1: 439, 444.

8. See John Dominic Crossan, *Who Killed Jesus? Exposing the Roots of Anti-Semitism in the Gospel Story of the Death of Jesus* (San Francisco: HarperSanFrancisco, 1995).

9. On the role of the Judenrat, see Lucille Eichengreen and Rebecca Fromer, *Rumkowski and the Orphans of Lodz* (San Francisco: Mercury House, 2000); POJ Filmproduction AB and Swedish Television (SVTI), *The Story of Chaim Rumkowski and the Jews of Lodz*, video-recording (1982).

CHAPTER 12

1. Cf. Joseph A. Fitzmyer, "Crucifixion in Ancient Palestine, Qumran Literature, and the New Testament," *Catholic Biblical Quarterly* 40 (1978): 493–515; Martin Hengel, *Crucifixion in the Ancient World and the Folly of the Message of the Cross*, trans. John Bowden (London: SCM Press, 1977).

2. There are numerous attempts to reconstruct the historical trial. In addition to commentaries on the Passion narrative, see, for example, Haim Hermann Cohn, *The Trial and Death of Jesus* (New York: Harper & Row, 1971); Ernst Bammel, *The Trial of Jesus: Cambridge Studies in Honour of C.F.D. Moule,* Studies in Biblical Theology, 2d Ser., 13 (London: SCM Press, 1970), Paul Winter, T. Alec Burkill, and Geza Vermes, *On the Trial of Jesus,* 2d ed. (Berlin: De Gruyter, 1974).

3. The representative of Rome in Judea was a procurator only from 44–66 CE. Until 41, the representative was a prefect; 41–44 was a brief period of direct rule by Herod Agrippa II. Gerd Theissen and Annette Merz, *The Historical Jesus: A Comprehensive Guide* (Minneapolis: Fortress, 1998), 455. According to Theissen (ibid., 457), the legal proceedings against Jesus before Pontius Pilate could have been either a *coercitio* or *cognitio*. A *coercitio* allows the Roman governor to employ all compulsions which are necessary to maintain public order; a *cognitio* is a formal legal procedure that includes an accusation, interrogation, confession, and verdict.

4. Pilate's handwashing was intended to emphasize both Pilate's own innocence in Jesus' death and thereby also his assessment that Jesus was innocent. According to Bammel, this act in fact implicated Pilate in that it suggests that Pilate knowingly condemned an innocent man to death. Ernst Bammel and C. F. D. Moule, *Jesus and the Politics of His Day* (Cambridge: Cambridge University Press, 1985), 447.

5. In recent decades, however, documents such as *Nostra Aetate,* from the Catholic Church (1965), and *Bearing Faithful Witness,* from the United Church of Canada (2003), repudiate the notion that all Jews, for all time, are responsible for Jesus' death. *Nostra Aetate,* for example, states, "what happened in His Passion cannot be charged against all the Jews, without distinction, then alive, nor against the Jews of today."

6. On the deicide charge in the history of anti-Semitism, see Robert S. Wistrich, *Antisemitism: The Longest Hatred* (New York: Pantheon, 1991). The charge persists. Film critic Dwight MacDonald was taken to task for a chance comment he made about Jewish responsibility for Jesus' death. His response was as follows:

When I made my gaffe two years ago, I took it for granted, as a WASP by upbringing, that the biblical account of the trial and crucifixion of Jesus was correct. Since then, I've learned, by the chancy methods that journalists learn things, that a good case can be made out that the Gospel writers, for propagandist reasons, played down the part of the Romans in the tragedy and played up that of the Jews. So I'm willing to agree that the matter is obscure and that the hundred or so readers who wrote in objecting to my remarks may have been right about the historical fact. But I'm not willing to admit...that my error—if it was such—was evidence of racial prejudice. We live in a time when the pendulum of social justice has swung back too far, when certain racial groups are sacrosanct, so that when one states, depending on the New Testament, that certain Jews two thousand years ago wanted Jesus killed, one is accused of denouncing all Jews today as "Christ killers."
Dwight Macdonald, *Dwight Macdonald on the Movies* (New York: Prentice-Hall, 1969), 428.

7. John Dominic Crossan, *Who Killed Jesus? Exposing the Roots of Anti-Semitism in the Gospel Story on the Death of Jesus* (San Francisco: HarperSanFrancisco, 1995), 162.

8. E. P. Sanders, *The Historical Figure of Jesus* (London: Penguin, 1993), 273–274.

9. Crossan, *Who Killed Jesus?*, 147–148.

10. Translations from the German are my own.

11. On the persistent association of Jews with the devil in western culture, to which the vague hornlike appearance of Caiaphas' headgear in *Der Galiläer* alludes, see Joshua Trachtenberg, *The Devil and the Jews: The Medieval Conception of the Jew and Its Relation to Modern Antisemitism* (Philadelphia: Jewish Publication Society, 1993).

12. Babington and Evans, *Biblical Epics*, 122.

13. Cecil B. DeMille and Donald Hayne, *The Autobiography of Cecil B. DeMille* (New York: Garland, 1985), 282–84.

14. Bruce Babington and Peter Williams Evans, *Biblical Epics: Sacred Narrative in the Hollywood Cinema* (Manchester: Manchester University Press, 1993), 102, 127.

15. See Ralph Berets, "Changing Images of Justice in American Films," *Legal Studies Forum* 20 (1996): 473–480; Ann M. Algeo, *The Courtroom as Forum: Homicide Trials by Dreiser, Wright, Capote, and Mailer* (New York: P. Lang, 1996).

16. Lloyd Baugh, *Imaging the Divine*, 37–38.

17. Zeffirelli testifies to having been deeply moved by *Nostra Aetate*, the declaration of Vatican II absolving the Jews as a people of collective guilt in the death of Jesus. Zeffirelli, *Franco Zeffirelli's Jesus*, 6.

18. Walsh, *Reading the Gospels in the Dark*, 107.

19. For the text of this introduction, see chapter 2. As a member of the advisory committee, I endorsed this text as the only means of "damage control" possible under the circumstances. Yet I doubt that a few lines scrolled during the opening seconds of a long film can have much impact upon the viewer's interpretation of and response to a set of scenes that occur near the end of the film nearly three hours later.

20. For critical reflections on Gibson's use of this verse, see David Klinghoffer, *"His Blood Be on Us": Mel Gibson and Matthew 27:25.* http://www.beliefnet.com/story/140/story_14043_1.html. August 8, 2005.

21. Zwick, "Antijüdische Tendenzen im Jesusfilm," 227.

CHAPTER 13

1. George F. Custen, *Bio/Pics: How Hollywood Constructed Public History* (new Brunswick, N.J.: Rutgers University Press, 1992), 2.

2. One question, beyond the scope of this study but of tremendous interest to the media and general public alike, is the personal viewpoints of the filmmakers themselves. The issue of anti-Semitism, for example, came to the fore in the period before the release of Mel Gibson's *The Passion of the Christ*. For some, the question was resolved in the summer of 2006, when Gibson was arrested for drunk driving and allegedly uttered anti-Semitic remarks to a police officer. The most entertaining and a propos commentary on this event that I have seen was a poem entitled "The Parable of

Mel" by John Allemang, published in The Globe and Mail, Saturday August 5, 2006, which I quote in full below.

And Jesus said: "Don't think it wise,
When traffic cops inspect your eyes
For signs that you're impaired by booze,
To blame your troubles on the Jews.
A certain man of Malibu,
Who'd clearly had a drink or two,
Instead of acting mild and meek
Became the right-wing Jesus freak
Who turns his Christian-soldier sword
On those who don't think Christ's the Lord.
"His words were vile. And then came worse:
He tried to blame tequila's curse
For all the demons in his brain
That drove him instantly insane,
And promised he'd do all it took
To get back in the Jews' good book:
'I'll say that Auschwitz was no hoax,
And never make priest/rabbi jokes,
Provided you don't crucify
A poor soul nailed for DUI.'
"Humility and sacrifice
Might help a sinner seem more nice,
But God demands a higher cost
Than lessons in the Holocaust –
For pious Pharisees like Mel,
The hot tequila bar of hell.
His films may quote from Holy Writ,
But life unmasks the hypocrite
Who cries for mercy from rehab –
Next time, shut up and take a cab."
                jallemang@globeandmail.com

3. Ibid., 122.

Bibliography

Alexander, Edward. *The Holocaust and the War of Ideas*. New Brunswick, N.J.: Transaction Publishers, 1994.

Algeo, Ann M. *The Courtroom as Forum: Homicide Trials by Dreiser, Wright, Capote, and Mailer*. New York: P. Lang, 1996.

Amishai-Maisels, Ziva. "Demonization of the 'Other' in the Visual Arts." In *Demonizing the Other: Antisemitism, Racism & Xenophobia*, edited by Robert S. Wistrich, 44–72. Amsterdam: Harwood Academic, 1999.

Apostolos-Cappadona, Diane. "The Art of 'Seeing': Classical Paintings and *Ben Hur*." In *Image and Likeness: Religious Visions in American Film Classics*, edited by John R. May, 104–115. Mahwah, N.J.: Paulist Press, 1992.

Applegate, Judith K. " 'And She Wet His Feet with Her Tears': A Feminist Interpretation of Luke 7.36–50." In *Escaping Eden: New Feminist Perspectives on the Bible*, edited by Harold C. Washington, Susan Lochrie Graham, and Pamela Lee Thimmes, 69–90. Sheffield, England: Sheffield Academic Press, 1998.

Arnal, William E. "Making and Re-Making the Jesus-Sign: Contemporary Markings on the Body of Christ." In *Whose Historical Jesus?* edited by William E. Arnal and Michel R. Desjardins, 308–319. Published by Canadian Corporation for Studies in Religion. Waterloo, Ontario: Wilfrid Laurier University Press, 1997.

Babington, Bruce, and Peter William Evans. *Biblical Epics: Sacred Narrative in the Hollywood Cinema*. Manchester: Manchester University Press, 1993.

Baker, James T. "The Red-Haired Saint." *The Christian Century* 94 (1977): 328–332.

Bammel, Ernst, and C. F. D. Moule. *Jesus and the Politics of His Day.* Cambridge: Cambridge University Press, 1985.

Bammel Ernst. *The Trial of Jesus: Cambridge Studies in Honour of C.F.D. Moule*, Studies in Biblical Theology, 2d Ser., 13. London: SCM Press, 1970.

Baugh, Lloyd. *Imaging the Divine: Jesus and Christ-Figures in Film, Communication, Culture and Theology.* Kansas City: Sheed & Ward, 1997.

Baumgarten, Albert I. *The Flourishing of Jewish Sects in the Maccabean Era: An Interpretation, Supplement to the Journal for the Study of Judaism, 55.* New York: Brill, 1997.

Becker, Adam H., and Annette Y. Reed, eds. *The Ways that Never Parted: Jews and Christians in Late Antiquity and the Early Middle Ages.* Tübingen: Mohr-Siebeck, 2003.

Berets, Ralph. "Changing Images of Justice in American Films." *Legal Studies Forum* 20 (1996): 473–480.

Berlin, Andrea, and Jodi Magness. *Two Archaeologists Comment on "The Passion of the Christ."* http://www.archaeological.org/pdfs/papers/Comments_on_The_Passion .pdf, 2003. August 28, 2005.

Birnbaum, Philip. *Ha-Sidur Ha-Shalem.* New York: Hebrew Publishing Co., 1949.

Boer, Esther de. *The Gospel of Mary: Beyond a Gnostic and a Biblical Mary Magdalene, Supplement to the Journal for the Study of the New Testament, 260.* London: T & T Clark International, 2004.

Bonaventure, Isa Ragusa, and Rosalie B. Green. *Meditations on the Life of Christ: An Illustrated Manuscript of the Fourteenth Century.* Princeton Monographs in Art and Archaeology, 35. Princeton, N.J.: Princeton University Press, 1961.

Bond, Helen K. *Caiaphas: Friend of Rome and Judge of Jesus?* 1st ed. Louisville, Ky.: Westminster John Knox Press, 2004.

Borg, Marcus J. *Jesus in Contemporary Scholarship.* Valley Forge, Pa.: Trinity Press International, 1994.

Boys, Mary C. *Has God Only One Blessing? Judaism as a Source of Christian Self-Understanding.* Mahwah, N.J.: Paulist Press, 2000.

Brown, Dan. *The Da Vinci Code.* New York: Doubleday, 2003.

Brown, Raymond Edward. *The Birth of the Messiah: A Commentary on the Infancy Narratives in the Gospels of Matthew and Luke.* Updated ed., Anchor Bible Reference Library. New York: Doubleday, 1993.

———. *The Community of the Beloved Disciple.* New York: Paulist Press, 1979.

———. *The Death of the Messiah: From Gethsemane to the Grave; A Commentary on the Passion Narratives in the Four Gospels.* 2 vols., Anchor Bible Reference Library. New York: Doubleday, 1994.

———. *The Gospel According to John.* 1st ed., 2 vols. Garden City, N.Y.: Doubleday, 1966.

Brunette, Peter. *Roberto Rossellini.* Berkeley: University of California Press, 1996.

Buby, Bertrand. *Mary of Galilee: A Trilogy of Marian Studies.* 3 vols. New York: Alba House, 1994.

Carter, Everett. "Cultural History Written with Lightning: The Significance of *the Birth of a Nation*." In *Hollywood as Historian: American Film in a Cultural Context*, edited by Peter C. Rollins, 9–19. Lexington: University of Kentucky Press, 1983.

Cartlidge, David R., and J. K. Elliott. *Art and the Christian Apocrypha*. New York: Routledge, 2001.

Christianson, Eric S., Peter Francis, and William R. Telford. *Cinéma Divinité: Religion, Theology and the Bible in Film*. London: SCM Press, 2005.

Clark, Elizabeth. *The Roles for Women*. http://www.pbs.org/wgbh/pages/frontline/shows/religion/first/roles.html. August 7, 2005.

Cohn, Haim Hermann. *The Trial and Death of Jesus*. New York: Harper & Row, 1971.

Collins, John J. *The Scepter and the Star: The Messiahs of the Dead Sea Scrolls and Other Ancient Literature*. 1st ed., Anchor Bible Reference Library. New York: Doubleday, 1995.

———. *The Apocalyptic Imagination: An Introduction to Jewish Apocalyptic Literature*. 2d ed., Biblical Resource Series. Grand Rapids, Mich.: Eerdmans, 1998.

Corley, Kathleen E., and Robert L. Webb. *Jesus and Mel Gibson's "The Passion of the Christ": The Film, the Gospels and the Claims of History*. New York: Continuum, 2004.

Croly, George, William David Davies, Eric M. Meyers, David Roberts, and Sarah Schroth. *Jerusalem and the Holy Land Rediscovered: The Prints of David Roberts (1796–1864)*. Durham, N.C.: Duke University Museum of Art, 1996.

Crossan, John Dominic. "Hymn to a Savage God." In *Jesus and Mel Gibson's "The Passion of the Christ": The Film, the Gospels and the Claims of History*, edited by Kathleen E. Corley and Robert L. Webb, 8–27. New York: Continuum, 2004.

———. *The Historical Jesus: The Life of a Mediterranean Jewish Peasant*. 1st ed. San Francisco: HarperSanFrancisco, 1991.

———. *Who Killed Jesus? Exposing the Roots of Anti-Semitism in the Gospel Story of the Death of Jesus*. San Francisco: HarperSanFrancisco, 1995.

Cuneo, Michael W. *American Exorcism: Expelling Demons in the Land of Plenty*. 1st ed. New York: Doubleday, 2001.

Custen, George F. *Bio/Pics: How Hollywood Constructed Public History*. New Brunswick, N.J.: Rutgers University Press, 1992.

———. "The Mechanical Life in the Age of Human Reproduction: American Biopics, 1961–1980." *Biography* 23 (2000): 127–159.

D'Angelo, Mary Rose. "A Critical Note: John 20:17 and Apocalypse of Moses 31," *Journal of Theological Studies* 4 (1990): 529–536.

———. "Reconstructing 'Real' Women in Gospel Literature." In *Women and Christian Origins*, edited by Ross Shepard Kraemer and Mary Rose D'Angelo, 105–128. New York: Oxford University Press, 1999.

Dart, John. *The Jesus of Heresy and History: The Discovery and Meaning of the Nag Hammadi Gnostic Library*. 1st ed. San Francisco: Harper & Row, 1988.

Dean, William D. *The American Spiritual Culture: And the Invention of Jazz, Football, and the Movies*. New York: Continuum, 2002.

DeMille, Cecil B., and Donald Hayne. *The Autobiography of Cecil B. DeMille*. New York: Garland, 1985.

Denby, David. "Nailed: Mel Gibson's 'The Passion of the Christ.'" *New Yorker*, March 1, 2004. http://www.newyorker.com/printale/?critics/040301crci.

Denny, Don. *The Annunciation from the Right: From Early Christian Times to the Sixteenth Century*. Outstanding Dissertations in the Fine Arts. New York: Garland, 1977.

Donahue, John R., and Daniel J. Harrington. *The Gospel of Mark*. Collegeville, Minn.: Liturgical Press, 2002.

Donin, Hayim. *To Pray as a Jew: A Guide to the Prayer Book and the Synagogue Service*. New York: Basic Books, 1980.

Doré, Gustave. *The Doré Bible Illustrations*. New York: Dover Publications, 1974.

Douglas, Lloyd C. *The Robe*. Toronto: Thomas Allen, 1942.

Ehrman, Bart D. *The Lost Gospel of Judas Iscariot: A New Look at Betrayer and Betrayed* (New York: Oxford University Press, 2006).

———. *Truth and Fiction in the Da Vinci Code: A Historian Reveals What We Really Know About Jesus, Mary Magdalene, and Constantine*. New York: Oxford University Press, 2004.

Eichengreen, Lucille, and Rebecca Fromer. *Rumkowski and the Orphans of Lodz*. San Francisco: Mercury House, 2000.

Epstein, Isidore, ed. *The Babylonian Talmud, Seder Mo'ed* 1. London: Soncino Press, 1938.

Erens, Patricia. *The Jew in American Cinema, Jewish Literature and Culture*. Bloomington: Indiana University Press, 1984.

Federation of Reconstructionist Congregations and Havurot. *Kol Haneshamah: Shabbat Ve-hagim*. 3d ed. Wyncote, Pa.: Reconstructionist Press, 1994.

Finkelstein, Louis, ed. *The Cambridge History of Judaism, Volume 3: The Early Roman Period*. Cambridge: Cambridge University Press, 1999.

Fitzmyer, Joseph A. "Crucifixion in Ancient Palestine, Qumran Literature, and the New Testament." *Catholic Biblical Quarterly* 40 (1978): 493–515.

———. *The Gospel According to Luke: Introduction, Translation, and Notes*. 2d ed. 2 vols. Garden City, N.Y.: Doubleday, 1983.

Forshey, Gerald Eugene. *American Religious and Biblical Spectaculars* Media and Society Series. Westport, Conn.: Praeger, 1992.

Fox, Richard Wightman. *Jesus in America: Personal Savior, Cultural Hero, National Obsession*. 1st ed. San Francisco: HarperSanFrancisco, 2004.

Fredriksen, Paula. *Jesus of Nazareth, King of the Jews: A Jewish Life and the Emergence of Christianity*. 1st ed. New York: Knopf, 1999.

———. "What You See Is What You Get: Context and Content in Current Research on the Historical Jesus." *Theology Today* 52 (1995): 75–95.

Freyne, Sean. *Galilee and Gospel: Collected Essays*. Tubingen: Mohr Siebeck, 2000.

———. *Galilee, Jesus, and the Gospels: Literary Approaches and Historical Investigations*. Dublin: Gill and MacMillan, 1988.

Gallagher, Tag. *The Adventures of Roberto Rossellini: His Life and Films*. New York: Da Capo Press, 1998.

Gaventa, Beverly Roberts. "Standing Near the Cross: Mary and the Crucifixion of Jesus." In *Blessed One: Protestant Perspectives on Mary*, edited by Beverly Roberts Gaventa and Cynthia L. Rigby, 47–56. Louisville, Ky.: Westminster John Knox, 2002.

Goa, David J. "The Passion, Classical Art and Re-Presentation." In *Jesus and Mel Gibson's "The Passion of the Christ": The Film, the Gospels and the Claims of History*, edited by Kathleen E. Corley and Robert L. Webb, 151–159. New York: Continuum, 2004.

Gombrich, E. H., Leonardo, Pietro C. Marani, and Palazzo Reale di Milano. *Il Genio E Le Passioni: Leonardo Da Vinci E Il Cenacolo: Precedenti, Innovazioni, Riflessi Di Un Capolavoro*. Firenze: Artificio, 2001.

Goodacre, Mark. *The Case against Q: Studies in Markan Priority and the Synoptic Problem*. Harrisburg, Pa.: Trinity Press International, 2002.

———. "The Power of the Passion: Reacting and Over-Reacting to Gibson's Artistic Vision." In *Jesus and Mel Gibson's "The Passion of the Christ": The Film, the Gospels and the Claims of History*, edited by Kathleen E. Corley and Robert L. Webb, 28–44. New York: Continuum, 2004.

Grindon, Leger. *Shadows on the Past: Studies in the Historical Fiction Film, Culture and the Moving Image*. Philadelphia: Temple University Press, 1994.

Haas, N. "Anthropological Observations on the Skeletal Remains from Giv'at Hamivtar." *Israel Exploration Journal* 20 (1970): 38–59.

Haskins, Susan. *Mary Magdalen: Myth and Metaphor*. London: HarperCollins, 1993.

Hengel, Martin. *Crucifixion in the Ancient World and the Folly of the Message of the Cross*. Trans. John Bowden. London: SCM Press, 1977.

Herford, R. Travers. *Christianity in Talmud and Midrash*. London: Williams, 1903; reprint, New York: Ktav, 1975.

Higashi, Sumiko. *Virgins, Vamps and Flappers: The American Silent Movie Heroine*, Monographs in Women's Studies. St. Albans, Vt.: Eden Press Women's Publications, 1978.

Hornsby, Teresa J. "Why Is She Crying? A Feminist Interpretation of Luke 7:36–50." In *Escaping Eden: New Feminist Perspectives on the Bible*, edited by Harold C. Washington, Susan Lochrie Graham, and Pamela Lee Thimmes, 91–103. Sheffield, England: Sheffield Academic Press, 1998.

Jansen, Katherine Ludwig. *The Making of the Magdalen: Preaching and Popular Devotion in the Later Middle Ages*. Princeton, N.J.: Princeton University Press, 2000.

———. "Maria Magdalena: Apostolorum Apostola." In *Women Preachers and Prophets through Two Millennia of Christianity*, edited by Beverly Mayne Kienzle and Pamela J. Walker, 57–96. Berkeley: University of California Press, 1998.

Johnson, E. Elizabeth. *Truly Our Sister: A Theology of Mary in the Communion of Saints*. New York: Continuum, 2003.

———. "'Who Is My Mother?' Family Values in the Gospel of Mark." In *Blessed One: Protestant Perspectives on Mary*, edited by Beverly Roberts and Cynthia L. Rigby Gaventa, 32–46. Louisville, Ky.: Westminster John Knox, 2002.

Johnson, Luke Timothy. *The Real Jesus: The Misguided Quest for the Historical Jesus and the Truth of the Traditional Gospels*. San Francisco: HarperSanFrancisco, 1996.

Josephus, Flavius, H. St. J. Thackeray, and Ralph Marcus. *Josephus: With an English Translation by H. St. J. Thackeray*. 9 vols. Cambridge: Harvard University Press, 1958.

Kazantzakis, Nikos. *The Last Temptation. A Novel*. 1st English ed. Oxford: B. Cassirer, 1961.

King, Karen L. *The Gospel of Mary of Magdala: Jesus and the First Woman Apostle*. Santa Rosa, Calif.: Polebridge Press, 2003.

Kinnard, Roy, and Tim Davis. *Divine Images: A History of Jesus on the Screen*. New York, N.Y.: Carol Publishing Group, 1992.

Kirschenbaum, Aaron. *Self-Incrimination in Jewish Law*. New York: Burning Bush Press, 1970.

Klassen, William. *Judas: Betrayer or Friend of Jesus?* Minneapolis: Fortress, 1996.

Klinghoffer, David. *"His Blood Be on Us": Mel Gibson and Matthew 27:25*. http://www.beliefnet.com/story/140/story_14043_1.html. August 8, 2005.

Kozloff, Sarah. *Invisible Story-Tellers: Voice-over Narration in American Fiction Film*. Berkeley: University of California Press, 1988.

Kuryluk, Ewa. *Veronica and Her Cloth: History, Symbolism, and Structure of a "True" Image*. Oxford: Blackwell, 1991.

Leff, Leonard J., and Jerold Simmons. *The Dame in the Kimono: Hollywood, Censorship, and the Production Code from the 1920s to the 1960s*. New York: Doubleday, 1990.

Levine, Lee Israel. *The Ancient Synagogue: The First Thousand Years*. New Haven: Yale University Press, 2000.

———. "Herod the Great." In *The Anchor Bible Dictionary*, edited by David Noel Freedman, 161–169. New York: Doubleday, 1992.

Litwack, Len F. *"The Birth of a Nation."* In *Past Imperfect: History According to the Movies*, edited by Mark C. Carnes, 136–141. New York: H. Holt, 1996.

Lytton, Edward Bulwer. *Last Days of Pompeii*. London: R. Bentley, 1834.

Maccoby, Hyam. *Jesus the Pharisee*. London: SCM Press, 2003.

———. *Judas Iscariot and the Myth of Jewish Evil*. (London: Peter Halban, 1992.)

Macdonald, Dwight. *Dwight Macdonald on the Movies*. New York: Prentice-Hall, 1969.

Malbon, Elizabeth Struthers. *In the Company of Jesus: Characters in Mark's Gospel*. 1st ed. Louisville, Ky.: Westminster John Knox Press, 2000.

Malvern, Marjorie M. *Venus in Sackcloth: The Magdalen's Origins and Metamorphoses*. Carbondale: Southern Illinois University Press, 1975.

Marcus, Joel. *Mark 1–8: A New Translation with Introduction and Commentary*. Edited by William Foxwell Albright and David Noel Freedman. Vol. 27, *The Anchor Bible*. New York: Doubleday, 2000.

Marjanen, Antti. *The Woman Jesus Loved: Mary Magdalene in the Nag Hammadi Library and Related Documents*, Nag Hammadi and Manichaean Studies, 40. New York: Brill, 1996.

Marsh, Clive, and Gaye Ortiz, eds. *Explorations in Theology and Film: Movies and Meaning*. Oxford: Blackwell, 1998.

Mason, Steve. *Understanding Josephus, Journal for the Study of the Pseudepigrapha. Supplement Series, 32*. Sheffield: Sheffield Academic Press, 1998.

McGehee, Michael. "A Less Theological Reading of John 20:17," *Journal of Biblical Literature* 105 (1986): 299–302.

Medved, Michael. *Hollywood Vs. America: Popular Culture and the War on Traditional Values*. 1st ed. New York: HarperCollins, 1992.

Meier, John P. *A Marginal Jew: Rethinking the Historical Jesus*. Anchor Bible Reference Library. New York: Doubleday, 1991.

Mellinkoff, Ruth, and Universitah ha-°Ivrit bi-Yerushalayim. Merkaz le-omanut Yehudit. *Antisemitic Hate Signs in Hebrew Illuminated Manuscripts from Medieval Germany*. Jerusalem: Center for Jewish Art, Hebrew University of Jerusalem, 1999.

———. "Judas's Red Hair and the Jews." *Journal of Jewish Art* 9 (1982): 31–46.

———. *Outcasts: Signs of Otherness in Northern European Art of the Late Middle Ages*. 2 vols., California Studies in the History of Art, 32. Berkeley: University of California Press, 1993.

Miles, Margaret Ruth. *Seeing and Believing: Religion and Values in the Movies*. Boston: Beacon Press, 1996.

Miller, John W. *Jesus at Thirty: A Psychological and Historical Portrait*. Minneapolis: Fortress, 1997.

Neusner, Jacob, and Bruce D. Chilton, eds. *In Quest of the Historical Pharisees*. Waco, Texas: Baylor University Press, 2006.

Paffenroth, Kim. "Film Depictions of Judas." *Journal of Religion and Film* 5 (2001): 1–11.

———. *Judas: Images of the Lost Disciple*. Louisville, Ky.: Westminster John Knox Press, 2001.

Parales, Heidi Bright. *Hidden Voices: Biblical Women and Our Christian Heritage*. Macon, Ga.: Smyth and Helwys, 1998.

Parish, James Robert. *Prostitution in Hollywood Films: Plots, Critiques, Casts, and Credits for 389 Theatrical and Made-for-Television Releases*. Jefferson, N.C.: McFarland, 1992.

Pelikan, Jaroslav Jan. *Mary through the Centuries: Her Place in the History of Culture*. New Haven: Yale University Press, 1996.

Perkins, Pheme. "Mary in Johannine Traditions." In *Mary, Woman of Nazareth: Biblical and Theological Perspectives*, edited by Doris Donnelly, 109–122. New York: Paulist Press, 1989.

Phipps, William E. *Was Jesus Married? The Distortion of Sexuality in the Christian Tradition*. 1st ed. New York: Harper & Row, 1970.

Plaskow, Judith. "Anti-Judaism in Feminist Christian Interpretation." In *Searching the Scriptures*, edited by Elisabeth Schèussler Fiorenza, 117–129. New York: Crossroad, 1993.

POJ Filmproduction AB and Swedish television (SVTI). *The Story of Chaim Rumkowski and the Jews of Lodz*. Video-recording, 1982.

Prothero, Stephen R. *American Jesus: How the Son of God Became a National Icon.* 1st American ed. New York: Farrar, Straus, and Giroux, 2003.

Reinhartz, Adele. "A Fork in the Road or a Multi-Lane Highway? New Perspectives on 'The Parting of the Ways' Between Judaism and Christianity." *The Changing Face of Judaism, Christianity and Other Greco-Roman Religions in Antiquity.* Studien zu den Jüdischen Schriften aus hellenistisch-römischer Zeit, Bd 2, Gütersloh: Gütersloher Verlagshaus GmbH, 2005.

———. "'And the Word Was Begotten': Divine Epigenesis in the Gospel of John." *Semeia* 85 (1999): *God the Father in the Gospel of John,* ed. Adele Reinhartz, 83–103.

———. "A Nice Jewish Girl Reads the Gospel of John." *Semeia 77: Ethics and Reading the Bible,* edited by Gary Phillips and Danna Nolan Fewell. Atlanta: Scholars Press, 1998.

———. "From Narrative to History: The Resurrection of Mary and Martha." In *"Women Like This": New Perspectives on Jewish Women in the Greco-Roman World,* edited by Amy-Jill Levine, 161–84. Atlanta: Society of Biblical Literature, 1991.

———. "'Jews' and Jews in the Fourth Gospel." In *Anti-Judaism and the Fourth Gospel: Papers of the Leuven Colloquium, 2000,* edited by Reimund Bieringer, 341–56. Assen: Van Gorcum, 2001.

———. "To Love the Lord: An Intertextual Reading of John 20." In *The Labour of Reading: Desire, Alienation, and Biblical Interpretation,* edited by Fiona C. Black, Erin Runions, and Roland Boer, 53–69. Atlanta: Society of Biblical Literature, 1999.

Ricci, Carla. *Mary Magdalene and Many Others: Women Who Followed Jesus.* Minneapolis: Fortress, 1994.

Richardson, Peter. *Herod: King of the Jews and Friend of the Romans,* Studies on Personalities of the New Testament. Columbia: University of South Carolina Press, 1996.

Rohner, Ronald P., and Robert A. Veneziano. "The Importance of Father Love: History and Contemporary Evidence." *Review of General Psychology* 5, no. 4 (2001): 382–405.

Ruether, Rosemary Radford. *Mary, the Feminine Face of the Church.* London: SCM Press, 1977.

Russell, Jeffrey Burton. *The Devil: Perceptions of Evil from Antiquity to Primitive Christianity.* Ithaca, N.Y.: Cornell University Press, 1977.

———. *Satan: The Early Christian Tradition.* Ithaca, N.Y.: Cornell University Press, 1981.

Safrai, Hannah. "Women and the Ancient Synagogue." In *Daughters of the King: Women and the Synagogue,* edited by Susan Grossman and Rivka Haut, 39–49. Philadelphia: Jewish Publication Society, 1992.

Saldarini, Anthony J. *Pharisees, Scribes and Sadducees in Palestinian Society: A Sociological Approach,* The Biblical Resource Series. Cambridge: Eerdmans, 2001.

Sanders, E. P. *The Historical Figure of Jesus.* London: Penguin, 1993.

————. "Jesus and the First Table of the Jewish Law." In *Jews and Christians Speak of Jesus*, edited by Arthur E. Zannoni, 55–73. Minneapolis: Fortress, 1994.

————. *Jesus and Judaism*. 1st Fortress Press ed. Philadelphia: Fortress, 1985.

————. *Jewish Law from Jesus to the Mishnah: Five Studies*. London/Philadelphia: SCM Press; Trinity Press International, 1990.

Sanders, E. P. and Margaret Davies. *Studying the Synoptic Gospels*. London/ Philadelphia: SCM Press; Trinity Press International, 1989.

Saramago, José. *The Gospel According to Jesus Christ*. Trans. Giovanni Pontiero. 1st Harvest ed., Harvest in Translation. San Diego: Harcourt Brace, 1994.

Sarna, Jonathan D. *American Judaism: A History*. New Haven: Yale University Press, 2004.

Sawicki, Marianne. "Magdalenes and Tiberiennes: City Women in the Entourage of Jesus." In *Transformative Encounters: Jesus and Women Re-Viewed*, edited by Ingrid Rosa Kitzberger, 181–202. Leiden: Brill, 2000.

Schaberg, Jane. "Fast Forwarding to the Magdalene." In *Semeia 74: Biblical Glamour and Hollywood Glitz*, edited by Alice Bach, 33–45. Atlanta: Society of Biblical Literature, 1996.

————. *The Illegitimacy of Jesus: A Feminist Theological Interpretation of the Infancy Narratives*, Biblical Seminar, 28. Sheffield: Sheffield Academic Press, 1995.

————. *The Resurrection of Mary Magdalene: Legends, Apocrypha, and the Christian Testament*. New York: Continuum, 2002.

Schiffman, Lawrence H. *From Text to Tradition: A History of Second Temple and Rabbinic Judaism*. Hoboken, N.J.: Ktav Publishing House, 1991.

————. "The Jewishness of Jesus: Commandments Concerning Interpersonal Relations." In *Jews & Christians Speak of Jesus*, edited by Arthur E. Zannoni, 37–53. Minneapolis: Fortress, 1994.

Schnackenburg, Rudolf. *The Gospel According to St. John*. New York: Seabury Press, 1980.

Schneemelcher, Wilhelm, and R. McL Wilson. *New Testament Apocrypha*. Rev. ed. 2 vols. Louisville, Ky.: Westminster John Knox Press, 1991.

Schneiders, Sandra M. "John 20:11–18: The Encounter of the Easter Jesus with Mary Magdalene—A Transformative Feminist Reading." In *What Is John? Readers and Readings of the Fourth Gospel*, edited by Fernando F. Segovia, 155–168. Atlanta: Scholars Press, 1996.

Schottroff, Luise. "Women as Followers of Jesus in New Testament Times." In *The Bible and Liberation: Political and Social Hermeneutics*, edited by Norman K. Gottwald and Richard A. Horsley, 453–461. Maryknoll, N.Y.: Orbis Books, 1993.

Schreckenberg, Heinz. *The Jews in Christian Art: An Illustrated History*. New York: Continuum, 1996.

Schürer, Emil, Geza Vermes, and Fergus Millar. *The History of the Jewish People in the Age of Jesus Christ (175 B.C.–A.D. 135)*. Rev. ed., vol. 1 (Edinburgh: T.&T. Clark, 1973.)

Shapiro, James S. *Oberammergau: The Troubling Story of the World's Most Famous Passion Play*. New York: Pantheon, 2000.

Shuler, Philip L. *A Genre for the Gospels: The Biographical Character of Matthew.*
    Philadelphia: Fortress, 1982.

Simon, John Ivan. "Christ in Concrete." In *Private Screenings*, 150–154. New York:
    Macmillan, 1967.

Skinner, James M. *The Cross and the Cinema: The Legion of Decency and the National
    Catholic Office for Motion Pictures, 1933–1970.* Westport, Conn.: Praeger, 1993.

Sklar, Robert. *Movie-Made America: A Cultural History of American Movies.* Rev. and
    updated ed. New York: Vintage, 1994.

Smith, D. Moody. *John among the Gospels.* 2d ed. Columbia: University of South
    Carolina Press, 2001.

Smith, Morton. *Jesus the Magician.* 1st ed. New York: Harper and Row, 1978.

Solomon, Jon. *The Ancient World in the Cinema.* Rev. and expanded ed. New Haven:
    Yale University Press, 2001.

Stack, Oswald, and Pier Paolo Pasolini. *Pasolini on Pasolini: Interviews with Oswald
    Stack.* London: Thames & Hudson, 1969.

Steinberg, Leo. *The Sexuality of Christ in Renaissance Art and in Modern Oblivion.* 2d ed.
    Chicago: University of Chicago Press, 1996.

Stemberger, Günter. *Jewish Contemporaries of Jesus: Pharisees, Sadducees, Essenes.*
    Minneapolis: Fortress, 1995.

Stern, Richard C., Clayton N. Jefford, and Guerric DeBona. *Savior on the Silver Screen.*
    New York: Paulist Press, 1999.

Tatum, W. Barnes. *Jesus at the Movies: A Guide to the First Hundred Years.* Santa Rosa,
    Calif.: Polebridge Press, 1997.

———. *Jesus at the Movies: A Guide to the First Hundred Years.* Rev. and expanded ed.
    Santa Rosa, Calif.: Polebridge Press, 2004.

Telford, William R. "'His Blood Be Upon Us, and Our Children': The Treatment
    of Jews and Judaism in the Christ Film." In *Cinéma Divinité: Religion, Theol-
    ogy and the Bible in Film,* edited by Eric S. Christianson, Peter Francis, and
    William R. Telford, 266–309. London: SCM Press, 2005.

———. "Jesus Christ Movie Star: The Depiction of Jesus in the Cinema." In
    Explorations in Theology and Film: Movies and Meaning, edited by Clive Marsh and
    Gaye Ortiz, 115–139. Malden, Mass.: Blackwell, 1998.

Theissen, Gerd, and Annette Merz. *The Historical Jesus: A Comprehensive Guide.*
    Minneapolis: Fortress, 1998.

Tissot, James Jacques Joseph. *The Life of Our Saviour Jesus Christ: Three Hundred and
    Sixty-Five Compositions from the Four Gospels, with Notes and Explanatory
    Drawings.* London: Sampson Low, Marston & Company, 1899.

Trachtenberg, Joshua. *The Devil and the Jews: The Medieval Conception of the Jew and
    Its Relation to Modern Antisemitism.* Philadelphia: Jewish Publication Society,
    1993.

VanderKam, James C. *From Joshua to Caiaphas: High Priests after the Exile.* Assen: Van
    Gorcum, 2004.

Vermes, Geza. *Jesus and the World of Judaism.* London: SCM Press, 1983.

Wallace, Lew. *Ben Hur: A Tale of the Christ.* New York: Harper and Brothers, 1901.

Walsh, Richard. *Reading the Gospels in the Dark: Portrayals of Jesus in Film*. Harrisburg, PA: Trinity Press International, 2003.

Webb, Robert L. "*The Passion* and the Influence of Emmerich's *the Dolorous Passion of Our Lord Jesus Christ*." In *Jesus and Mel Gibson's "The Passion of the Christ": The Film, the Gospels and the Claims of History*, edited by Kathleen E. Corley and Robert L. Webb, 160–172. New York: Continuum, 2004.

Winsor, Ann Roberts. *A King Is Bound in the Tresses: Allusions to the Song of Songs in the Fourth Gospel*, Studies in Biblical Literature, 6. New York: P. Lang, 1999.

Winter, Paul, T. Alec Burkill, and Gâeza Vermáes. *On the Trial of Jesus*. 2d ed. New York: De Gruyter, 1974.

Wistrich, Robert S. *Antisemitism: The Longest Hatred*. 1st American ed. New York: Pantheon, 1991.

Wooden, Cindy. "Pope Never Commented on Gibson's 'Passion' Film, Says Papal Secretary." *Catholic News Service*, January 19, 2004.

Wrede, William. *The Messianic Secret: Library of Theological Translations*. Greenwood, S.C.: Attic Press, 1971.

Wright, N. T. *Christian Origins and the Question of God*. 2 vols. 2d impression with corrections. London: SPCK, 1993.

Wyke, Maria. *Projecting the Past: Ancient Rome, Cinema, and History*, The New Ancient World. New York: Routledge, 1997.

Zeffirelli, Franco. *Franco Zeffirelli's Jesus: A Spiritual Diary*. Transl. Willis J. Egan. San Francisco: Harper & Row, 1984.

Zwick, Reinhold. "Antijüdische Tendenzen im Jesusfilm." *Communicatio Socialis* 30 (1997): 227–46.

———. *Evangelienrezeption im Jesusfilm: Ein Beitrag Zur Intermedialen Wirkungsgeschichte Des Neuen Testaments*, Studien Zur Theologie Und Praxis Der Seelsorge, 25. Würzburg: Seelsorge/Echter, 1997.

Filmography

Barabbas. Dir. Richard Fleischer. Video. Columbia Pictures, 1962.

Ben-Hur. Dir. Fred Niblo. Video. Metro-Goldwyn-Mayer, 1925.

Ben-Hur. Dir. William Wyler. Video. Metro-Goldwyn-Mayer, 1959.

The Big Fisherman. Dir. Frank Borzage. Video. Metro-Goldwyn-Mayer, 1959.

The Birth of a Nation. Dir. D.W. Griffith. Video. Epoch Film, 1915.

Christus. Dir. Guilio Antamoro. Video. Cines, 1917.

The Crown of Thorns. Dir. Robert Wiene. Video. Kinematrade, 1934.

The Da Vinci Code. Dir. Ron Howard. Film. Columbia Pictures, 2006

Der Galiläer. Dir. Dimitri Buchowetzki. Video. Express-Films, 1921.

From the Manger to the Cross. Dir. Sidney Olcott. Video. Kalem, 1912.

Godspell. Dir. David Greene. Video. Columbia Pictures, 1973.

Golgotha. Dir. Julien Duvivier. Video. Metro-Goldwyn-Mayer, 1943.

The Gospel According to St. Matthew. Dir. Pier Pablo Pasolini. Video. Arco Films, 1964.

The Gospel of John. Dir. Philip Saville. DVD. Toronto Film Studios, 2003.

The Greatest Story Ever Told. Dir. George Stevens. Video. United Artists, 1965.

He Who Must Die. Dir. Jules Dassin. Video. Kassler Films, 1957.

Il Messia. Dir. Roberto Rossellini. Video. 20th Century Fox, 1975.

I.N.R.I.. Dir. Robert Wiene. Video. Bayerische Film, 1923.

Intolerance: Love's Struggle Through the Ages. Dir. D.W. Griffith. Video. Triangle, 1916.

Jesus. Dir. John Krish and Peter Sykes. Prod. John Heyman. Video. Warner Brothers, 1979.

Jesus. Dir. Roger Young. DVD. Lions Gate, 1999.

Jesus Christ Superstar. Dir. Norman Jewison. Video. Universal Pictures, 1973.

Jesus of Montreal. Dir. Denys Arcand. Video. Orion Classics, 1989.

Jesus of Nazareth. Dir. Franco Zeffirelli. Video. National Broadcasting, 1977.

The King of Kings. Dir. Cecil B. DeMille. Video. Cinema Corporation of America, 1927.

King of Kings. Dir. Nicholas Ray. Video. Metro-Goldwyn-Mayer, 1961.

The Last Temptation of Christ. Dir. Martin Scorsese. Video. Universal Studios, 1988.

The Life of Brian. Dir. Terry Jones. DVD. Orion Pictures, 1979.

The Master and Margareth. Dir. Yuri Kara. Video. Tvorcheskaya Assotsiatsiya Mezhdunarodnykh Programm, 1994.

The Milky Way. Dir. Luis Buñuel. Video. American Cinematheque, 1969.

The Miracle Maker. Dir. Derek W. Hayes and Stanislav Sokolov. Video. American Broadcasting Company, 2000.

The Nativity Story. Dir. Catherine Hardwicke. Forthcoming. New Line Cinema, 2006.

Pale Rider. Dir. Clint Eastwood. Video. Warner Brothers, 1985.

The Passion of the Christ. Dir. Mel Gibson. Film. Icon Productions, 2004.

The Passion Play at Oberammergau. Dir. Henry C. Vincent. Video. Edison Manufacturing Company, 1898.

Quo Vadis. Dir. Mervyn LeRoy. Video. Metro-Goldwyn-Mayer, 1951.

The Robe. Dir. Henry Koster. Video. 20th Century Fox, 1966.

Salome. Dir. Charles Bryant. Video. Nazimova Productions, 1923.

Salome. Dir. William Dieterle. Video. Columbia Pictures, 1953

The Ten Commandments. Dir. Cecil B. DeMille. Video. Paramount Pictures, 1923.

The Ten Commandments. Dir. Cecil B. DeMille. Video. Paramount Pictures, 1956.

Index of Ancient Sources

Modern Author Index

Subject Index

This index is arranged alphabetically in letter-by-letter order. Page numbers in *italics* indicate illustrations.

Film Index